DUBLIN

DUBLIN BAY

RATHMINES

Rathmines

Rathmines

Séamas Ó Maitiú

**Irish Historic Towns Atlas
Dublin suburbs No. 2**

Series editors: Colm Lennon and Jacinta Prunty
Cartographic editor: Sarah Gearty
Editorial assistant: Angela Byrne

IRISH HISTORIC TOWNS ATLAS
Editors: H.B. Clarke, Raymond Gillespie, Michael Potterton and Jacinta Prunty
Consultant editor: Anngret Simms
Cartographic editor: Sarah Gearty
Editorial assistants: Jennifer Moore, Frank Cullen

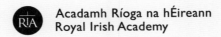

Acadamh Ríoga na hÉireann
Royal Irish Academy

Rathmines

First published in 2021 by the Royal Irish Academy
in association with Dublin City Council

Maps prepared in association with Ordnance Survey Ireland

Irish Historic Towns Atlas
Royal Irish Academy
19 Dawson Street
Dublin 2

www.ria.ie
www.ihta.ie

Text © 2021 Séamas Ó Maitiú
Copyright © The Royal Irish Academy

ISBN 978-1-911479-78-9

Thanks are due to the institutions mentioned in the captions and in the list of maps (pp 85–6) and illustrations (pp 130–1) for permission to reproduce material in their custody.

Maps 1–6, 18, 19, 25–7, 29 and photography for Plate 1 © Ordnance Survey Ireland/Government of Ireland, copyright permit no. 9252.

Figures 1–9 drawn by Sarah Gearty and Frank Cullen.

Design: Fidelma Slattery
Printed in Italy by Printer Trento

5 4 3 2 1

Front endpaper: Rathmines Road Lower, looking north, c. 1910 (National Library of Ireland)
Back endpaper: Ordnance Survey, Dublin, popular edition, scale 1:25,000, 1959. © Ordnance Survey Ireland/Government of Ireland
Previous pages: 'Hen and Chicken Lane, Harold's Cross', looking east to Rathmines, 1817, by C.M. Nairn (National Library of Ireland)

DIGITAL VERSION: the Topographical information section and further study maps are downloadable and available for research via www.ria.ie/dublin-suburbs-digital-content, click the 'Rathmines' panel and use the code 'rathmines02' to access the material.

A NOTE FROM THE PUBLISHER
We want to try to offset the environmental impacts of carbon produced during the production of our books and journals. For the production of our books this year we will plant 45 trees with Easy Treesie.

The Easy Treesie – Crann Project organises children to plant trees. Crann – 'Trees for Ireland' is a membership-based, non-profit, registered charity (CHY13698) uniting people with a love of trees. It was formed in 1986 by Jan Alexander, with the aim of "Releafing Ireland". Its mission is to enhance the environment of Ireland through planting, promoting, protecting and increasing awareness about trees and woodlands.

Contents

Acknowledgements vi

Preface vii

Introduction 1

The topographical development of Rathmines 7

Topographical information 35

Maps 83

Further notes 127

List of illustrations 130

Selected bibliography and key to abbreviations 132

General abbreviations 137

Acknowledgements

The author and editors of this atlas owe a debt of gratitude to many individuals, archives, libraries and institutions that assisted in its preparation and publication. Research carried out with the IHTA as part of the Maynooth University (MU) Summer Programme for Undergraduate Research (SPUR) 2016–21 proved helpful for Rathmines and thanks are due to the following MU students who contributed: Róisín Byrne, Ben Callan, Evan Dwyer, Jack Flood, Keith Harrington, Ryan Heerey, Cora McDonagh and Daniel O'Dwyer. We would also like to acknowledge Ruth McManus and Jonathan Wright who were appointed to the IHTA editorial board in April 2021 and who provided comments on the printers' proofs.

Special thanks are due to Mary Clark, former Dublin City Archivist, and her team at Dublin City Library and Archive. We are most grateful to John Brabazon, earl of Meath, who made part of the Meath papers available in the National Archives of Ireland and to Brian Donnelly who kindly facilitated access to the papers. The late Gregory O'Connor was also of unfailing assistance in the National Archives. The staff of the Hartley Library of the University of Southampton provided access to the Palmerston papers relating to Ireland. Thanks are extended to the staff of the National Library of Ireland, especially Mary Broderick; the staff of the Representative Church Body Library, in particular Bryan Whelan; Paul Ferguson and Paul Mulligan in the Glucksman Map Library, Trinity College, Dublin; Jane Nolan, University College Dublin Library; and Alan Phelan in the Erasmus Smith Schools Archive. Thomas Curran and Sean McDermott provided copies of maps from the Land Surveying and Mapping Department, Dublin City Council. Andrew Bonar Law generously supplied images of several of the maps that are included. In the Royal Irish Academy, the staff in the library have, as always, given every assistance as have colleagues throughout the institution. The Academy's publication department continues to provide valuable support and assistance. The project has been supported from the outset by Dublin City Council and thanks are due to Charles Duggan, Heritage Officer, for facilitating this collaboration.

Séamas Ó Maitiú would like to acknowledge local information provided by members of the Rathmines, Ranelagh and Rathgar Historical Society, especially Tom Harris, Angela O'Connell, Jed Walsh and the late Noel Healy. Elizabeth Smith's work on Belgrave Square and her direction to several maps were of great assistance. Wemmechien Hofman is thanked for information obtained in her history of Harold's Cross Cottages. The local knowledge of Séamus Greene, David Costello and Dermot and Gerard Matthews was also drawn on. Séamas Ó Maitiú acknowledges the unfailing support of his wife Gráinne and children Aoife and Connla.

Preface

Since 1986 the Irish Historic Towns Atlas, as part of an international project, has published atlases of representative types of Irish town. The aim has been to explore the morphological development of towns as a reflection of their underlying social, economic, cultural and political structures. In most cases each town has fitted neatly into one atlas, but for the larger towns and cities it has proved necessary to concentrate on urban cores. While this has many practical advantages, it means that suburbs have received less attention than they deserve. As well as having their own identity and personality, suburbs contribute to the multi-centred nature of the nineteenth-century city. This tension between local identity and the forces of urbanisation will serve to show the dynamic interdependence of suburb and metropolis. Organised along Irish Historic Towns Atlas lines, this series of suburban atlases allows us to capture a different aspect of the urban experience and to engage in comparative study of suburban life. Complementary to the main atlas series, it deserves as much attention as the more extended coverage of urban cores and should promote an exciting and expansive approach to the Irish urban past.

H.B. Clarke, Raymond Gillespie, Michael Potterton, March 2021

Overleaf: South side of city, *c.* 1935, from *Plan of Dublin, Baile Átha Cliath*, by Geographia Ltd (University College Dublin Library)

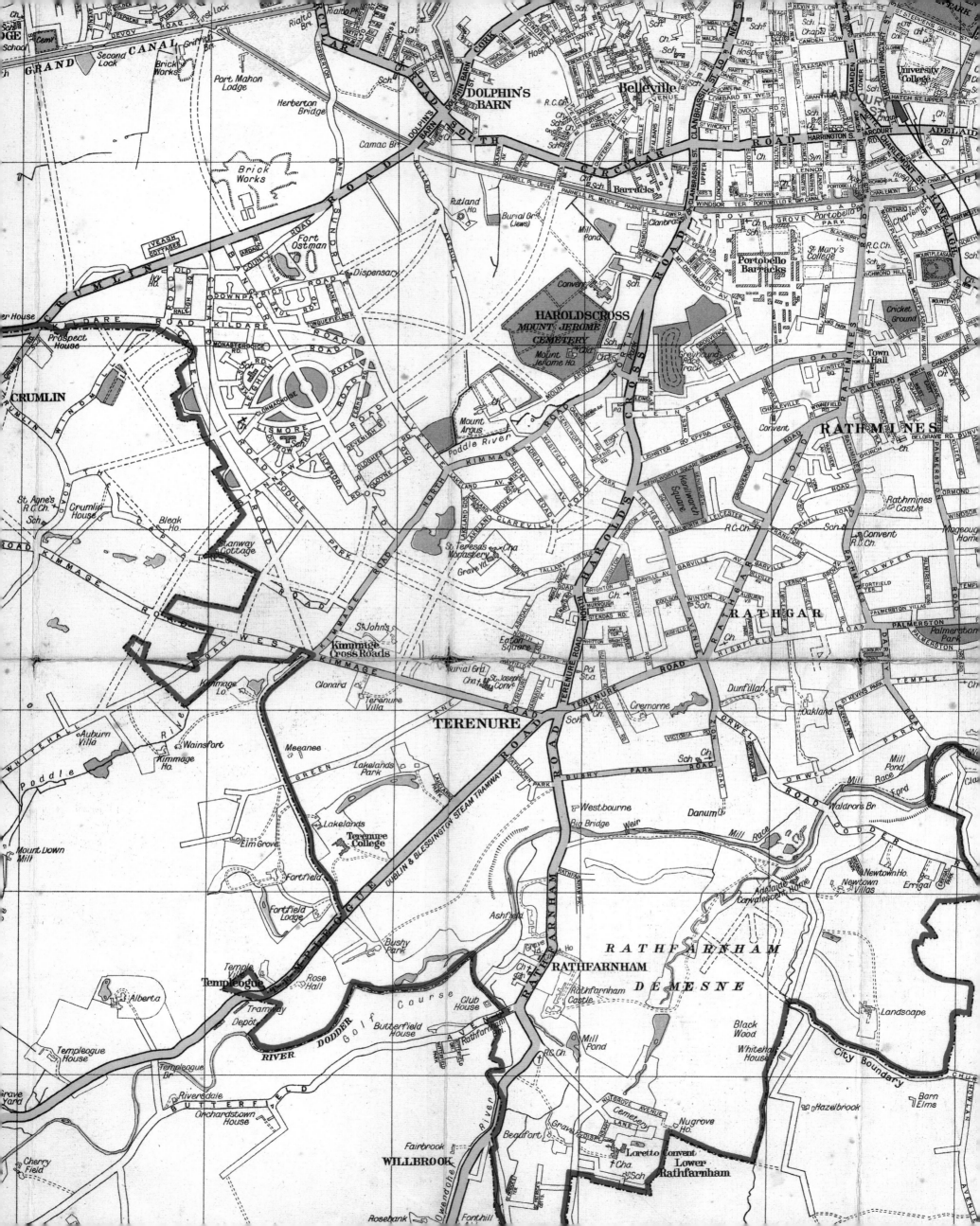

Introduction

The success of the Irish Historic Towns Atlas (IHTA) project over the past forty years is attested to by its ongoing series of town atlases (thirty of which have appeared to date) and its many ancillary publications. The atlas has also, through its fascicles and annual conferences, encouraged the comparative study of towns within Ireland, Britain and across the continent of Europe, in harmony with the recommendations of the International Commission for the History of Towns. Many experts in cartography, historical geography, archaeology and urban history in Ireland have served both on the editorial board and as advisers and authors of individual fascicles in the towns atlas series. The enterprise to date has resulted in the compilation of huge resources of information for the interpretation of topographical history and has helped to conceptualise the study of comparative urban development over a *longue durée*.

While the capital city of Ireland has been accorded special treatment, in that its atlas has been divided into separate parts, the same organising principles as govern those of other towns have characterised the fascicles of Dublin that have been published to date. Thus, the three parts of *Dublin* provide long views of urban growth and contain the same core elements of maps and texts as the other town atlases. The first part of *Dublin* traces the topographical history down to 1610, the second to 1756 and the third to 1847, while the fourth will eventually bring it down to the twentieth century. Although comparatively vast in its physical extent, for the purposes of the atlas, Dublin city incorporates only the area bounded by the circular roads and the two canals, the Royal to the north and the Grand to the south. As is evident from the principal map in *Dublin, part III*, based on the Ordnance Survey of 1847, the built-up area of the city was already expanding into districts outside these perimeters.

Although extramural quarters were a feature of the immediate neighbourhood of Dublin from the late Middle Ages, it was in the nineteenth century that the phenomenon of suburbanisation resulting from the settlement of large populations in the urban hinterland took hold. The migration, which was driven by political, social and

1

economic factors, impinged on what had been out-lying villages on the urban periphery. Communities of older inhabitants and newcomers together were faced with forming new topographical and munici-pal identities. The most complete form of suburban integration in the Dublin region was through the constitution of townships, self-governing enclaves that had devolved powers of local taxation and administration. In all, nine of these suburban town-ships evolved in the Victorian period – Rathmines and Rathgar, Pembroke, Blackrock, Kingstown, Dalkey, Killiney, Kilmainham, Drumcondra and Clontarf. The last-mentioned trio were absorbed within the municipal boundaries of Dublin in 1900, while the rest, by then urban district councils, were abolished in 1930. Districts within the present-day Dublin City Council boundary are the first to be dealt with in this series of suburban atlases.

Even in those Dublin suburbs that did not evolve into townships in the nineteenth century, there were issues of local topographical, cultural and social identification. Municipal boundaries, forms of transportation and the lure of the seaside to excur-sionists, for example, were among the factors that affected relations between the metropolis and tra-ditional village centres. Bray, Co. Wicklow, already the subject of a town atlas by K.M. Davies (no. 9 in the IHTA series), provides a valuable case study of a suburban town in which development was thus shaped through the symbiosis of city and locality.

In this series, a number of townships and suburbs within the area that comprised the county of Dublin (now administered by Dublin City Council, as well as the local authorities of Fingal, South County, and Dún Laoghaire-Rathdown) are the subject of atlases, organised along IHTA lines. As well as establishing the distinctive topographical identity of the individual village or suburb, each unit of the series will explore the relationship between city and district in so far as this has shaped the pattern of settlement through the ages. In respect of the former aim, the roots of suburban communities will be examined by showing the evolution over

time of modern-day topographical features, includ-ing streets and roads, waterways, religious sites and substantial houses. This process necessarily entails the delineation of localities, which could be cross-cut by several sets of boundaries, including those of manor, parish, townland and estate ownership, and in some cases will allow for natural combina-tions of smaller settlements to be defined as areas for study. As to the elucidation of aspects of the history of the city through suburban studies, the series will analyse the dynamics of residential areas aspiring to preserve their ambience in the face of the expansion of metropolitan borders, maritime and public utilities, and recreational facilities in the neighbourhood of Dublin. In thus considering the balance of interests of traditional village centres and estate cores on the one hand and the munici-pality and port of Dublin on the other, the suburbs series should complement parts I–IV of the IHTA atlas of Dublin city.

In this regard, the proven composition and meth-odology of the atlas in terms of a combination of maps and texts are carried over into the suburbs series. As with the main town series, there are maps common to all of the atlases presented in large format followed by facsimile reproductions, as the cartographical heritage allows. This section is com-pleted by the provision of base maps to encourage further study. The textual element is introduced by an extended essay interpreting the maps and evidence for settlement history from the first emer-gence of a recognisable village or suburb down to the late twentieth century. The essay also contains text maps and other illustrations as appropriate. As with the atlases of towns, there is a gazetteer section entitled Topographical information, collating data down to about 1970 under the standard twenty-two headings of the IHTA, in so far as this is feasible and relevant to each place, with standardised references and abbreviations. The selected bibliography lists important works devoted to a township or suburb for the period, especially those of topographical relevance, and is not necessarily confined to works cited in the footnotes. Other sources mentioned in the footnotes are not separately tabulated, except where their titles have been abbreviated in a way that requires explanation. Abbreviations of more general application for the whole series are listed after the bibliography at the end of the volume.

The atlas expresses the belief that, within the context of the comparative analysis of the topography of European towns, a suburban series makes a valuable contribution to studying the changes associated with modern urban expansion and the interdependency of city and suburbs. As such, it should be useful not only to students and teachers of history, geography, archaeology and architecture, but also to planners, conservationists and local government officers, and thus directly or indirectly to all residents and visitors in the township or suburban areas concerned.

Colm Lennon, Jacinta Prunty, December 2020

Overleaf: Rathmines Road Lower, looking north, c. 1910 (National Library of Ireland)

The topographical development of Rathmines

What has become known as Rathmines today is bounded on the south by the River Dodder and on the north by the Grand Canal. Its salient feature is the Rathmines Road/Dartry Road axis, creating a long north–south central spine. Its eastern and western boundaries are now delineated by arterial roads running from the city of Dublin, Mountpleasant Avenue/Belgrave Square East/Palmerston Road to the east and Harold's Cross Road to the west (Map 3, Plate 1). Rathmines has over the centuries shifted north. What is still referred to as Old Rathmines, its ancient core, was centred on a *ráth*, known only from placename evidence, and a later castle situated beside what is now Palmerston Park.

The designation Rathmines once covered ground both north and south of the River Dodder. In the medieval period, Meinierath, a contemporary variant of the name of Rathmines, was described as lying on both sides of the river.[1] Indeed, the present townlands of Rathmines Great and Rathmines Little are to the south of the Dodder, but are regarded as parts of Churchtown today and are not included in this study. For the purposes of this volume, Rathmines is defined as the area covered by the five townlands of Harold's Cross East, Portobello, Rathmines East, Rathmines South and Rathmines West.

The topography of Rathmines has been determined by its physical geography. The Lower Carboniferous limestone bedrock between the Dodder and the Grand Canal is covered by fertile and relatively dry grey-brown podzolic soils left behind after the retreat of the ice at the end of its last glaciation.[2] From ancient times, much of this land was covered by a forest known as Cullenswood. Although the name is restricted to a part of Ranelagh today, it formerly stretched as far west as Harold's Cross, taking in much of Rathmines. The name Castlewood Avenue in Rathmines is probably an echo of its former existence there. Two rivers, the Dodder and the Swan, shaped the area. The main branch of the Swan, now underground, enters

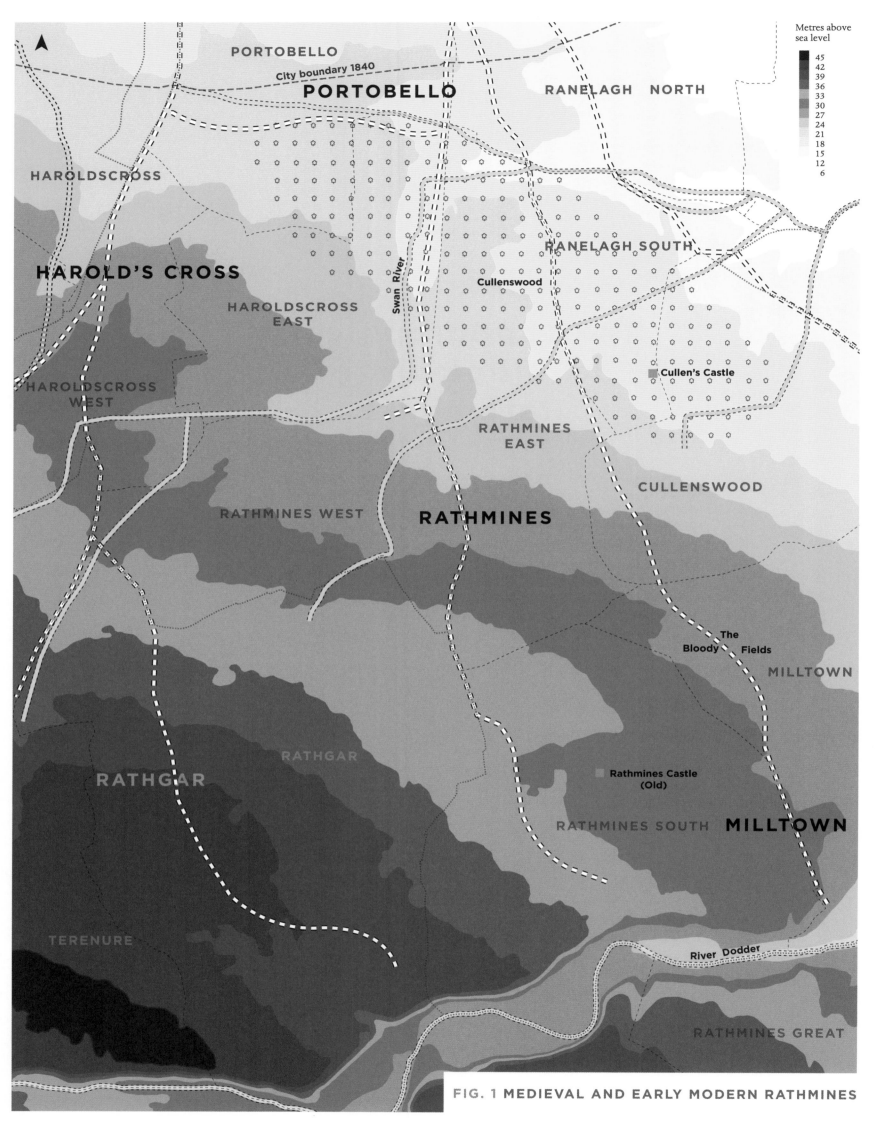

PORTOBELLO

City boundary 1840

PORTOBELLO

RANELAGH NORTH

HAROLDSCROSS

HAROLD'S CROSS

HAROLDSCROSS
EAST

RANELAGH SOUTH

Cullenswood

Swan River

HAROLDSCROSS
WEST

RATHMINES
EAST

Cullen's Castle

RATHMINES WEST

RATHMINES

CULLENSWOOD

**The
Bloody Fields**

MILLTOWN

RATHGAR

RATHGAR

□ Rathmines Castle
(Old)

RATHMINES SOUTH

MILLTOWN

TERENURE

River Dodder

RATHMINES GREAT

FIG. 1 MEDIEVAL AND EARLY MODERN RATHMINES

Metres above
sea level

45
42
39
36
33
30
27
24
21
18
15
12
6

═ ═ ═ ═ ═ ═ Road or pathway

------------ River or stream (Sweeney)

See also note on pp 127–8

------------ City boundary 1840

.... Parish boundary (1843 OS)

------------ Townland boundary (1843 OS)

RATHMINES EAST
RATHMINES

Townland name (1843 OS)
Placename (1760 Rocque)

Scale 1:10,000

0   Metres   400

the area from the south-west, flows along the west side of the present Rathmines Road Lower, before making a sharp turn east alongside the present Richmond Hill. In medieval times, the Dodder formed the boundary of the civil parish of St Peter in which much of Rathmines lay, and was the southern boundary of the later Rathmines township. The Dodder also influenced the first known settlement pattern (Fig. 1).

The land of Rathmines rises gently from the valley of the Liffey to high ground overlooking the Dodder; from 23 m above sea level at the canal at Portobello to 37 m at Palmerston Park. It then falls to the Dodder. Placename evidence points to a line of ringforts on this ridge overlooking the Dodder. Ringforts or *ráthanna* are typically found on low, well-drained slopes, such as on the eastern flanks of the Dublin Mountains in the nearby Rathdown barony, where many occur. These usually indicate areas of pastoral farming in early Ireland that were converted to arable use with the arrival of the Anglo-Normans.[3] This line of early settlements overlooking the Dodder consisted of ringforts at Baggotrath, Rathmines, Rathgar and, on the far side of the river, Rathfarnham (Map 1). Each of these ringforts later had a castle built adjacent to it. Indicating this elevated ridge, the sites of the *ráthanna* at Rathmines and Rathgar are joined today by the tellingly named Highfield Road.

The distinctive curved southern boundary of Palmerston Park may be a vestige of the ringfort that gave Rathmines its name; the site seems plausible, as it is adjacent to old Rathmines Castle. Rathgar, very close along the ridge to the ringfort at Rathmines, also had a castle. Finally Rathfarnham, on the far side of the river, boasted the most spectacular castle of all. Rathfarnham Castle, still extant, was built by Archbishop Adam Loftus in *c.* 1560.[4]

Ringforts, protected by superstition, usually survived as landscape features in the countryside. George Petrie stated in 1856 that he remembered the demolition of the *ráth* at Baggotrath. The circular 'fort of Rathgar' is clearly marked on John

Taylor's *Map of the environs of Dublin* (1816) and it is likely that the *ráth* of Rathmines survived until the land was converted to houses and roads (Map 12).[5] According to Patrick W. Joyce, the pioneer of Irish placename study and resident of Leinster Road, the *ráth* survived in the cultural legacy of Rathmines. Writing in the 1860s, he commented:

> It is worthy of remark, however, that the peasantry living in or near these places, to whom the names have been handed down orally and not by writing, generally preserve the correct pronunciation; of which Rathmines, Rathgar, Rathfarnham and Rathcoole are good examples, being pronounced by the people of the localities Ra-mines, Ra-gar, Ra-farnham and Ra-coole.[6]

The *ráth* at what later came to be called Rathmines was part of the ancient territory of Cualu, an extensive area whose boundary is uncertain as it fluctuated over time. The name is retained in eighteenth- and nineteenth-century documents relating to Rathmines in the form Cullenswood or more commonly Cullen's Farm. For instance, land on the west side of Rathmines Road leased in 1791 was described as being in Cullenswood and records in the Meath estate usually refer to its land in Rathmines as being part of Cullen's Farm.[7] By the sixteenth century the lands of the archbishop were parcelled out into units called 'farms' and this term was used rather than the usual 'townlands'. The old Colonia or Cullenswood (or part of it) became Cullen's Farm.[8]

No early Irish church site has been identified in Rathmines, the major centre being Tallaght with a possible small ecclesiastical foundation at nearby Rathfarnham.[9] By AD 1000, following the Scandinavian invasions, Rathmines had become part of the extensive Hiberno-Norse hinterland of Dublin known as *Dyflinnarskíri* (Dublinshire).[10] Despite the apparent absence of an early Irish ecclesiastical site, the church greatly influenced the development of Rathmines as it came to form a part of the patrimony of the archbishops of Dublin from pre-Anglo-Norman times.[11] With the Anglo-Norman invasion, these lands were confirmed to the archbishop and, perhaps, augmented. In 1185, for instance, Lord John on his visit to Ireland made a grant of a carucate of land adjacent to St Kevin's Church to Holy Trinity Church (Christ Church Cathedral).[12] The area was erected into the manor of St Sepulchre. It had formerly been called the manor of Colonia, a Latinised version of the old name Cualu. The change of name appears to have taken place during the reign of Edward I (1272–1307).[13]

The manor was directly farmed by the archbishop and formed an important part of his demesne possessions. Apart from its woodland, which then covered just 66 acres (an acre at this time in the Dublin area was about 2.125 times the size of a statute acre), this demesne land of the archbishop contained much arable land, consisting in the fourteenth century of 50 acres of wheat, 48 acres of oats and 68 acres that lay fallow. Much of it was probably tilled by hired labour. Freeholders and small tenants were also found on the land of the manor. They paid about 6d. per acre in rent but there were wide variations; they ranged from 2s. near the city to 3d. on the far margins.[14]

The area received an unsavoury reputation in the minds of the inhabitants of Dublin when, on Easter Monday 1209, a group of the newly arrived colonists were massacred there as they were enjoying a day in the countryside. The actual massacre may be remembered in the spot known as the Bloody Fields, just outside the area under study here. The citizens paraded to the scene every year thereafter, the commemoration being held by the Dublin merchants' guild as late as 1722.[15] Mountpleasant Avenue and Milltown Path, formerly referred to as 'the ancient path to Milltown', may have formed the route of the march. The earliest reference to roads in the area is an entry in Archbishop Alen's register of c. 1396, in which two highways in the archbishop's demesne, one to Colon and the other to Milltown, are mentioned.[16] It is difficult to

say which of the three modern routes are being referred to here – Ranelagh Road, Mountpleasant Avenue or Rathmines Road.

In 1315, a little over a century after the massacre at Cullenswood, a band of O'Tooles availed themselves of the shelter of the wood on the eve of an attack on the city. It is no surprise to learn that an extent of the manor made eleven years later depicts a house in a sorry state, later known as Cullenswood Castle, belonging to the archbishop's farm at Cullenswood: 'A hall with stone walls now prostrate, a chamber for the archbishop, with a chapel annexed to the chamber, roofed with shingles; also there were a kitchen formed of wood, a grange, stable, and granary covered with boards, now totally prostrate to the ground'.[17] Apart from the chronic problem of the native hillsmen, other factors may have contributed to the dereliction, such as the Bruce invasion (1315–18), environmental deterioration and the neglect of the archbishops.

Amidst this scene of desolation, Rathmines enters the historical record as 'le Rath' when, on 22 May 1313, the justiciar John Wogan granted to Richard de Welton one hundred acres of arable land and five acres of pasture he already had leased from the late archbishop of Dublin, Richard de Ferings (1299–1306).[18] De Welton would not long remain in possession and was displaced by the upwardly mobile De Meones family. William de Meones, the first member of the family that would give its name to Rathmines, came to Ireland from East Meon in Hampshire in 1279–80 in the entourage of John de Derlington, archbishop of Dublin.[19] William became chief baron of the Irish exchequer in 1311. He acquired the lands in the manor of St Sepulchre that became known first as Meonesrath and later as Rathmines, i.e., the *ráth* of De Meones. A close associate of the archbishop, he probably acquired the land during the archbishopric of De Derlington, between 1279 and 1284.[20] William died in 1325 and his property passed to Gilbert de Meones, a soldier, the son of his brother Geoffrey.[21] In an extent of the manor of St Sepulchre made in 1326, Gilbert held 160 acres at le Rath and Frythiay for 44s. with suit of court. The family flourished. John de Meones was mayor of Dublin in 1331–2 and 1337–8, and Robert de Meones held the same office in 1351–2. Nicholas de Meones was appointed a judge of the court of king's bench (Ireland) in 1374.

The grant to the De Meones at Rathmines included a mill on the Dodder. The presence of a mill, and the fact that the family was granted a site with a history of previous settlement in the form of a *ráth*, would lead us to expect, perhaps, that a new manor was set up here. Indeed, Archbishop Alen states that there was a manor at Rathmines and in 1399 Rathmines is described as a 'demesne'.[22] The De Meones family at this time were the chief tenants in the manor of St Sepulchre and as such they would have been expected to build a castle in an area bordering on that of the native Irish. While no documentary evidence has come to light, one piece of visual evidence may point to the existence of a medieval castle at Rathmines. A depiction of a house, known as Rathmines Castle, which was erected by Sir George Radcliffe between 1633 and 1639, suggests that it incorporated two older structures. This house, now demolished, should not to be confused with a later 'castle' farther north that would become the Church of Ireland College of Education. 'Rathmines Castle Old' was situated on or near the southern curved boundary of the present Palmerston Park (Fig. 1). A single-storey building on one side and a corner tower are quite clearly of a much older appearance than the rest of the structure.[23]

Within forty years of the De Meones family coming into the possession of the *ráth*, the Anglo-Norman colony was under severe pressure from the effects of the Bruce invasion and the increased presence of the native Irish. The subsequent arrival of the Black Death also took its toll. In the 1326 extent, Colonia was said to be 'near evildoers'. This must have been even more so in the case of Meonesrath, which was on the periphery of the demesne, straddling the Dodder.[24] In 1357 Gilbert de Meones was made *custos* of the peace to protect the Leinster marches, with power to muster men for their defence. Meonesrath must have been a very suitable place from which to organise such operations. Gilbert had previously been constable of the castles at Arklow and Newcastle, Co. Wicklow. In 1382 a second William de Meones was lord of Meonesrath. By the early fifteenth century the De Meones name seems to disappear from the records.[25]

In the years that followed, the further alienation of land belonging to the see of Dublin would bring new landowners to the Rathmines area, in particular the Brabazon family, ennobled as the earls of Meath. Individual archbishops had only a life interest in the land and often succumbed to the temptation to make a quick profit by letting it out on long renewable leases. As early as the fifteenth century a statute described the archbishop's patrimony as 'decayed and diminished'. This process, coupled with the reformation and the availability in the Dublin area of large tracts of former ecclesiastical land, both episcopal and monastic, enriched members of a coterie close to the establishment.[26]

George Browne, the reforming archbishop of Dublin (1536–54), disposed of some see lands, Myles Ronan commenting that 'he evidently found it inconvenient and troublesome to look after them'.[27] They were usually leased and an annual rent paid. In *c.* 1543 he conveyed land to various named people, all of Thomas Court and the village of Rathlande 'to hold forever to the use of William Brabazon, his heirs and assigns at the yearly rent of 13*s*. 4*d*.' This was the beginning of the presence of the Brabazon family, later the earls of Meath, in the suburban area of south Dublin.[28]

William Brabazon was the son of a Leicestershire landowner who entered the royal service as a protégé of Thomas Cromwell. In 1534 he was appointed vice-treasurer in Ireland and was to remain at the centre of Irish affairs for the rest of his life.[29] In March 1545 Brabazon was granted the lands of the abbey of St Thomas, Dublin, with all its jurisdictions, liberties and privileges. This grant was confirmed in 1609 to Sir Edward, his son. This liberty extended far into south Dublin. Adjoining it was the manor of St Sepulchre and the earls of Meath eventually extended their landownership here and in much of what became known as Upper and Lower Rathmines (Map 7).[30]

Once long leases were obtained from the archbishop they could be sold on, and this led to land changing hands before the original lease expired.[31] Around the time that the Brabazon family was obtaining possession of land in Rathmines we find in a document dated to between 1529 and 1534 that Fercath, 'a parcel of Menes Rath', near the Dodder in Upper Rathmines was in the possession of the lord of Howth.[32] Less than a century later, in 1611, it was recorded that the barons of Howth 'suffered a recovery' of Rathmines, that is, conveyed the land, but to whom is not known. It would not be long before Rathmines changed hands again.[33]

As Lower Rathmines to the north became dominated by the Meath estate, so the southern section or Upper Rathmines came into the possession of the Radcliffe, and later the Palmerston, estate. George Radcliffe (1593–1657) was one of the many place-seekers and fortune-hunters attracted to Ireland in the sixteenth and seventeenth centuries. From Overthorpe in the parish of Thornhill, Yorkshire, Radcliffe was a close associate of Thomas Wentworth, earl of Strafford. Wentworth sent him to Ireland as an administrator in January 1633, to prepare for the latter's arrival as deputy.[34] Radcliffe was knighted within months of his arrival in Dublin and was returned as an MP for Armagh in the Irish parliament of 1634. Moreover, he sat on Wentworth's 1634 commission for defective titles, 'a position from which, it has been suggested, it may have been possible to acquire land "on cheap terms"'.[35] Having now the means at his disposal, Radcliffe began a spate of land acquisitions including 586 acres in Rathmines, in the vicinity of the ancient *ráth*.

In 1636 Wentworth began building his massive mansion at Jigginstown, Co. Kildare, and his protégé Radcliffe soon followed suit on his newly acquired land in Rathmines. The house was described by a contemporary as a 'stately thing'; Radcliffe, emulating his patron's extravagance at Jigginstown, spent £7,000 on it, an enormous sum. For a time, Radcliffe directed Irish affairs from his new residence. On 24 September 1639 he wrote a letter from Rathmines to Lord Conway and Killultagh stating that he was acting for the lord deputy in his absence and requesting information as to the policy to be pursued in Ireland.[36] Like Strafford at Jigginstown, Radcliffe did not have much time to enjoy his new luxurious residence. His star fell with that of Strafford and he spent most of the civil war in Oxford. Rathmines Castle, as his new house was called, survived the immediate impact of 1641 and was inhabited for a short while in the following year by the earl of Ormond and his family when he was commanding the army in Ireland. In August 1642 Ormond moved to Dublin and three days later the house was burnt, some implicating the caretaker, whose wife was found dead there.[37]

The most famous event in the history of Rathmines took place on 2 August 1649, when the earl of Ormond failed in an attempt to take Dublin from the parliamentary forces. Ormond, encamped at Rathmines, sent a detachment to fortify Baggotrath Castle. This force was attacked and fled to Rathmines, pursued by Col. Michael Jones. Some idea of the topography of Rathmines and the surroundings of the castle at the time may be had from eyewitness accounts of the battle. The contested terrain was depicted as one of fields bounded by hedges and crossed by a series of rough paths and tracks.[38] In the parliamentarian Edmund Ludlow's *Memoirs*, Col. Jones, pursuing Royalists, marched 'up to the walls of Rathmines [Castle], which were about sixteen feet high, and containing about ten acres of ground, where many of the enemy's foot had shut up themselves'.[39]

During the ensuing Cromwellian period, the restored Rathmines Castle contained six hearths. The lands of Rathmines were still owned by Sir George Radcliffe, while the house and sixty acres of demesne land were occupied by Capt.

William Shore. Shore may well have seen action at the Battle of Rathmines and come to know the mansion through this. According to F. Elrington Ball, Sir Henry Brooke (ancestor of the baronets of that name) also had an interest in the house and land of Rathmines. Both Shore and Brooke were married to daughters of Henry Docwra of Culmore.[40] The 'census' of 1659 recorded twelve taxpayers in Rathmines, evenly divided into six Irish and six English. The number may seem small, but it is comparable to neighbouring Rathgar. William J. Smyth characterises the population of Rathgar at this time as a gentry household standing alone in its townland. Rathmines may well have been the same, with the total population being associated with the big house and its demesne.[41]

George Radcliffe died in 1657. Under Charles II, after a lengthy legal battle, his son Thomas recovered the estates in Ireland that he had inherited on the death of his father. When Capt. Shore died in 1668, his representatives and Thomas Radcliffe engaged in legal proceedings over the lands at Rathmines, but Radcliffe remained in possession. Thomas Radcliffe died at Rathmines Castle in 1679 without issue. Rathmines ended up in the hands of his aunt, Margaret Trappes. In a will of 1698 she left all of her land in Ireland to Sir John Temple. He came into possession of the lands on her death in 1701 and was the first of a family who would have a major impact on the development of Upper Rathmines. In 1666 he purchased the Palmerston estate in Chapelizod and so associated his family with the name under which they would be ennobled. His eldest son, Henry, would become Viscount Palmerston in 1722.[42] In 1702, the year after the death of Margaret Trappes, an older proprietorial presence re-emerged. An act relating to the purchase of forfeited estates in Ireland was passed and Narcissus Marsh, archbishop of Dublin, hastened to put forward his ancient claim to his head rents payable out of the lands of Rathmines. His case was put before trustees acting under the act and was upheld.[43] The rent may have amounted to no more than a nominal sum, however. In the early 1790s it was stated to be £1 14s. annually.[44]

In the late eighteenth and early nineteenth centuries, Rathmines fulfilled the function of a retreat from Dublin. Numerous writers depict it as a desirable resort for those fleeing the supposed unhealthy environment of the city under the prevailing theory of the miasmatic spread of disease. In 1795 Charles Barry, the headmaster of the then school in Old Rathmines Castle, explained that 'the air from the sea, being meliorated by that from the mountains of Wicklow', was beneficial to those 'of a consumptive disposition'. Such people could resort to this area, which was quite close to the city, 'in preference to a more distant situation'. The later village of Rathmines in 1822 was said to be chiefly inhabited by invalids, in consequence of the supposed purity and wholesome quality of the atmosphere.[45] Ironically, in the same year, a death notice for John Thorpe, attorney of French Street in the city, stated that he had gone to Rathmines to recover his health.[46]

This therapeutic and tranquil atmosphere was on the verge of change. In Lower Rathmines, the new Circular Line of the Grand Canal was completed as far as Portobello by the end of 1790, and Portobello Bridge was built in 1791 to maintain the link between the present Rathmines Road Lower and the city (Map 14).[47] A road and pathway from the present core of Rathmines northwards is depicted on John Rocque's 1760 map and labelled as 'Rathmines Path' (Map 9). The new straight line of Rathmines Road was laid out in the summer of 1800. Described in the *Statistical survey of County Dublin* (1801), the old road was said to be 'situated so low, as to be overflowed upon any extraordinary rain or snow, and also narrow and winding'. The old road had taken a wide curve west, probably following a meander of a branch of the Swan River. This may be seen faintly on John Taylor's map (1816) alongside the new straight line (Map 12). It is marked as 'old road' on an 1810 plan of part of the Meath estate (Map 11).[48] In 1760, Rocque depicted a path running alongside the road to the east. Later, this side of the road from Portobello Bridge to Castlewood Avenue was edged by what Meyler's reminiscences called an 'ugly ditch' and an occasional thorn hedge.[49] The new, straight line of road would facilitate the building of terraced brick housing, which was to be a feature of Rathmines (Fig. 4).[50]

On John Taylor's map of 1816, Rathmines Castle is labelled as a school. This was a boarding school run by Charles Barry and begun in the 1790s. It was an ambitious project and Barry published a prospectus of the school that went through a number of reprints. It seems to have specialised in preparing students for Trinity College Dublin. Barry highlighted the healthy environs of Rathmines and the spaciousness of the building, with each student having his own bed. There was an extensive playground and one side had a 'piazza', a veranda or porch where the pupils could exercise in bad weather. The whole contained a farm of twenty-two acres surrounded by a nine-feet-high wall. Could this be the same supposedly sixteen-feet-high wall behind which the royalist soldiers took refuge in 1649?[51] Barry died in 1822 and the castle was described in 1833 as 'an irregular, uninteresting building' that had been so modernised as to give it the appearance of an old whitewashed farmhouse. It was at that time used as a boarding house for invalids and those suffering from consumption.[52]

No settlement appears to have developed around the castle. The Catholic priest, Fr Henry Young, gives a sense of its rural character before suburban development:

> In the years 1815–17, when I was a curate in St Nicholas, Francis Street, I used in my turn, on Sundays to celebrate Mass [at 9 o'clock] in Harold's Cross chapel, and then, a second Mass [at 11 o'clock] in Milltown, returning home through the fields.[53]

He would have criss-crossed an area clearly without roads, with occasional stiles at walls and boundaries to facilitate travel – much the same landscape as described at the time of the Battle of Rathmines in 1649.[54] However, 1.2 km away, where the Swan River takes a sharp turn north from its easterly course, a small village grew up that heralded the first shift in the centre of gravity of Rathmines. The road from the city followed the course of this north-flowing section of the river (Fig. 2). The turn allowed a road to diverge to the west from Rathmines to Rathgar. At this fork in the road the village of Rathmines grew up. This point was also the boundary marker between what was known as, and still is, tellingly, Old or Upper Rathmines and Lower Rathmines to its north. Alexander Taylor's map of c. 1802 shows the beginnings of the road to Rathgar, but it appears to have petered out into a track (Map 10). The building of a new straight road to Rathgar must have boosted the village enormously. It is mentioned in an advertisement of September 1815 as 'the new road to Rathgar' and its impressive length is labelled 'new road' on John Taylor's map of 1816 as it heads through the fields southwards.[55]

At the heart of the village was an area known as The Chains, consisting of a set of chains and bollards (one of which is still in place), possibly fencing the stream off from the small houses that grew up there (Map 22). A small village green fronting the river may also have existed.[56] At the turn of the nineteenth century, this small rural settlement was described as 'a pleasant fine village, one mile and a half S. of the castle of Dublin; it is extremely rural and healthy, and well wooded and watered'.[57] W.T. Meyler, writing in 1822, describes the surrounding area as being 'laid out in meadow and dairy fields'.[58]

An 1836 survey of the earl of Meath's estate shows the tenurial situation in Rathmines as a major surge in suburbanisation got under way (Map 15). The estate owned two blocks of land in Rathmines. One, in Lower Rathmines beginning just south of the Grand Canal, took in Portobello (Cathal Brugha) Barracks and all of the land to the east of that, on which many villas had been built. It also took in Lower Rathmines as far as the junction with Leinster Road and all the land to the east of that, including a stretch of Mountpleasant Avenue as far as Ranelagh Road.[59] The second block took

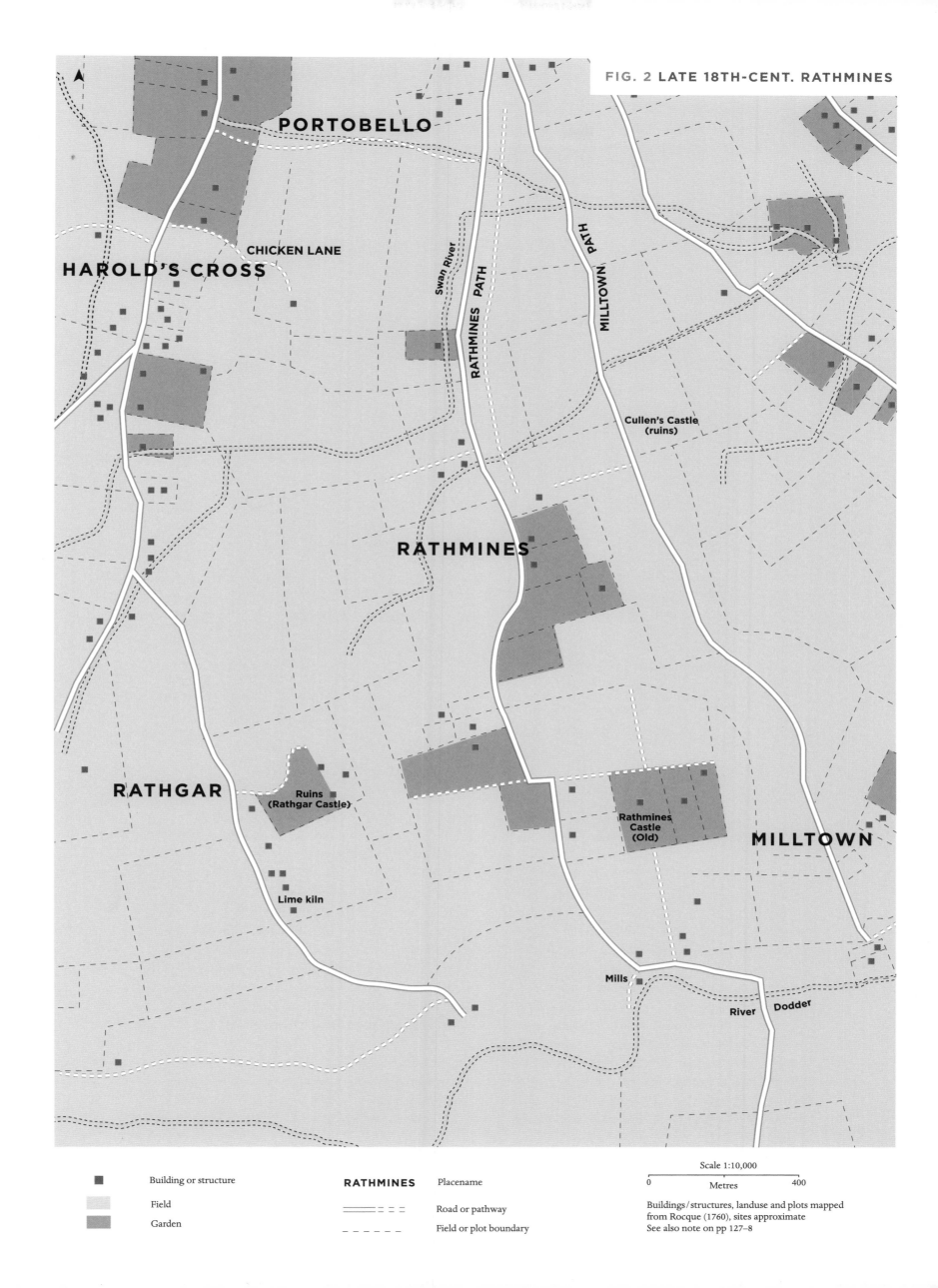

FIG. 2 LATE 18TH-CENT. RATHMINES

PORTOBELLO

CHICKEN LANE

HAROLD'S CROSS

Swan River

RATHMINES PATH

MILLTOWN PATH

Cullen's Castle
(ruins)

RATHMINES

RATHGAR

Ruins
(Rathgar Castle)

Rathmines
Castle
(Old)

MILLTOWN

Lime kiln

Mills

River Dodder

Scale 1:10,000

0   Metres   400

■	Building or structure
	Field
	Garden

RATHMINES   Placename

———— = = = Road or pathway

– – – – – – Field or plot boundary

Buildings / structures, landuse and plots mapped
from Rocque (1760), sites approximate
See also note on pp 127–8

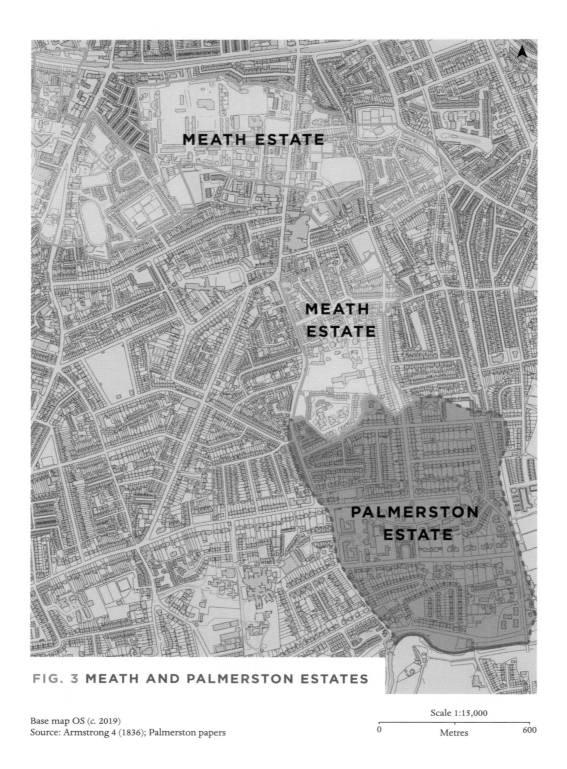

FIG. 3 MEATH AND PALMERSTON ESTATES

Base map OS (*c.* 2019)
Source: Armstrong 4 (1836); Palmerston papers

Scale 1:15,000

0   Metres   600

in the east side of Rathmines Road Upper, from its beginning at the junction with Rathgar Road, stretching east to what would become Belgrave Square East and Palmerston Road. It bordered on the Palmerston estate close to Tranquilla House in Upper Rathmines.[60] The estate had let out the bulk of this land on perpetual leases or for long periods of time. Of the forty-two holders of this land in 1836, thirty-three held leases that were 'renewable forever', one for four hundred years, five for one hundred years and the few remaining for shorter periods.[61] Shortly after 1800, the property market in Rathmines began to show signs of a surge. The

main beneficiaries of development would be the Palmerston estate in Upper Rathmines and the Meath estate in Lower Rathmines, although the latter was prevented from gaining maximum benefit as much of its land was let out on long fixed leases. On the fringes and in between, smaller owners and speculators such as the earl of Howth, Sir Robert Shaw and the earl of Milltown benefited (Fig. 3).[62]

In 1810–15, the building of a large cavalry barracks (later Cathal Brugha Barracks) on land belonging to the earl of Meath on the west side of Rathmines Road Lower, stretching to Harold's Cross, must have greatly increased traffic on the new road and raised the profile of the area.[63] By 1837, enormous change had taken place in the surroundings of the pleasant, rural, secluded village of 1800:

> Twelve years since Rathmines was only known as an obscure village; it now forms a fine suburb, commencing at Portobello Bridge, and extended in a continued line of handsome houses, with some pretty detached villas, for about one mile and a half.[64]

The 'line of handsome houses' was a series of terraces extending along the east side of Rathmines Road. Susan Galavan has pointed out that the model of the city terrace was extended into the suburbs and that, while villas were also built, the terrace dominated in Rathmines more than in other suburbs.[65] While nearly all the terraces were subsequently built on the east side of Rathmines Road, one of the first terraces was on the west side, erected on the land of William Bernard shortly after 1800 and bearing the same name as his villa, Williams Park.[66]

The map evidence is that terrace-building was piecemeal rather than an ordered march of sequential house-building from the city along Rathmines Road (Maps 16, 17). Perhaps not unexpectedly, the first terrace built on the east side appears to be opposite the village of Rathmines as seen on Alexander Taylor's map of *c.* 1802 (Map 10). This became known simply as Rathmines Terrace. By the publication of John Taylor's *Map of the environs of Dublin* (1816) and Duncan's map of 1821, a line of houses appeared between Richmond Hill and Castlewood Avenue (Maps 12, 13). This included what would become known as Rathmines Mall and Newington Terrace. By 1816, some houses had been built on Richmond Hill and its eastern end was completed in 1827, as indicated by a contemporary wall plaque. As described in Lewis's *Topographical dictionary*, terraces were beginning at Portobello Bridge by 1837. These are depicted on the first-edition Ordnance Survey map of 1843 and include Fortescue Terrace

and Berry's Buildings, to the north and south respectively of the Catholic chapel.

The west side of Rathmines Road was a different matter. While the Swan River and its tributary were the key factors in the very location of Rathmines Road, they also had a major impact on the development of the west side of the road up to the present day (Fig. 4). Apart from the danger of flooding, there was little room between road and river for a house, back and front gardens, coach house and back lane, Williams Park being an exception. On the west side were a number of villas on the low ridge running parallel to the Swan, with large gardens extending down to the river. The earliest were Mount Anthony, built by Anthony Clavell, and Williams Park, situated well back from the stream (Map 16). The Swan was 'comparatively dry' during the summer months, but sudden autumnal showers caused flooding in its immediate vicinity.[67]

In the area between Blackberry Lane – a very old lane that for a time served as a service entrance to Portobello (Cathal Brugha) Barracks – and the barracks' main entrance at the end of Military Road were Lissonfield House and Lark Hill, the nucleus of St Mary's College. In 1810 Major Alexander Taylor of the Irish Engineers leased Lissonfield from the earl of Meath for one hundred years. He was the author of a map of the environs of Dublin in *c.* 1802. A notable large house in Upper Rathmines was 'new' Rathmines Castle, built by Robert Wynne, possibly on the site of an earlier house depicted on John Taylor's map of 1816.[68]

With the terraces on the main artery well in hand, a series of cross roads were built through the fields, linking the main roads from the city. Highfield Road was constructed during the period of Chief Justice Yorke's residence at Rathmines Castle – between 1746 and 1763 – thus linking Rathgar to Rathmines.[69] Richmond Hill also probably originated as a path from Rathmines Road to the Milltown Path along the bank of the Swan River. Exceptionally long gardens kept the houses well back from the south bank of the flood-prone stream.

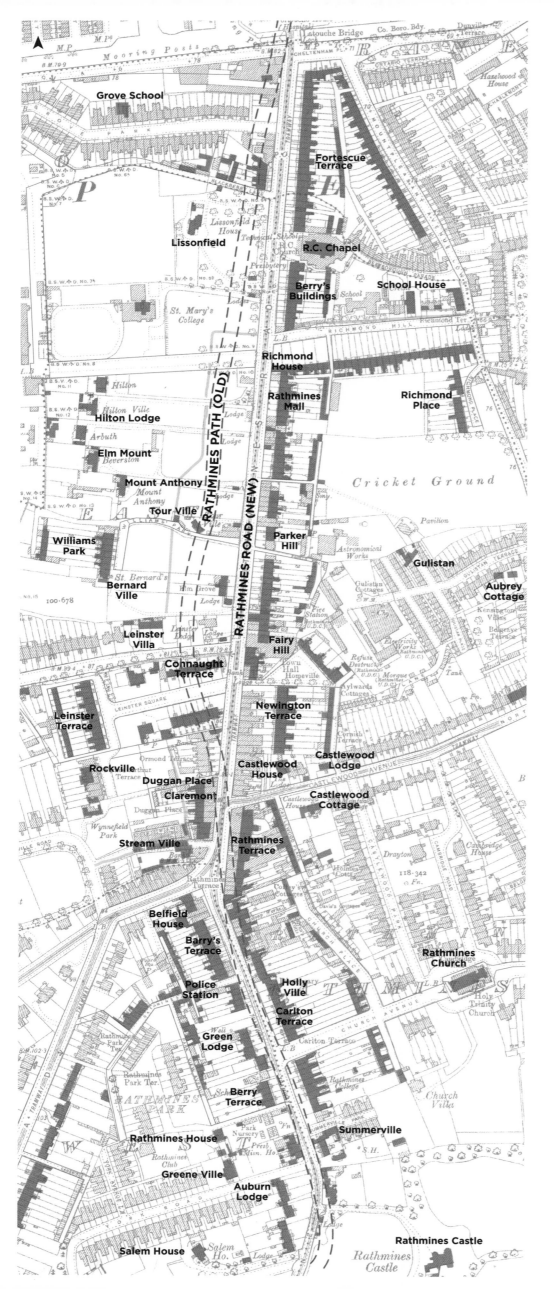

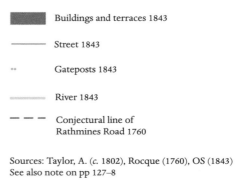

FIG. 4 RATHMINES ROAD VILLAS AND TERRACES

▆	Buildings and terraces 1843
—	Street 1843
••	Gateposts 1843
—	River 1843
– – –	Conjectural line of Rathmines Road 1760

Sources: Taylor, A. (*c.* 1802), Rocque (1760), OS (1843)
See also note on pp 127–8

Scale 1:4000

0   Metres   200

Blackberry Lane probably began as a path along the banks of the branch of the Swan flowing southeast from the Portobello area (Map 8). Castlewood Avenue, said in 1822 to be 'a narrow lane without a house or a cabin', may have originated as a path to Cullenswood Castle (which probably stood near where Cullenswood House now stands) and linked Ranelagh with Rathmines.[70] Leinster Road, originally part of Mowld's farm, was completed by the developer Frederick Jackson in *c*. 1840 to connect Harold's Cross Road and Rathmines Road Lower.[71]

The demand for suburban housing can be inferred from the regularity with which Rathmines occurs in the Registry of Deeds. Before 1800, Rathmines crops up infrequently, but there is a huge surge in land transactions from the first decade of the nineteenth century that continued into the 1820s and 1830s. Many villa-owners in the area began selling off land for housing. William Bernard of Williams Park began disposing of whole fields, and two acres of meadow came on the market between Rathmines Road and Mountpleasant Avenue in 1817. Grimwood's, a large nursery concern at the junction of Rathmines Road and Rathgar Road, sold off for house-building the greater part of their nursery land fronting the road, as a result selling off thousands of oak, elm, ash, beech and fruit trees.[72] A number of notable speculative builders and developers were associated with particular areas: these were William Bernard (Williams Park), John Butler (Leinster Square), Frederick Jackson and Frederick Stokes (Leinster Road area); John Holmes (Holmeville and Castlewood Avenue), Michael Murphy (Kenilworth Square) and Patrick Plunkett (Belgrave and Palmerston Roads).

As the link roads were built, a process of infilling with houses took place, with further adjacent roads opening up more land (Maps 18, 19). This also facilitated the creation of squares, a notable feature of Rathmines. Mountpleasant Square (outside the extent of this study), developed by Terence Dolan, was the first in the area. This was followed by Leinster Square, begun in the 1830s, and Belgrave Square begun in the mid-1840s (Map 21).[73] Kenilworth Square followed in the 1850s

and Grosvenor Square from the mid-1850s to the mid-1870s (Map 20). Some squares and roads were gated, such as Mountpleasant Square, Leinster Square and Leinster Road. In 1867, John Butler wrote to the Rathmines township commissioners requesting that they take charge of the roads in Leinster Square. They agreed on the condition that he remove the gates and provide a financial contribution, citing a precedent set when they took over Leinster Road from its developers.[74]

A major step in the completion of a middle-class enclave was taken in 1867 when the township commissioners ordered that all the remaining thatched cabins and wooden sheds in the township were to be removed and due notice given to their owners.[75] With its proliferation of squares and fine roads, in 1869 the *Irish Builder* referred to Rathmines as the 'Dublin Belgravia'.[76] House building reached a peak in the 1850s and 1860s. Unlike the neighbouring Pembroke township, which had a more uniform, patrician air owing to building clauses laid down in the leases by the Pembroke estate, Rathmines had a rather more free enterprise regime owing to the long-lease policy of its major landlord. Houses in Rathmines were built in a variety of sizes and roof heights, as one speculation gave way to another. They were described in 1859 as being in many instances of a first-class character, 'seldom degenerating beyond what are professionally known as third-rate structures', and of 'every variety of plan'(Map 2).[77]

In the early nineteenth century, the Swan River was being promoted as an asset. In 1814 Rathmines was advertised as one of the handsomest and healthiest districts in the neighbourhood of the city with the river being an added attraction. Land was on offer at Williams Park with seven acres of choice ground and two acres of lawn 'divided by a mountain river running through it'.[78] Valuable insights into the mechanics of suburbanisation can be obtained from the correspondence between Lord Palmerston and his Dublin agent relating to the development of Upper Rathmines at this time. Henry John Temple, third Viscount Palmerston, who would become prime minister in 1859, inherited his father's title and estates in Dublin, Sligo and England in 1802. Since the estates he inherited were heavily encumbered, Palmerston was constantly in debt in his early years and up to middle age was somewhat obsessed with his personal finances. For this reason, the Dublin estates were very important to him. The greatest part of his income was derived from Dublin, outstripping what he earned from his Sligo estate and indeed his estate in England, and as demand for housing grew its potential was quickly realised.[79] Palmerston knew little of Ireland at first, but educated himself through extensive reading and a number of visits, beginning in 1808. Self-interest and a paternal, Whiggish interest in his tenants led him to follow keenly the day-to-day doings on his estates.[80]

As early as 1809 there were expressions of interest in developing Upper Rathmines. Developers were especially keen to build villas on what was described as the 'natural bare sod'.[81] While too far from the city for terrace building at this time, the potential for the building of villas was growing. In 1809 a Mr Miller had his land divided into small lots 'proper for an advantageous letting of them to citizens for country villas'.[82] It was not only builders who were interested in the newly opened-up land. The Palmerston agent reported that he had inquiries from dairymen, butchers and keepers of livery stables.[83] The opening up of fields by road-building or the improvement of existing roads were vital first steps in facilitating development. The correspondence records that the estate expected rents to double when roads were driven through fields.[84] Patrick Hayes, writing from Westmoreland Street in central Dublin in the summer of 1812, sought improved terms from Lord Palmerston. His eight acres fronted the road from Dr Darby's demesne wall to the River Dodder – a very narrow road with a dangerous ditch at its side. He had built a gate lodge and as soon as he had cut the harvest of grass he hoped to 'build a house or two on it'.[85]

The need for a completely new road to the Dodder became evident. To the present day, Rathmines Road Upper ends in a T-junction where a kink then links it to Dartry Road. It is likely that the road once ended here, where it turned left into the gate to old Rathmines Castle. The highly deficient Dartry Road to Classon's Bridge perhaps originated in a track to the Dodder. This is the road that the estate sought to improve. By August 1814, considerable progress was reported. A dangerous ditch was eliminated at extra expense and the road was brought into better alignment with Classon's Bridge. Improvements were made to the bridge itself and works completed to eliminate the flooding of the road near the river, which tended to happen in winter. The agent reported that all had been 'done in a manner that will, I trust, give satisfaction' to Lord Palmerston. He stated that a map of the lands had been put up in 'our commercial coffee house' and had been advertised in the newspapers, but he pointed out that the new road must be completed.[86] A number of problems arose, however. Lord Palmerston's improvements could extend only to the boundary of his estate. The usefulness of the new road would be diminished by difficulties experienced in getting the neighbouring landowner, a Mr Davies, to give over the land to extend it over Classon's Bridge.[87] By 1816, Lord Palmerston was becoming somewhat exasperated by lack of development on the extension to the road, recognising that the economic downturn caused by the ending of the French wars was, as he wrote to his Dublin agent, not a time for villa building.[88]

Not all were happy with the improvements. It is rare to hear the voice of the indigenous inhabitants of the rapidly suburbanising areas, but they looked upon road building with suspicion. Daniel Mallea, a small-time middleman, absconded owing rent, claiming that his own tenants would not pay him as they believed that the new road had left their plots open to trespassers.[89] As development gradually gathered pace again, opposition re-emerged among the indigenous population. The agent reported in June 1824 that the tenants were withholding rents as an ancient prophecy led them to believe that they would become the owners of the soil in 1825. A newcomer named Hutton, who had taken land in the area, communicated his plight to the estate. The agent explained to Lord Palmerston that Hutton had suffered much at the hands of impoverished tenants who held their land on yearly terms. They were 'enraged that a stranger should come amongst them taking the land at a higher rent than they would give for it'.[90] They had killed or stolen Hutton's cattle and he complained that 'scarcely a week passes that his gates are not broken and carried off'. The agent's solution was that, if the delayed road was made, the land could be let in lots for villas.[91]

Twenty years later, old Rathmines Castle fell victim to Lord Palmerston's desire to cash in on the resurgent villa-building market. The estate agent had taken Lord Palmerston to see the house and the land in October 1841. The agent felt that the castle could be let out for a few years more, as desired by the occupier, one John Arthur, a relative of Chief Justice Yorke who had lived there in the eighteenth century. As the agent wrote, however, 'your lordship seemed to think that they [castle and outbuildings] ought to be taken down'.[92] His lordship reiterated that the land was suitable for villas and the decision was made to demolish it. In July 1843 a Mrs Richardson, widowed sister of John Arthur, asked if she could remain in the house until it was pulled down. On 6 April 1844 Palmerston's agent reported that the old castle at Rathmines had been razed to the ground and a road made for a terrace of houses to the front of the site (Palmerston Park); the pleasure ground also to the front (the site of the later public park) had been laid out and planted. He went on to say that 'should your lordship wish to visit the property he will find a great change in its appearance'.[93] In June of the following year, villa plots were available to let on the site of the castle at £20 per acre and ground for terraces was also available.[94]

Although a certain amount of infilling was still taking place (Castlewood Park, for instance, was laid out in the 1870s and 1880s), the last major road and house-building development took place on the Palmerston estate in Upper Rathmines (Fig. 5). Although begun in the 1860s, Palmerston Road and the roads that lead from it did not reach completion for another two decades; Temple Villas, for instance, was built in the 1880s. A major developer here was Patrick Plunkett, especially on Palmerston Road.[95] Palmerston Road did not fully

follow the ancient Milltown Path, but the commissioners disallowed any encroachment on the path, leaving it intact when houses were built. It weaves its narrow way between houses to the present day. The whole area to the west of the Palmerston estate acquired the name Dartry. It was called after a house and lands of twelve acres of the same name that was the residence of Hugh McMahon and was put up for sale in 1820, some time after his death. Described as a new house with handsome gardens stocked with the choicest fruit trees on the banks of the Dodder adjoining Willan's mills, it was probably called after the townland of Dartry in Co. Monaghan, a stronghold of the McMahon family.[96] It later became the residence of William Martin Murphy, the employer of 1913 lock-out fame.

To cater for the needs of the new population, retail outlets began to appear. In 1859 it was reported that 'at the junction of Rathmines with Rathgar and Rathmines Upper, a "business town" has sprung up within the last few years, wherein all the requirements of the outward man may be satisfied'.[97] The phenomenon of shops sprouting up in front gardens to the line of the railings, with narrow alleyways between them to give access to the terraced houses behind, became a feature of Rathmines seen to the present day. No planning authority existed to oppose this practice, which was often decried. Even the Rathmines township board, from its establishment in 1847, had weak powers relating to such developments as long as they complied with sanitary regulations. The commissioners usually requested that the developer flag the pavement in front of the new structures, as when in 1867 Mr John Butler objected to 'the projection of the new building at Duggan Place' – a shop – being built by Mr Holmes; the commissioners allowed it go ahead as long as the footpath was flagged.[98]

The new residents flocking to Victorian Rathmines, as with their counterparts elsewhere, increasingly expected services for their new homes such as paved streets, public and domestic gas lighting, running water and an adequate and sanitary sewerage system. A scheme was proposed in 1839 to set up a body to provide public lighting, but was said to

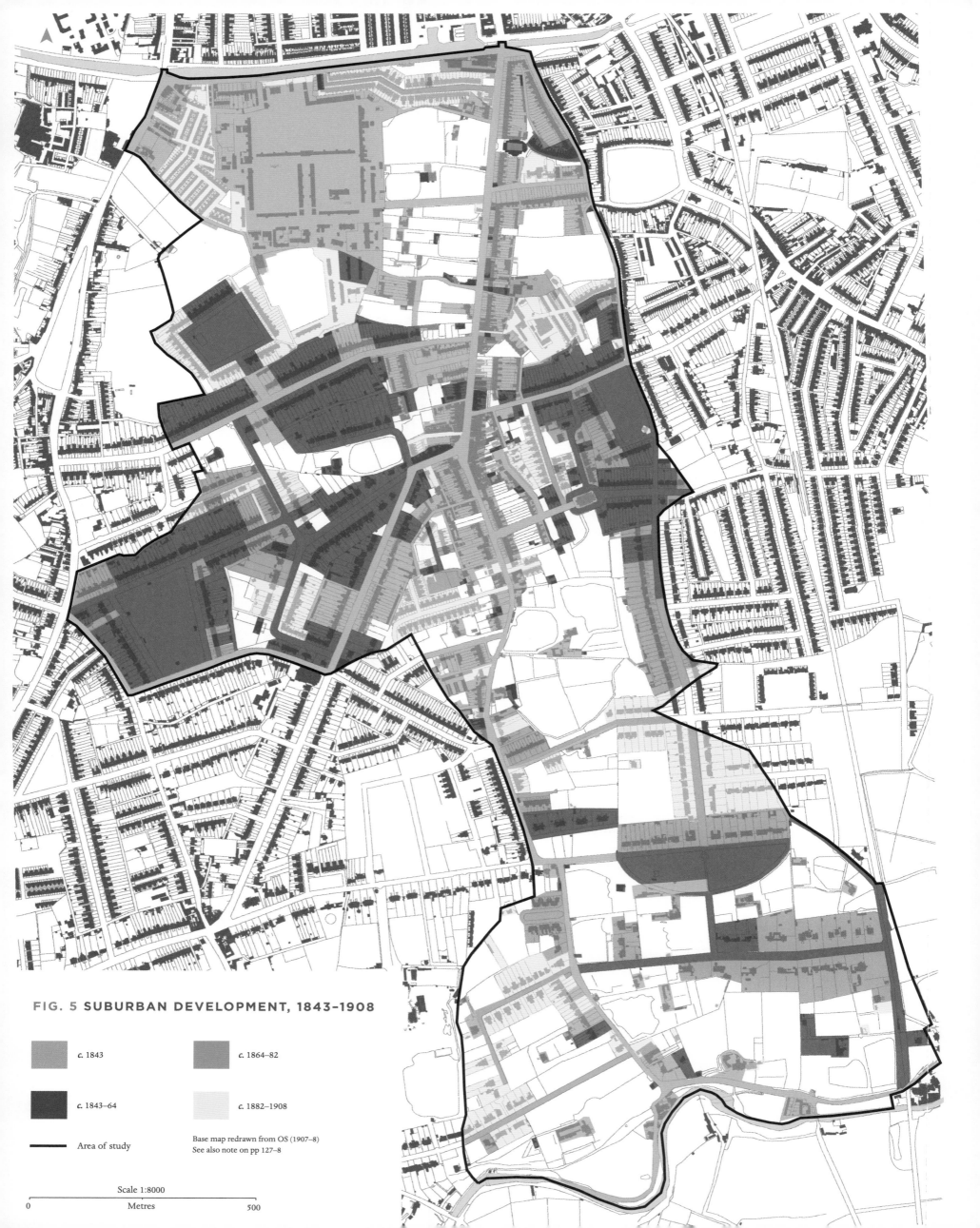

FIG. 5 SUBURBAN DEVELOPMENT, 1843–1908

| | *c.* 1843 | | *c.* 1864–82 |
| | *c.* 1843–64 | | *c.* 1882–1908 |

Area of study

Base map redrawn from OS (1907–8)
See also note on pp 127–8

Scale 1:8000

0   Metres   500

have been rejected by four hundred inhabitants of the area. A similar proposal was rejected in 1843.[99] The year 1847 might not seem like a propitious year to make another such proposal, but in fact the Great Famine made little difference to the ongoing influx of the middle classes to Rathmines. There was some distress, however, among the indigenous population. A relief committee was established and a soup kitchen set up on Rathmines Avenue. Relief roadworks for the distressed indigenous population were also carried out on Rathmines Road Lower under the Labour Rate Act (1846). Meanwhile, speculative building continued apace. The *Freeman's Journal* reported in September 1847 that houses were selling in Upper Rathmines for over £550 – thirteen years' purchase – and that there was 'anything but a diminution in the value of houses in this area'.[100]

The fashionable flight to the suburbs moved down the social scale: at first the upper classes built villa-type dwellings, followed by the middle classes moving into semi-detached and terraced houses. This put areas such as Rathmines under increasing infrastructural pressure. The existing local authority, the grand jury, a rural *ad hoc* body that met only twice a year, was totally unequal to the requirements of suburbanisation. In 1847 Rathmines township was set up under a private act of parliament (10 & 11 Vict., c. 253) championed by speculative builders, in particular Frederick Stokes, a major developer. The board of commissioners of the township would have a major impact on the topographical development of the area. Under the 1847 act, the commissioners obtained planning powers of a very general nature. For example, terraces had to be at least thirty feet from the middle of a new road, where the sewer would run. Roads were to be properly gravelled with well-formed footpaths, according to a sketch prepared by the township surveyor, before they would be taken over by the commissioners (Fig. 6). Apart from condemning dangerous buildings, the powers of the commissioners were weak, as seen in their response to the proliferation of shops.[101]

When the Rathmines township was established, public lighting was almost non-existent. The commissioners had obtained powers in the 1847 act to build their own gasworks and provide public lighting, but never availed themselves of this. Instead, almost immediately after their establishment, they contracted the Alliance and Dublin Consumers' Gas Company, which provided lighting for the city, to light the area. The first agreement required the company to provide one thousand perches of mains and two hundred lamps, 152 of which had been erected by 1852. Frequent complaints were made that the area was not lit on an equitable basis, with streets in the more affluent areas obtaining a greater concentration of lamps or ones of greater luminosity. An exception was made for lanes that were reputedly used for immoral purposes.[102] Rathmines ended its contract with the gas company and switched to electricity in 1900, building its own electricity works for the purpose. This was on land behind the town hall and close to Gulistan artisans' dwellings. Enough electricity was generated to light up to 30,000 lamps in consumers' homes, 108 arc lamps on the principal thoroughfares and 230 shorter posts on side streets. By October 1900, it was reported that two-thirds of the area had electric public lighting.[103]

The 1850s and 1860s saw huge infrastructural development, spearheaded by the Rathmines commissioners. One of the first tasks of the commissioners was the culverting of the Swan River. By 1858 the river had been largely culverted in an arched tunnel as far as the Carmelite convent ground in Ranelagh.[104] Material used on roads by the commissioners was usually dry macadam, unbound compacted stones set into the ground, and asphalt on footpaths. This material gave rise to roads that were a sea of mud in winter and were choked by clouds of dust when a vehicle passed in dry weather. As a consequence, the commissioners obtained water carts to keep down dust and erected crossings, raised sets that allowed pedestrians to cross mud-free.

Attempts by Dublin Corporation to introduce piped water to the Rathmines area had been a major catalyst in the setting up of the township, and the provision of running water was high on the commissioners' agenda. This involved an ambitious

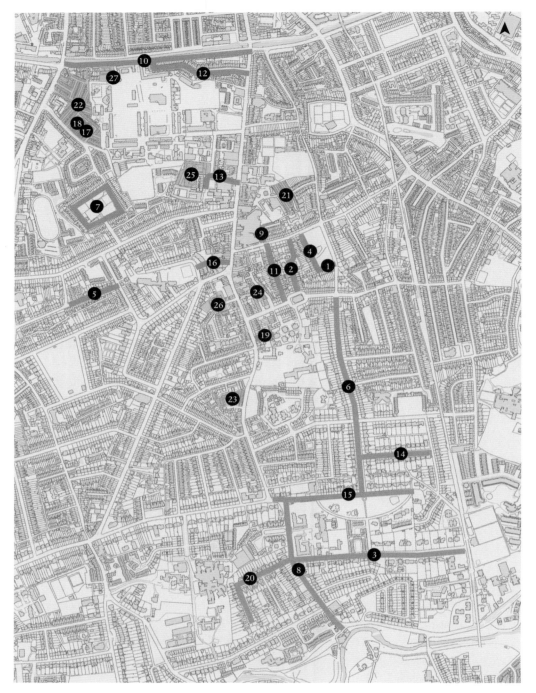

FIG. 6 STREETS ADOPTED BY UDC AND HOUSING DEVELOPMENTS

Streets adopted by Rathmines and Rathgar township commissioners/Rathmines and Rathgar Urban District Council, 1862–1922

1. Belgrave Square South, 1862
2. Cambridge Road, 1863
3. Temple Road, 1866
4. Belgrave Square West, 1871
5. Effra Road, 1871
6. Palmerston Road, 1874
7. Grosvenor Square, 1882
8. Dartry Park Road, 1882
9. Newington Lane, 1883
10 Grove Road, 1886
11. Castlewood Park, 1888
12. Grove Park Road, 1890
13. Williams Park, 1891
14. Temple Gardens, 1894
15. Palmerston Park, 1894
16. Wynnefield Road, 1898
17. Ashworth Place, 1899
18. Drummond Place, 1899
19. Summerville Park, 1903
20. St Kevin's Gardens, 1922

Source: RRTA, descriptive list by Mary Clark, appendix 1. Dates refer to when streets were adopted by township commissioners and UDC and do not indicate their initial laying out. See also note on pp 127–8

Public housing schemes

21. Gulistan Cottages, Rathmines and Rathgar UDC, 1894
22. Harold's Cross Cottages, Dublin Artisans' Dwelling Company, 1884–5
23. Hollyfield Buildings, Rathmines and Rathgar UDC, 1903–c. 1980
24. Church Gardens, Rathmines and Rathgar UDC, 1928
25. Mount Anthony Flats, Iveagh Trust, 1962
26. Rathmines Avenue Flats, Dublin Corporation, 1962
27. Grove Road Flats, Dublin Corporation, 1963

Source: dates are of first reference from Topographical information

Scale 1:15,000

0   Metres   600

and expensive engineering feat completed in 1863. A reservoir was built on the eighth lock of the Grand Canal at Gallanstown, mains laid and the water piped the 8 km to houses in Rathmines. Complaints about the quality and pressure of the water led to the provision of a replacement supply. The River Dodder was dammed at Bohernabreena in the Dublin mountains and the water was turned on in Rathmines in 1887. The scheme proved enormously costly owing to engineering complexities at the site and litigation brought by Dodder mill owners, forcing the commissioners to postpone other capital projects such as the building of a new town hall.[105]

The introduction of running water exacerbated sewage problems as more and more householders installed water closets. Up to then, human waste was disposed of in cess pits under dry closets in back gardens. These pits were cleaned out by night soil men but were often neglected, resulting in human waste entering the soil and water courses. The Swan River became an open sewer and then a culverted one as the density of houses increased. The culverting of the Swan River and the embanking of the Dodder improved drainage, but by the 1860s a bolder approach was required. A main drainage scheme, however, would be expensive. Lying between Rathmines and the sea was the

Pembroke township (founded in 1863), both areas being in the basin of the Dodder and the Swan. Pembroke was also in need of drainage, so a joint scheme was proposed and agreed upon. Under legislation, a Rathmines and Pembroke main drainage board was established and a drainage system was completed in 1879. The higher ground in Rathmines was drained through the Swan sewer and on through Pembroke, where it was then pumped and discharged into Dublin Bay near the South Bull Wall at ebb tide.[106]

The pace of improvements in transport and communications quickened in the 1850s and 1860s. The arrival of omnibuses heralded the era in which those commuting regularly to the city for business no longer required a private means of transport to do so. Omnibuses became very popular in the 1850s, when a number of competing companies such as Anderson's, Wilson's and the Shamrock Company plied the Rathmines route. By 1850, omnibuses from the General Post Office passed up Rathmines Road every fifteen minutes.[107] The importance of Rathmines as a growing suburb can be seen in the fact that the first tramway in the city was opened in 1872, linking the city centre with Garville Avenue in the enlarged township, which had been extended to include Rathgar in 1862 (Map 23).[108] A notable development was the building of the first line in the Dublin area that did not go to the city centre, but linked Upper Rathmines to Ballsbridge. This was grandly known as the 'Rathmines to the Sea' project. The tramway was electrified in 1900 (Map 24).

It has been shown that railways had only a limited impact on suburban development, omnibuses and trams being the major factor as far as transport was concerned. During the railway mania in Ireland in the 1850s and 1860s, many schemes for trains to traverse the Rathmines township were put before the commissioners. The only one ever built was the inland line of the Dublin, Wicklow and Wexford line, which ran from Harcourt Street to Bray and opened in 1854. This had little impact on commuting to and from Rathmines, as Milltown station, opened in 1860, was too remote from the main commuting area and the more convenient Rathmines and Ranelagh station was not opened until 1896.[109]

In 1857 an application was made to the post office to have pillar boxes erected on the leading roads in the township. The following year, the commissioners agreed to have a finger post erected at the junction of Grosvenor, Charleville and Rathgar Roads pointing the way to Kenilworth Square. The area was surveyed for sites for similar signage. Between 1864 and 1866, telegraph poles were erected and a temporary telegraph office set up in the town hall.[110]

By the 1880s the activity of private developers was slackening as much of the area had been built on (Map 4). The period to about 1910 was characterised by increased activity by the township commissioners. While the purpose of the creation of the township had been to facilitate residential development by the upper and middle classes, there was a constant need for manual workers as domestic servants, stablemen and various other unskilled roles. While some travelled to the suburb on a daily basis, many wished to live near their employment. This need was usually met by building small rows and terraces of cottages in lanes behind the big houses, where they were kept out of sight and out of mind, such as Aylwards Cottages, Castlewood Terrace and Coffey's Cottages at Church Place. As public transport – usually at first patronised by the wealthy – developed, the need to keep horses declined and many stables began to be turned into dwellings for the working classes. Stables often had a residential role as mews, that is, with the stableman or coachman living above the stable at the end of the back gardens of the larger houses. As early as 1809, a Hugh Holmes entered a legal transaction concerning a house, garden and a small house formerly a stable in Rathmines.[111] From the mid-1850s, a time that saw a huge increase in the availability of omnibuses, the commissioners began to receive numerous complaints of stables being converted to dwellings without permission.[112]

FIG. 7 VALUATION OF BUILDINGS IN RATHMINES, *c.* 1900

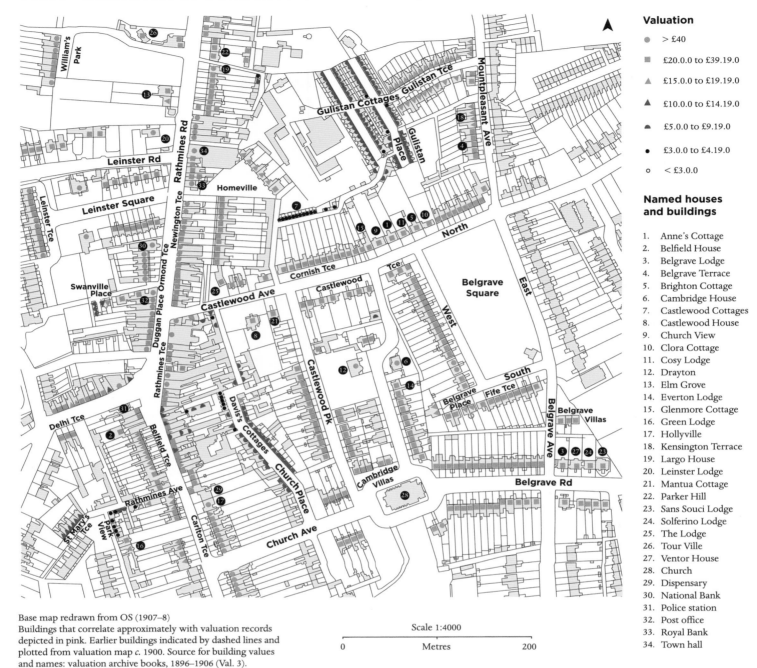

Valuation

● > £40

■ £20.0.0 to £39.19.0

▲ £15.0.0 to £19.19.0

▲ £10.0.0 to £14.19.0

◆ £5.0.0 to £9.19.0

● £3.0.0 to £4.19.0

○ < £3.0.0

Named houses and buildings

1. Anne's Cottage
2. Belfield House
3. Belgrave Lodge
4. Belgrave Terrace
5. Brighton Cottage
6. Cambridge House
7. Castlewood Cottages
8. Castlewood House
9. Church View
10. Clora Cottage
11. Cosy Lodge
12. Drayton
13. Elm Grove
14. Everton Lodge
15. Glenmore Cottage
16. Green Lodge
17. Hollyville
18. Kensington Terrace
19. Largo House
20. Leinster Lodge
21. Mantua Cottage
22. Parker Hill
23. Sans Souci Lodge
24. Solferino Lodge
25. The Lodge
26. Tour Ville
27. Ventor House
28. Church
29. Dispensary
30. National Bank
31. Police station
32. Post office
33. Royal Bank
34. Town hall

Base map redrawn from OS (1907–8)
Buildings that correlate approximately with valuation records depicted in pink. Earlier buildings indicated by dashed lines and plotted from valuation map *c.* 1900. Source for building values and names: valuation archive books, 1896–1906 (Val. 3).

Scale 1:4000

0   Metres   200

In 1884 the Dublin Artisans Dwelling Company constructed 120 artisans' cottages in Harold's Cross and in 1887 Rathmines applied for loans under the 1885 Housing Act also with the intention of building artisans' dwellings.[113] This was a break with the past, as the township had been set up to cater for middle-class households. A house known as Gulistan, occupied by a family called Hallinan and located just behind the commissioners' town hall and yard, became available. In 1895–8, the commissioners built artisans' dwellings there, but not without opposition. Residents in the adjacent Gulistan Terrace, shopkeepers on Rathmines Road and the nearby Leinster Cricket Club all objected, and the agent for the Meath estate had reservations about building housing of this class in such a prominent part of Rathmines (Fig. 7). Despite such powerful opposition, the scheme went ahead and sixty-three cottages were built.[114] Further schemes saw the completion of what were termed labourers' dwellings in Hollyfield in Upper Rathmines in 1903 and in 1921, after the hiatus of the First World War, the commencement of slum clearances at Church Place and the building of small houses.[115]

The lack of recreational, cultural and education facilities had been pointed out in 1868:

> It is singular that in the great township of Rathmines there is neither a hotel, clubhouse, public library or concert room. Would it not be wise to induce the young people to take amusement near home, and save journeys to and from the city?[116]

In fact, in the previous year, the commissioners built a modest town hall on their premises, which could be used for 'every useful public purpose' except public worship.[117] In the latter part of the nineteenth century, the municipality began to cater for wider leisure and cultural needs. The Rathmines commissioners adopted the Public Libraries Act (1855) in 1887 to celebrate the diamond jubilee of Queen Victoria and opened a public library at 53 Rathmines Road. Owing to increased demand, it moved to larger premises at 67 Rathmines Road in 1899. When generous grants for building libraries became available from the Andrew Carnegie Trust, Rathmines erected a fine library on a prestigious site opposite the town hall at the corner of Rathmines Road and Leinster Road.[118]

The new library building had attached to it the College of Commerce and both were opened in 1913. The new college was part of a government movement to promote technical education and local government bodies were used to that end. Rathmines involvement began when the commissioners established a school in the recently closed premises of Dr Charles Benson's well-known Rathmines School on Rathmines Road, founded in 1858. Attempting to cater for the social and occupational requirements of the area, Rathmines technical school was especially geared towards those entering the commercial world, particularly accounting, banking and insurance.[119] A later notable educational presence that endured until very recently was the Church of Ireland College of Education on the grounds of 'new Rathmines Castle' in Upper Rathmines. Its move from Kildare Place in 1963 had led to the demolition of the castle.[120] The Rathmines commissioners were also conscious of the large number of domestic servants working in the area and the need to provide opportunities to help them to improve their skills. Under the technical education legislation, a school of cookery and domestic economy was opened at Carleton Terrace in 1908. It relocated to the new technical school on Rathmines Road Lower in 1913.

There was a growing interest in the latter part of the nineteenth century in opening up green spaces as amenities for the urban public. Landscaped gardens and fresh air were regarded as having moral and health benefits, especially among the working classes. While the middle-class area of Rathmines, with its large back and front gardens, was less in need of this than the overcrowded city, the commissioners were nevertheless anxious to open public parks. In the 1870s, efforts to obtain Kenilworth Square as a public park foundered on the objections of a small number of vocal residents of the area. In 1881 Lady Mount Temple's agents offered six acres adjacent to the site of old Rathmines Castle for use as a public park to be known as Palmerston Park. The council agreed, but Lord Mount Temple died shortly afterwards and negotiations stalled. The land was left untended and in 1891, after complaints from residents about its wild state, the council took up the matter again with Lady Mount Temple. This effort succeeded and the park was opened in 1895.

Complementing the efforts of the township, numerous private sporting organisations and clubs for tennis and other sports opened in the area's large open squares. Of particular note is the Leinster Cricket Club, which was founded in 1852 in Grosvenor Square and moved to Rathmines Road Lower in 1865, where it has remained ever since, admirably declining the blandishments of developers with an eye on its potentially lucrative ground. Cinema productions were shown in the new Rathmines Town Hall in its early years, but the silver screen really took off in the area with the building in 1913 of Ireland's first purpose-built cinema, The Princess, on Rathmines Road Lower, to be followed by The Stella cinema and ballroom in 1923.[121]

The skyline of Rathmines was changed forever when a magnificent new town hall was built on the somewhat restricted footprint of the old one in 1897. Where the commissioners could not go wide, they went up. A four-faced clock by Chancellors of Dublin was placed in a soaring sandstone tower. The new clock tower quickly rivalled the massive

FIG. 8 **CIVIC NUCLEUS**

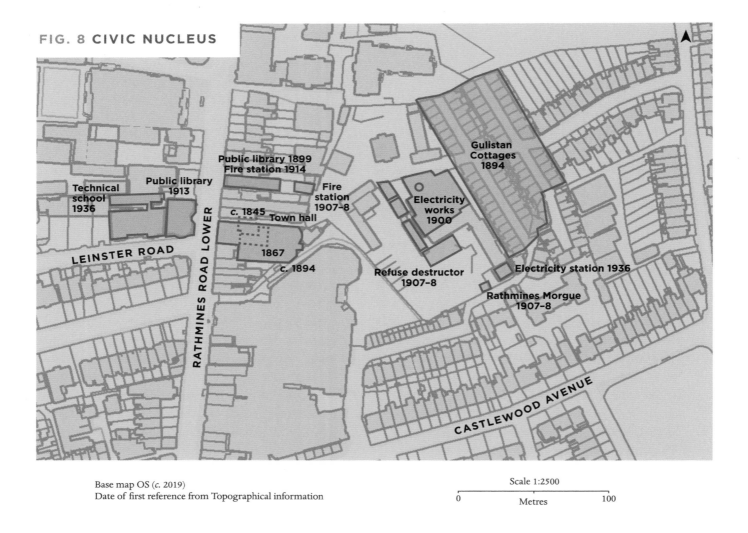

Base map OS (*c.* 2019)
Date of first reference from Topographical information

Scale 1:2500

0   Metres   100

dome of the Catholic church on Rathmines Road Lower (built in the 1850s and restored after a devastating fire in 1922) as an emblem of Rathmines.[122] The energetic activity of the township in the late nineteenth and early twentieth centuries led to a cluster of municipal buildings around the town hall in Rathmines Road Lower, shifting the centre of gravity of the area farther north for the second time. This cluster consisted of a new town hall, public library and commercial college opposite it, a fire station alongside, large yard, electricity works, refuse destructor and artisans' dwellings behind and morgue adjacent (Fig. 8).[123]

One notable non-residential development was a feature of twentieth-century Rathmines. Industry had been present in the world-famous Grubb's astronomical works in Observatory Lane, which moved from Ranelagh to Rathmines in the 1860s. The 1930s saw the development of a small industrial sector (Map 5). Some of this was related to British firms setting up production in Ireland in response to the economic war. These enterprises clustered in a zone on the west side of Rathmines Road Lower, from Portobello Bridge to the Williams Park junction. G.A. Brittain's motor works took up a site on the former Grove House to assemble Morris and Riley cars. Mackintosh's manufactured confectionery on Ardee Road, farther up Rathmines Road. The nearby Kelso laundry, built in 1914, was the first modern industrial building in the area and Kodak cameras started production in a fine Art Deco building in 1930. Another industry, probably set up owing to the economic war, was the Rathmines Paper Manufacturers Ltd at Parker Hill, which later became the Dublin Box Company. Manufacture of the famous Tayto crisps began off Mountpleasant Avenue in 1956.

The period of the War of Independence saw significant decline of the Unionist and Protestant population, which had been a feature of Rathmines for many years. In 1918 the area returned the only Unionist member of parliament outside Ulster and the two members elected for the University of Dublin. The Unionists finally lost control of the now urban district council (the commissioners were constituted as such in 1898) in the local government elections of 1920. One reason for the exodus of the upper-middle class, largely Protestant, population

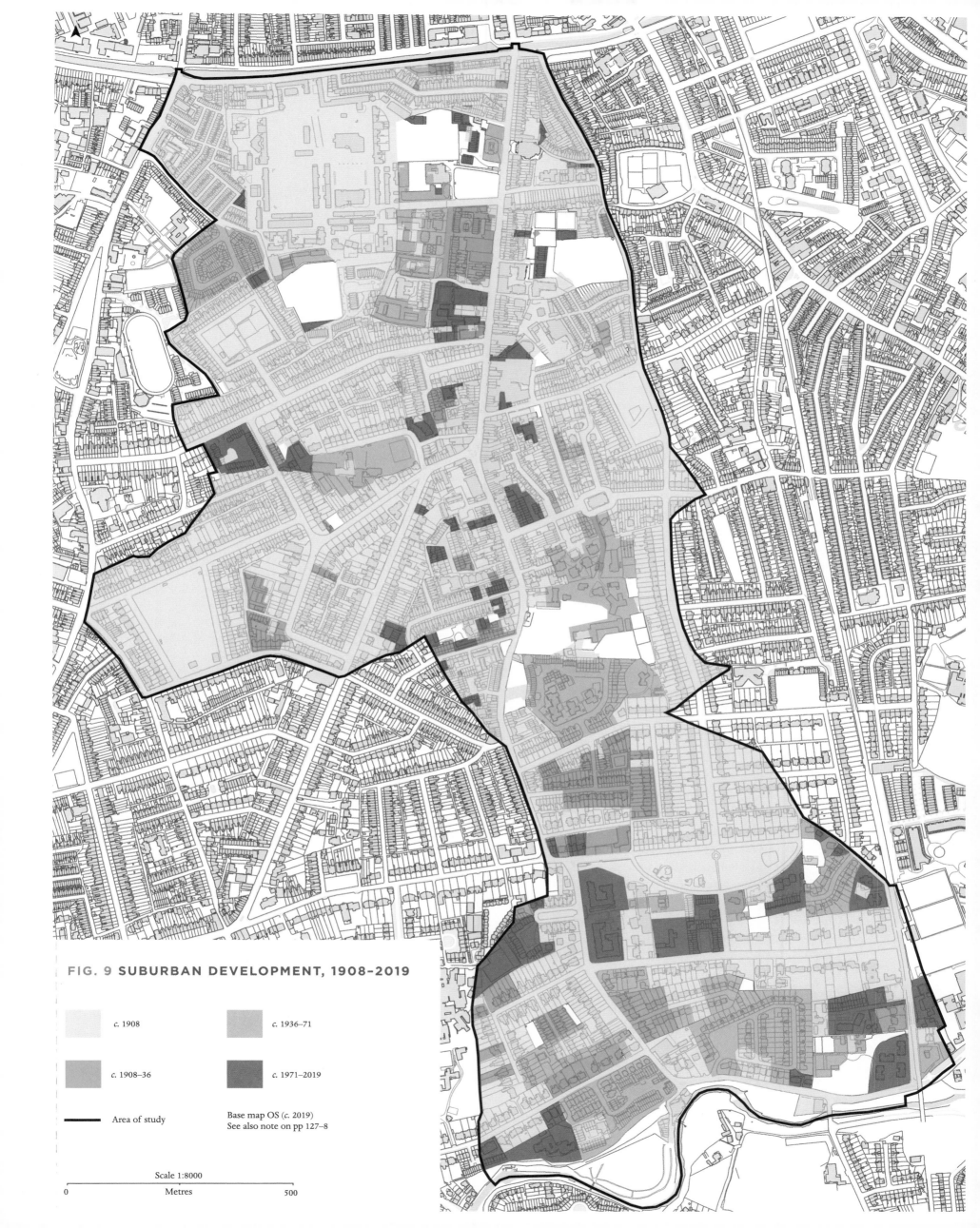

FIG. 9 SUBURBAN DEVELOPMENT, 1908–2019

c. 1908

c. 1936–71

c. 1908–36

c. 1971–2019

Area of study

Base map OS (c. 2019)
See also note on pp 127–8

Scale 1:8000

0   Metres   500

was a feeling of alienation in post-independence Ireland as a whole, leading to resettlement in Britain. Other factors included the increased cost of maintaining large and often decaying houses, and the disappearance of the cheap labour required to run them on a day-to-day basis. The arrival of the motor car brought more modern and compact houses farther from the city within range of commuters.[124] Their place was taken by a new class of young civil servants, teachers, nurses and students from the country who found flats and bedsits convenient to the city centre in the newly vacated terraces of big houses in Lower Rathmines. This trend continued into the 1950s and 1960s as landlords acquired multiple properties to subdivide, leading to a proliferation of even smaller flats, bedsits and boarding houses (Maps 25–7).[125]

In 1930, under the Free State government, the township was swept away, seen as an anachronism from colonial times, and Rathmines came under the administration of Dublin Corporation. While Upper Rathmines escaped much of the move to multiple occupancy and retained many family homes, the rise of the area as Dublin's main 'flatland' continued apace (Fig. 9). The increase in the number of young, single office workers and students, and the decline in young families, saw a two-tier situation develop with a cosmopolitan, shifting, young population living side-by-side with an aging, more indigenous cohort. The Victorian shops were replaced by convenience stores and supermarkets, and by fast-food outlets often catering to a late-night clientele. This trend culminated in the arrival of the landmark Swan Shopping Centre in 1983.

The revival of a civic spirit related to pride in locality and the attempted resurrection of the so-called 'villages' of Dublin since the 1960s has had a limited impact on Rathmines (Map 6). The recent influx of non-Irish born residents has given new life to many of the old terraces on the east side of Rathmines Road and elsewhere. The long-term dilapidated condition of many of these – among them Rathmines' oldest houses – gives cause for concern, however. The return to single-family use of houses, championed especially by the late activist Deirdre Kelly in the 1970s, has failed to materialise to any appreciable degree. Many are just too big for such adaptation to be economically feasible, but the overall cosmopolitan vibrancy of present-day Rathmines, witnessed especially as one wanders down its long central thoroughfare on weekend nights, lends hope for the future.

Notes

[1] *Alen's reg.*, p. 295.
[2] Murphy and Potterton, pp 33–6.
[3] Geraldine Stout and Matthew Stout, 'Patterns in the past: County Dublin, 5000 BC–1000 AD' in Aalen and Whelan, pp 16–19.
[4] Ball, ii, p. 118.
[5] J. Huband Smith, 'On the castle and manor of Baggotrath' in *PRIA*, vi (1853–7), p. 311.
[6] P.W. Joyce, 'On changes and corruptions in Irish topographical names' in *PRIA*, ix (1864–6), p. 226.
[7] Hampshire Record Office, Winchester, MS 43M48/2839.
[8] Raymond Gillespie, 'Historical introduction: the archbishops of Dublin and their estate maps' in Refaussé and Clark, p. 28.
[9] Patrick Healy, *Pre-Norman grave-slabs and cross-inscribed stones in the Dublin region*, ed. Kieran Swords (Tallaght, 2009), p. 87.
[10] Bradley, pp 43–4.
[11] Paul MacCotter, 'The church lands of the diocese of Dublin: reconstruction and history' in Seán Duffy (ed.), *Medieval Dublin XIII: proceedings of the Friends of Medieval Dublin symposium 2011* (Dublin, 2013), p. 95.
[12] H.B. Clarke, 'External influences and relations, c. 1200 to c. 1500' in John Crawford and Raymond Gillespie (eds), *St Patrick's Cathedral, Dublin: a history* (Dublin, 2009), p. 74.
[13] *Court bk*, pp viii–ix.
[14] Murphy and Potterton, pp 179–92.
[15] H.F. Berry, 'The Merchant Tailors' Gild: that of St John the Baptist, Dublin, 1418–1841' in *JRSAI*, viii (1918), p. 52.
[16] *Alen's reg.*, p. 234.
[17] Mills, 1889a, p. 33.
[18] *Alen's reg.*, p. 164.
[19] F. Elrington Ball, *The judges in Ireland, 1221–1921* (2 vols, London, 1926), i, p. 58.
[20] Ball, ii, p. 100; Ball, *Judges*, i, p. 88.
[21] Mills, 1889a, p. 36.
[22] *Alen's reg.*, pp 172, 234.
[23] *The Gentleman's Magazine 1789*, p. 500.
[24] *Alen's reg.*, p. 170.
[25] Mills, 1889a, p. 36.
[26] Gillespie, 'Historical introduction', p. 22.
[27] Ronan, pp 297–8.
[28] Ibid.
[29] *DIB*, i, p. 752.
[30] Ronan, p. 199.
[31] Ibid., p. 24.
[32] *Alen's reg.*, p. 303.

33 The Law Dictionary, available at https://thelawdictionary.org/suffering-a-recovery/, last accessed 18 Aug. 2019; Ball, ii, p. 101; D'Alton, p. 391.

34 *DIB*, viii, pp 369–70.

35 L.J. Arnold, *The restoration land settlement in County Dublin, 1660–1688* (Dublin, 1993), p. 25; 'Radcliffe (Ratcliffe), George (1594–1657)', History of Parliament Online, available at www.historyofparliamentonline.org/volume/1604-1629/member/radcliffe-george-1594-1657, last accessed 18 Aug. 2019.

36 *Cal. SP Ire., 1633–47*, p. 224.

37 Ball, ii, p. 101.

38 Brunskill, p. 25.

39 Quoted in Joyce, p. 188.

40 Ball, ii, p. 106.

41 *Census, 1659*, pp 320–78; W.G. Smyth, 'Exploring the social and cultural topographies of sixteenth- and seventeenth-century County Dublin' in Aalen and Whelan, p. 165.

42 *DIB*, ix, pp 296–7.

43 Palmerston papers, BR 144/4/6.

44 Palmerston estate, Dublin rent book, 1790, 1791. NLI, MS 1566.

45 Barry, p. 6; G.N. Wright, *A guide to the county of Wicklow* (London, 1822), p. 146.

46 *FJ* 9.1.1822.

47 Kelly, p. 235; plaque *in situ*.

48 Armstrong 3.

49 Meyler, i, p. 43.

50 Archer, p. 117.

51 Barry, p. 7.

52 Joyce, p. 170.

53 M.V. Ronan, *An apostle of Catholic Dublin: Father Henry Young* (Dublin, 1944), p. 95.

54 *FJ* 6.5.1800.

55 Ibid. 11.9.1815.

56 Lavin, p. 26.

57 Archer, p. 117.

58 Meyler, i, p. 43.

59 Armstrong 4.

60 Ibid.

61 Ibid.

62 *FJ* 14.6.1823; Lavin, p. 19.

63 Kelly, p. 196.

64 Lewis, ii, p. 504.

65 Galavan, p. 13.

66 Little, p. 42.

67 RRTM, UDC/1/Min1/2, 5 Apr. 1854.

68 Little, pp 47–50.

69 Ball, ii, p. 107.

70 Meyler, i, p. 43.

71 Ibid., p. 44.

72 *FJ* 10.11.1829.

73 Smith, p. 18.

74 RRTM, UDC/1/Min 1/3, 13 Feb. 1867.

75 Ibid., 23 Jan. 1867.

76 *Ir. Builder* 1.11.1869.

77 Ibid. 1.8.1859.

78 *FJ* 24.3.1814.

79 David Brown, *Palmerston: a biography* (New Haven, 2010), p. 79.

80 Ibid., pp 87–8.

81 Palmerston papers, BR 144/1/10/1–2.

82 Ibid.

83 Ibid.

84 Palmerston papers, BR 144/1/8.

85 Ibid., BR 144/2/1/1–2.

86 Ibid., BR 144/3/4.

87 Ibid., BR 139/30.

88 Ibid., BR 139/131.

89 Ibid., BR 144/3/4.

90 Ibid., BR 144/6/1/8.

91 Ibid.

92 Ibid., BR 144/9/6/1–3.

93 Ibid., BR 144/9/29.

94 Ibid., BR 144/9/31/1–2.

95 Kelly, pp 223–33.

96 *FJ* 7.1.1820.

97 *Ir. Builder* 1.8.1859.

98 RRTM, UDC/1/Min 1/3, 28 Aug. 1867.

99 *FJ* 28.12.1843.

100 Ibid. 16.9.1847.

101 Ó Maitiú, p. 78.

102 Ibid., p. 103.

103 Ibid., pp 166–7.

104 RRTM, UDC/1/Min 1/2, 3.2.1858.

105 Ibid., pp 95–6.

106 Ibid., pp 101–2.

107 *FJ* 4.2.1851, 31.12.1852, 16.9.1854.

108 Ó Maitiú, p. 148.

109 Ibid., pp 146–7.

110 RRTM, UDC/1/Min/2, 1 July 1857, 2 June 1858, 15 June 1864, 11 Apr. 1866.

111 RD 609/566/423205.

112 RRTM, UDC/1/Min/2, 6 Sept. 1854.

113 Hofman, p. 60.

114 RRTM, UDC/1/Min 1/7, 6 Aug. 1890; RRTM, UDC/1/Min 1/7, 4 Aug. 1897.

115 Ó Maitiú, p. 157.

116 *Rathmines Free Press* 18.11.1922.

117 RRTM, UDC/1/Min 1/3, 30 Oct. 1867.

118 Ó Maitiú, pp 183–4.

119 Ibid., pp 175–7.

120 Parkes, p. 182.

121 Kelly, pp 197–201.

122 Ibid., pp 162–3.

123 Ó Maitiú, p. 187.

124 Kelly, p. 15.

125 Lavin, p. 9.

Overleaf: 'Cullen's Castle, near Cullen's wood', 1772, by Gabriel Beranger (National Library of Ireland)

Topographical information

From medieval times onwards references to the changing topography of Rathmines can be found in a wide range of documentary sources including maps. The following section, included across the suburbs series, draws from many of these sources, collecting information on topographical features that originated before *c.* 1970 and collating them under twenty-two standardised headings. The gazetteer format enables individual sites to be followed through over time, by theme, giving reference information in each case. The methodology upon which the gazetteer is constructed is introduced below with further notes on pp 128–9. These principles follow the pattern of the main Irish Historic Towns Atlas series, allowing links to be made between the city of Dublin and its suburbs.

The area covered by the Topographical information includes part of the former manor of Colonia/St Sepulchre and the parish of St Peter. It is bounded to the north by the Grand Canal, to the west by Harold's Cross Road, to the south by the River Dodder and to the east by Mountpleasant Avenue/Palmerston Road, and is framed by the existing network of townland boundaries. The area under study includes the townlands of Rathmines East, Rathmines West, Rathmines South, Portobello and Harold's Cross East. A portion of Ranelagh North has been included and a small part of Rathmines West has been excluded to follow the line of Mountpleasant Avenue Lower and Leicester Avenue respectively.

Sections **1–9** give information on the suburb as a whole including various placename forms, legal status and population figures. Section **10** tabulates streets by their present-day name in alphabetical order. Sections **11–22** are concerned with functions of the suburb, such as religion, manufacturing and education, with a select list of residences provided at the end. Entries in these sections are laid out chronologically by categories: for example, mills are listed before cloth manufactories, because the oldest mill predates the oldest cloth manufactory.

Sites are located, where possible, according to their orientation to the nearest street and by grid reference (these relate to the eastings and northings shown on Map 3, pp 88–9). Abbreviated source-references are explained in the bibliography and general abbreviations on pp 132–41.

1. NAME

Early spellings

Le Rath 1313 (*Alen's reg.*, 164).
Mean Rath 1326 (Mills, 1889b, 124).
Meen Rath 1326 (*Alen's reg.*, 172).
Raith 1326 (*Alen's reg.*, 171).
Menesrath 1399 (*Alen's reg.*, 234).
Moenesrath 1399 (*Alen's reg.*, 234).
Meinierath 1529–34 (*Alen's reg.*, 294).
Rathmayne 1550 (*Fiants, Edw. VI*, 653).
Rathmyne 1553 (*Fiants, Edw. VI*, 1242).
Meynsrath 1611 (D'Alton, 778).
Rathmynes 1649 (*Memorials*, ii, 161), 1659 (*Census, 1659*, 380).
Ramines 1661 (*Cal. SP Ire.*, *1660–62*, 223).
RatMaigan 1836 (OSN).
Ráth Ó Máine 1905 (Laoide, 108).

Current spellings

Ráth Maonais
Rathmines

Derivation

Ráth or ringfort in the possession of the De Meones family early 14th cent. (Mills, 1889a, 36).

2. LEGAL STATUS

Part of manor of Colonia/St Sepulchre of archbishop of Dublin 1171 (*Court bk*, vii).
Township 1847 (10 & 11 Vict., c. 253).
Urban District Council 1899 under Local Government (Ireland) Act 1898 (61 & 62 Vict., c. 37).
Part of Dublin municipal ward under Local Government (Dublin) Act 1930 (27/1930).

3. PARLIAMENTARY STATUS

Part of County Dublin constituency until 1885 (D'Alton, 14, 24; Walker 1, vii–viii).
Part of South County Dublin constituency 1885–1918 (Walker 1, ix).
Parliamentary constituency of Rathmines 1918–19 (Walker 2, 293).
Part of Dublin County constituency 1920 (Walker 2, 293).
Part of Dublin constituency 1923–34 (Walker 2, 294).
Part of Dublin Townships constituency 1935 (Walker 2, 298).
Part of Dublin South-East constituency 1947–74 (Walker 2, 298).
Part of Dublin South constituency 1980 (Walker 2, 299).
Part of Dublin South-East constituency 1983 (Walker 2, 299).
Part of Dublin Bay South constituency 2013 (Electoral Act, 2013).

4. PROPRIETORIAL STATUS

Richard de Welton granted 100 acres of arable land and 5 acres of pasture at 'le Rath' by John Wogan in 1313 (*Alen's reg.*, 164).
Ráth came into possession of De Meones family, from Richard de Welton, in early 14th cent. (Ball, ii, 100).
Part obtained by earls of Meath by 1600 (Ronan, 199).
Part obtained by George Radcliffe in 1630s (*Cal. SP Ire., 1633–47*, 224); inherited by Thomas Radcliffe in 1657 (*DIB*); inherited by Margaret Trappes in 1679 (Palmerston papers, BR 138/3/1–3); inherited by Sir John Temple 1701 (Palmerston papers, BR 138/8).

5. MUNICIPAL BOUNDARY

Township boundary, area of the barony of Uppercross in the parish of St Peter with exception of Milltown, defined 1847 (10 & 11 Vict., c. 253; Ó Maitiú, 36). Boundary marker of township of Rathmines, Dodder R. bank 1847 (plaque). Mapped in 1881 (*Mun. bound. comm.*, 56); Rathmines Township mapped in 1890 (Thom map).
Rathmines and Rathgar Urban District boundary mapped in 1907 (OS).

6. ADMINISTRATIVE LOCATION

Dyflinnarskíri (Dublinshire) *c.* 1000 (Bradley, 43–4).
County: Dublin, shired in 1210 (D'Alton, 12).
Barony: Uppercross 1837 (Lewis, ii, 503).
Civil parish: St Kevin's 1654–6 (*CS*, vii, 308); united parish of St Peter and St Kevin 1837 (Lewis, ii, 503). St Peter's 1843 (OS).
Townlands: Haroldscross East, Portobello, Rathmines East, Rathmines South, Rathmines West 1836 (OSN). Mapped in 1843 (OS).
Poor law union: South Dublin, formed in 1839 (*Annual rept*, 301).
Poor law electoral division: Rathmines 1849 (*Boundary comm.*, 18).
District electoral division: Rathmines and Rathgar UDC 1898 (61 & 62 Vict., c. 37). Rathmines UDC 1900 (63 & 64 Vict., c. 264). Pembroke-Rathmines 2013 (*Local electoral area rept 2013*, 41). Rathgar-Rathmines 2018 (*Local electoral area rept 2018*, 21).
Dublin Corporation 1930 (Local Government (Dublin) Act).

7. ADMINISTRATIVE DIVISIONS

Wards: Rathmines, Rathgar 1862 (25 & 26 Vict., c. 25); Rathmines East, Rathmines West 1885 (Ó Maitiú, 130). Rathmines East, Rathmines West, Rathfarnham 1936 (OS).

8. POPULATION

1659	12[1]	1901	19,269[9]	1979	33,799
1821	1,108[2]	1911	37,840	1981	33,293
1831	1,600[3]	1926	39,984	1986	32,006
1837	1,600[4]	1936	45,629[10]	1991	33,542
1841	4,721[5]	1946	43,269[11]	1996	35,069
1851	5,765	1951	42,959	2002	36,367
1861	8,853	1956	37,606	2006	35,567
1871	17,330[6]	1961	37,271	2011	36,260
1881	19,779[7]	1966	38,797	2016	38,212
1891	27,796[8]	1971	36,798		

(Source: *Census*, unless otherwise stated.)

NOTES

[1] *Census*, 1659, 380.
[2] Rathmines village (same for housing in 1821).
[3] Town of Rathmines.
[4] Lewis, ii, 503.
[5] For **8** Population and **9** Housing in 1841, 1851 and 1861, returns for Rathmines East, West and South, Harold's Cross East and West (computed as one in *Census*) and Portobello townlands have been added together.
[6] Rathmines Ward.
[7] Rathmines Ward.
[8] Rathmines and Rathgar Township.
[9] Rathmines and Rathgar Urban District 1901 to 1936 inclusive.
[10] Rathmines and Rathgar DED East and West have been added together.
[11] Rathmines East and West DED are added together from 1946 onwards.

9. HOUSING

Number of houses

	Inhabited	Uninhabited	Building	Total
1821	149	12	–	161
1831	213	7	8	228
1841	748	79	9	836
1851	838	56	15	909
1861	1,121	76	31	1,228
1871	2,552	132	14	2,698
1881	3,089	269	27	3,385
1891[1]	4,608	197	21	4,826
1901[2]	5,651	342	46	6,039
1911	6,533	94	16	6,643

	1st-class	2nd-class	3rd-class	4th-class	Unoccupied	Total
1841	207	463	69	9	79	827
1851	232	524	72	11	71	910
1861	322	724	75	–	107	1,228

Classes as defined in 1861 *Census*:
4th: predominantly mud cabins with 1 room and window only.
3rd: better, with 2–4 rooms and windows.
2nd: good, with 5–9 rooms and windows.
1st: all houses of a better description than classes 2–4.

(Source: *Census*, unless otherwise stated.)

NOTES

[1] Rathmines and Rathgar Township.
[2] Rathmines and Rathgar Urban District in 1901 and 1911.

10. STREETS

Ardee Road/Bóthar Bhaile Átha Fhirdhia (Rathmines Rd Lower W., 715468, 732037). Ardee Road 1920 (*Thom*), 1936–*c.* 2019 (OS). Ardee Road/Bóthar Bhaile Átha Fhirdhia 2021 (Logainm).

Armstrong Street/Sráid Armstrong (Harold's Cross Rd E., 714874, 732323). Armstrong Street 1898 (Thom map), 1907–*c.* 2019 (OS). Armstrong Street/Sráid Thréanlamhaigh 2021 (nameplate). Armstrong Street/Sráid Armstrong 2021 (Logainm).

Ashworth Place/Plás Ashworth (Harold's Cross Rd E., 714952, 732148). Ashworth Place 1899 (RRTM (7), 1.11.1899), 1907–*c.* 2019 (OS). Ashworth Place/Plás Aisbhoirt 2021 (nameplate). Ashworth Place/Plás Ashworth 2021 (Logainm).

Barrack Avenue Rathmines Rd Lower, site unknown, possibly same as Military Road (*q.v.*). Barrack Avenue 1847 (*FJ* 12.6.1847).

Belgrave Avenue/Ascaill Belgrave (Rathmines Rd Upper E., 715956, 731542). Belgrave Avenue 1852 (*Thom*), 1882–*c.* 2019 (OS). Belgrave Avenue/Ascal Belgrave 2021 (nameplate). Belgrave Avenue/Ascaill Belgrave 2021 (Logainm). See also Belgrave Square East.

Belgrave Place/Plás Belgrave (Rathmines Rd Upper E., 715875, 731572). Belgrave Place 1880 (*Thom*), 1882, 1907–8 (OS), 1913 (Electoral rolls), 1936–*c.* 2019 (OS). Belgrave Place/Plás Belgrave 2021 (nameplate; Logainm).

Belgrave Road/Bóthar Belgrave (Rathmines Rd Upper E., 715929, 731471). Path, unnamed 1760 (Rocque). Road, unnamed, leading to church (see **11 Religion: Holy Trinity Church**) 1843 (OS). Houses built from *c.* 1854 (O Brolchain). Section of Church Avenue from Holy Trinity Church to Dunville Avenue, Ranelagh renamed Belgrave Road 1856 (RRTM (2), 12.3.1856). Belgrave Road 1856 (*FJ* 8.7.1856); straightened, widened by 1874 (Thom map); 1882–*c.* 2019 (OS). Belgrave Road/Bóthar Belgrave 2021 (nameplate; Logainm).

Belgrave Square or Belgrave Square East/Cearnóg Belgrave Thoir (Rathmines Rd Lower E., 715927, 731685), partly on site of former Church Fields (see **14 Primary production**). Lane 1816 (Taylor, J.). Foot path 1821 (Duncan). Cullenswood Avenue Upper 1843 (OS). Belgrave Avenue renamed Belgrave Square 1856 (RRTM (2), 10.9.1856). Belgrave Square East 1857 (*Thom*). Unnamed 1874 (Thom map). Belgrave Square East 1882–*c.* 2019 (OS). Belgrave Square East/Cearnóg Belgrave Thoir 2021 (nameplate; Logainm).

Belgrave Square North/Cearnóg Belgrave Thuaidh (Rathmines Rd Lower E., 715852, 731748), partly on site of former Church Fields (see **14 Primary production**). Begun in mid-1840s (Smith, 18). Belgrave Square North *c.* 1864 (OS), 1874 (Thom map), 1882–*c.* 2019 (OS). Belgrave Square North/Cearnóg Belgrave Thuaidh 2021 (nameplate; Logainm).

Belgrave Square South/Cearnóg Belgrave Theas (Rathmines Rd Lower E., 715919, 731591), partly on site of former Church Fields (see **14 Primary production**). Begun in mid-1840s (Smith, 18). Belgrave Square 1857 (*Thom*). Belgrave Square South 1862 (RRTM (3), 3.4.1862), 1874 (Thom map), 1882–*c.* 2019 (OS). Belgrave Square South/Cearnóg Belgrave Theas 2021 (nameplate; Logainm).

Belgrave Square West/Cearnóg Belgrave Thiar (Rathmines Rd Lower E., 715849, 731652), partly on site of former Church Fields (see **14 Primary production**). Begun in mid-1840s (Smith, 18). Belgrave Square West 1859 (*Thom*), 1871 (RRTM (4), 3.5.1871), 1874 (Thom map), 1882–*c.* 2019 (OS). Belgrave Square West/Cearnóg Belgrave Thiar 2021 (nameplate; Logainm).

Bessborough Parade/Paráid Bessborough (Rathmines Rd Lower E., 715725, 732241). Bessborough Parade 1849 (*Thom*), 1850 (Val. 2), 1882–1908 (OS), 1913 (Electoral rolls). Bessborough Parade 1936, *c.* 2019 (OS). Bessborough Parade/Parád Beasbra 2021 (nameplate). Bessborough Parade/Paráid Bessborough 2021 (Logainm).

Blackberry Lane/Lána na Sméar (Rathmines Rd Lower W., 715542, 732336). Unnamed 1760 (Rocque). Blackberry Lane 1782 (Brownrigg), 1810 (Armstrong 3). Unnamed 1817 (Nairn 1), 1821 (Duncan). Blackberry Lane 1830 (Sherrard and Brassington). Blackberry 1849; Blackberry Lane 1850 (Thom; Val. 2). Unnamed 1874 (Thom map). Blackberry Lane 1882; gate depicted 1887; 1907–8; Blackberry Lane 1936, *c.* 2019 (OS). Blackberry Lane/Lána na Sméar 2021 (nameplate; Logainm).

Bushes Lane/Lána Bush (Rathgar Rd W., 715018, 731246). Unnamed *c.* 1864–1968; Bushes Lane *c.* 2019 (OS). Bushes Lane/Lána Bush 2021 (nameplate).

Cambridge Lane See Rathgar Place.

Cambridge Road/Bóthar Cambridge (Rathmines Rd Upper E., 715782, 731561). Cambridge Road 1863 (Thom; RRTM (3), 3.6.1863), 1874 (Thom map), 1882–*c.* 2019 (OS). Cambridge Road/Bóthar Cambridge/Bóthar Mac Ambróis 2021 (nameplate). Cambridge Road/Bóthar Cambridge 2021 (Logainm).

Cambridge Villas/Bailtíní Cambridge (Belgrave Rd W., 715782, 731475). Cambridge Villas 1870 (*Thom*). Unnamed 1882; Cambridge Villas 1907–*c.* 2019 (OS). Cambridge Villas/Bailtíní Cambridge 2021 (nameplate; Logainm).

Canal Road/Bóthar na Canálach (Rathmines Rd Lower E., 715751, 732495). Unnamed *c.* 1864–1907; Canal Road 1936, *c.* 2019 (OS). Canal Road/Bóthar na Canálach 2021 (nameplate; Logainm).

Castlewood Avenue/Ascaill Fhiodh an Chaisleáin (Rathmines Rd Lower E., 715680, 731682). 'A narrow lane without a house or a cabin' 1822 (Meyler, i, 43). Unnamed 1843 (OS). Castlewood Avenue 1845 (*Thom*), 1850 (Val. 2), 1874 (Thom map), 1882–*c.* 2019 (OS). Castlewood Avenue/Ascaill Choill an Chaisleáin 2021 (nameplate). Castlewood Avenue/Ascaill Fhiodh an Chaisleáin 2021 (Logainm).

Castlewood Lane See Castlewood Terrace.

Castlewood Park/Páirc Fhiodh an Chaisleáin (Rathmines Rd Upper E., 715716, 731561). Unnamed lane *c.* 1864 (OS). Castlewood Park 1874 (Thom map), 1882 (OS), 1888 (RRTM (6), 1.2.1888), 1907–*c.* 2019 (OS). Castlewood Park/Páirc Fheadha an Chaisleáin 2021 (nameplate). Castlewood Park/Páirc Fhiodh an Chaisleáin 2021 (Logainm).

Castlewood Place/Plás Fhiodh an Chaisleáin (Rathmines Rd Upper E., 715613, 731618). Unnamed *c.* 1864; Castlewood Place 1907–*c.* 2019 (OS). Castlewood Place/Plás Feadha an Cáisleáin 2021 (nameplate). Castlewood Place/Plás Fhiodh an Chaisleáin 2021 (Logainm).

Castlewood Terrace/Ardán Fhiodh an Chaisleáin [east] (Rathmines Rd Lower E., 715728, 731766). Castlewood Lane 1859 (*Thom*), 1863 (RRTM (3), 18.2.1863). Unnamed *c.* 1864, 1882; Castlewood Lane 1907–8 (OS). Castlewood Terrace 1913 (Electoral rolls), 1936–*c.* 2019 (OS). Castlewood Terrace/Árdán Feadha an Chaisleáin/Ardán Fhiodh an Chaisleáin 2021 (nameplate). Castlewood Terrace/Ardán Fhiodh an Chaisleáin 2021 (Logainm).

Castlewood Terrace/Ardán Fhiodh an Chaisleáin [south] (Rathmines Rd Lower E., 715660, 731717). Unnamed 1843 (OS). Castlewood Lane 1859 (*Thom*), 1863 (RRTM (3), 18.2.1863). Unnamed *c.* 1864, 1882 (OS). Newington Lane 1883 (RRTM (5), 5.9.1883). Castlewood Lane 1907–8 (OS). Castlewood Terrace 1913 (Electoral rolls), 1936–*c.* 2019 (OS). Castlewood Terrace/Árdán Feadha an Chaisleáin/Ardán Fhiodh an Chaisleáin 2021 (nameplate). Castlewood Terrace/Ardán Fhiodh an Chaisleáin 2021 (Logainm).

Chains, The (Rathmines Rd Lower W., 715512, 731588). Enclosed area associated with Swan R., locally known as The Chains 19th cent. (Kelly, 28, 172). The Chains 1889 (RRTM (6), 6.7.1889). Bollard extant 2021.

Charleville Close/Clós Charleville (Leinster Rd S., 715238, 731665). Unnamed *c.* 1864–1907; Charleville Close *c.* 2019 (OS). Charleville Close/Clós Ráth Luirc 2021 (nameplate). Charleville Close/Clós Charleville 2021 (Logainm).

Charleville Road/Bóthar Charleville (Leinster Rd S., 715270, 731584). Charleville Road *c.* 1864 (OS), 1874 (Thom map), 1882–*c.* 2019 (OS). Charleville Road/Bóthar Ráth Luirc/Bóthar Ráthluirc 2021 (nameplate). Charleville Road/Bóthar Charleville 2021 (Logainm).

Cheltenham Place/
Plás Cheltenham

(Rathmines Rd Lower E., 715647, 732481). Unnamed 1821 (Duncan). Cheltenham Place 1841 (*Thom*), 1850 (Val. 2), 1882–1908 (OS), 1913 (Electoral rolls), 1936, *c.* 2019 (OS). Cheltenham Place/Plás Seilteanam 2021 (nameplate). Cheltenham Place/Plás Cheltenham 2021 (Logainm).

Chicken Lane

See Mount Drummond Avenue.

Church Avenue/
Ascaill an
Teampaill

(Rathmines Rd Upper E., 715688, 731408). Unnamed 1843 (OS). Church Avenue 1850 (Val. 2), 1853 (*FJ* 1.12.1853), 1874 (Thom map), 1882–*c.* 2019 (OS). Church Avenue/Ascaill an Teampaill 2021 (nameplate; Logainm). See also Belgrave Road.

Church Gardens/
Gairdíní an
Teampaill

(Rathmines Rd Upper E., 715655, 731500). Unnamed 1843; Church Place 1882–1936; Church Gardens 1968, *c.* 2019 (OS). Church Gardens/Garraithe an Teampuil 2021 (nameplate). Church Gardens/Gairdíní an Teampaill 2021 (Logainm). See also **22** Residence.

Church Lane/Lána
an Teampaill

(Rathmines Rd Upper E., 715717, 731381). Unnamed 1843–1936; Church Lane *c.* 2019 (OS). Church Lane/Lána an Teampaill 2021 (nameplate; Logainm).

Church Place

See Church Gardens.

Cowper Mews/
Eachlann Cowper

(Rathmines Rd Upper E., 715646, 730903). Unnamed 1882–1936; Cowper Mews *c.* 2019 (OS). Cowper Mews/Eachlann Chóipéir 2021 (nameplate). Cowper Mews/Eachlann Cowper 2021 (Logainm).

Cowper Road/
Bóthar Cowper

(Rathmines Rd Upper E., 716020, 730954). Unnamed lane 1843, *c.* 1864; Cowper Road, extended to E. by 1882; Cowper Road 1907–*c.* 2019 (OS). Cowper Road/Bóthar Cowper 2021 (nameplate; Logainm).

Cullens Wood or
Cullenswood Road

See Mountpleasant Avenue Lower.

Cullenswood
Avenue Upper

See Belgrave Square East, Mountpleasant Avenue Upper.

**Darley Street/
Sráid Darley**

(Leinster Rd N., 714929, 732216). Darley
Street 1907–*c.* 2019 (OS). Darley Street/
Sráid Dárlaoi 2021 (nameplate). Darley
Street/Sráid Darley 2021 (Logainm).

**Dartry Cottages/
Iostáin Dhartraí**

(Dartry Rd S., 715956, 729997).
Unnamed 1843, *c.* 1864; Dartry Cottages
1879 (OS). Dartry Cottage 1890 (*Thom*).
Dartry Cottages 1907–*c.* 2019 (OS).
Dartry Walk 2021 (local information).
Dartry Cottages/Iostáin Dhartraí 2021
(Logainm).

**Dartry Park/Páirc
Dhartraí**

(Dartry Rd E., 715983, 730291). Dartry
Park 1936; extended to E., over site of
former Woodpark (see **22** Residence) by
1968; *c.* 2019 (OS). Dartry Park/Páirc
Dartraighe 2021 (nameplate). Dartry
Park/Páirc Dhartraí 2021 (Logainm).

**Dartry Park Road
or Dartry Road/
Bóthar Dhartraí**

(715801, 730348). Unnamed 1843
(OS). 'Road from Rathmines to the
Dodder' 1849 (*Thom*). Unnamed *c.*
1864, 1882 (OS). Dartry Park Road
1882, 1889 (RRTM (5), 2.11.1882;
RRTM (6), 6.2.1889). Dartry Road 1905
(RRTA 1/1/71), 1907–*c.* 2019 (OS).
Dartry Road/Bóthar Dartraighe 2021
(nameplate). Dartry Road/Bóthar
Dhartraí 2021 (Logainm).

Dartry Walk

See Dartry Cottages.

Dolly's Lane

Location unknown. Dolly's Lane (*FJ*
18.2.1860).

Doyle's Lane

(Rathmines Rd Lower W., 715484,
731583). Doyle's Lane 1850 (*Thom*).
Unnamed *c.* 1864 (OS). Doyle's Lane,
'four small dwelling houses' 1877 (OSN,
53); 1882 (OS), *c.* 1901 (Val. 3). Unnamed
1907, *c.* 2019 (OS).

**Drummond Place/
Plás Drummond**

(Leinster Rd N., 714932, 732172).
Drummond Place (RRTM (7),
1.11.1899), 1907–*c.* 2019 (OS).
Drummond Place/Plás Droman
2021 (nameplate). Drummond Place/
Plás Drummond 2021 (Logainm).

**Effra Road/
Bóthar Éafra**

(Leinster Rd S., 714987, 731473). Effra
Road 1871 (RRTM (4), 4.12.1871),
1876 (OS), 1880 (*Thom*), 1907–*c.* 2019
(OS). Effra Road/Bothar Eafra 2021
(nameplate). Effra Road/Bóthar Éafra
2021 (Logainm).

**Emmet Street/
Sráid Emmet**

(Harold's Cross Rd E., 714893, 732220).
Emmet Street 1907–*c.* 2019 (OS). Emmet
Street/Sráid Emmet 2021 (nameplate;
Logainm).

**Fitzgerald Street/
Sráid Mhic Gearailt**

(Leinster Rd N., 714998, 732155).
Fitzgerald Street 1907–*c.* 2019 (OS).
Fitzgerald Street/Sráid Mhic Ghearailt
2021 (nameplate). Fitzgerald Street/
Sráid Mhic Gearailt 2021 (Logainm).

**Fortescue Lane/
Lána Fortescue**

(Rathmines Rd Lower E., 715675,
732334). Unnamed 1843–1907; Fortescue
Lane *c.* 2019 (OS). Fortescue Lane/Lána
Fortescue 2021 (nameplate; Logainm).

**Fortfield Gardens/
Gairdíní Ghort an
Dúin**

(Rathmines Rd Upper E., 715796,
730836). Fortfield Gardens 1936, *c.* 2019
(OS). Fortfield Gardens/Gáirdíní Ghort
an Dúna 2021 (nameplate). Fortfield
Gardens/Gairdíní Ghort an Dúin 2021
(Logainm).

**Fortfield Terrace/
Ardán Ghort an
Dúin**

(Rathmines Rd Upper E., 715759,
730784). Fortfield Terrace 1870
(*Thom*), 1882–1936; extended E. by
1968; *c.* 2019 (OS). Fortfield Terrace/
Ardán Ghort an Dúna 2021
(nameplate). Fortfield Terrace/
Ardán Ghort an Dúin 2021 (Logainm).

**Greenfield Place/
Plás an Ghoirt
Ghlais**

(Leinster Rd N., 715003, 732124).
Greenfield Place 1907–*c.* 2019 (OS).
Greenfield Place 2021 (nameplate).
Greenfield Place/Plás an Ghoirt Ghlais
2021 (Logainm).

**Greenwich Court/
Cúirt Greenwich**

(Rathmines Rd Lower W., 715493,
731691). Unnamed *c.* 1864–1936;
Greenwich Court *c.* 2019 (OS).
Greenwich Court/Cúirt Greenwich
2021 (nameplate; Logainm).

**Grosvenor Lane/
Lána Grosvenor**

(Leinster Rd N., 715061, 731739).
Unnamed *c.* 1864–1936; Grosvenor
Lane 1967, *c.* 2019 (OS). Grosvenor
Lane/Lána Grosvenor 2021 (nameplate;
Logainm).

**Grosvenor Lodge/
Lóiste Grosvenor**

(Leinster Rd N., 715254, 731906).
Unnamed 1907, 1936; Grosvenor Lodge
c. 2019 (OS). Grosvenor Lodge 2021
(nameplate). Grosvenor Lodge/Lóiste
Grosvenor 2021 (Logainm).

Grosvenor Place/ Plás Grosvenor
(Leinster Rd S., 715087, 731522). Grosvenor Road *c.* 1864; Grosvenor Place 1876 (OS), *c.* 1901 (Val. 3), 1907–*c.* 2019 (OS). Grosvenor Place/Plás Gróbhanar 2021 (nameplate). Grosvenor Place/Plás Grosvenor 2021 (Logainm).

Grosvenor Road/ Bóthar Grosvenor [north]
(Rathmines Rd Upper W., 715310, 731441). Grosvenor Road *c.* 1864, 1874 (Thom map), 1882–*c.* 2019 (OS). Grosvenor Road/Bothar Grosvenor/ Bóthar Ghróbhanar 2021 (nameplate). Grosvenor Road/Bóthar Grosvenor 2021 (Logainm). See also previous entry, Grosvenor Place.

Grosvenor Road or Grosvenor Road West/Bóthar Grosvenor [south]
(Rathmines Rd Upper W., 715116, 731150). Grosvenor Road West 1874 (Thom map). Grosvenor Road 1882 (OS). Grosvenor Road West 1898 (Thom map). Grosvenor Road 1907–*c.* 2019 (OS). Grosvenor Road/Bothar Grosvenor/Bóthar Ghróbhanar 2021 (nameplate). Grosvenor Road/Bóthar Grosvenor 2021 (Logainm).

Grosvenor Square/ Cearnóg Grosvenor
(Leinster Rd N., 715009, 731831). Grosvenor Square 'recently planned surveyed and laid out', sites for 82 houses 1856 (*FJ* 10.5.1856). Grosvenor Square 1858 (*Thom*), 1876 (OS), 1882 (RRTM (5), 17.5.1882), 1907–*c.* 2019 (OS). Grosvenor Square/Cearnóg Grosvenor 2021 (Logainm).

Grosvenor Villas/ Bailtíní Grosvenor
(Rathmines Rd Upper W., 715059, 731192). Unnamed 1907; Grosvenor Villas 1936–*c.* 2019 (OS). Grosvenor Villas/Bailtíní Grosvenor 2021 (nameplate; Logainm).

Grove Avenue/ Ascaill an Gharráin
(Rathmines Rd Lower W., 714976, 732377). Grove Avenue 1907–*c.* 2019 (OS). Grove Avenue/Ascal an Gharráin 2021 (nameplate). Grove Avenue/Ascaill an Gharráin 2021 (Logainm).

Grove Park or Grove Park Road/Páirc an Gharráin
(Rathmines Rd Lower W., 715393, 732390). Unnamed, gates depicted *c.* 1864–87 (OS). Grove Park Road, laid out on former lane leading to Grove

GROSVENOR SQUARE, EARLY 20TH CENT.

School (see **20** Education) by 1890 (RRTM (6), 5.11.1890). Grove Park 1907–8, 1936, *c.* 2019 (OS). Grove Park/Páirc an Gharráin 2021 (nameplate; Logainm).

Grove Road/Bóthar an Gharráin	(Rathmines Rd Lower E., 715257, 732441). Unnamed 1811 (Campbell), 1816 (Taylor, J.), 1821 (Duncan), 1822 (Cooke), 1843–82 (OS). Toll bar erected by Grand Canal Co. in 1883 (RRTM (5), 4.6.1883). Canal bank taken over by Township Commissioners, to be named Grove Road 1886 (RRTM (6), 7.4.1886). Unnamed 1887; Grove Road 1907–*c.* 2019 (OS). Grove Road/Bóthar an Gharráin 2021 (nameplate; Logainm).
Gulistan Avenue	See Gulistan Terrace.
Gulistan Cottages	See **22** Residence.
Gulistan Place/ Plás Gulistan	(Mountpleasant Ave Upper W., 715787, 731853). Gulistan Place *c.* 1901 (Val. 3), 1907–*c.* 2019 (OS). Gulistan Place/Plás Gulistan 2021 (nameplate; Logainm).
Gulistan Terrace/ Ardán Gulistan	(Mountpleasant Ave Upper W., 715801, 731906). Gulistan Terrace 1847 (*Thom*), 1850 (Val. 2), *c.* 1864 (OS). Gulistan Avenue 1868 (RRTM (4), 8.1.1868). Gulistan Terrace 1874 (Thom map), 1882–1907 (OS). Gulistan Avenue 1913 (Electoral rolls). Gulistan Terrace 1936–*c.* 2019 (OS). Gulistan Terrace/ Árdán Gulistan 2021 (nameplate). Gulistan Terrace/Ardán Gulistan 2021 (Logainm).
Half Mile Road	See Mountpleasant Avenue Lower.
Harold's Cross or Haroldscross Road/Bóthar Chrois Araild	(714819, 732313). Road from Harold's Cross 1798 (Wilson). Harold's Cross Road 1811 (Campbell; *FJ* 30.8.1811). Unnamed 1821 (Duncan). To Harold's Cross, Terenure etc. 1822 (Cooke). Unnamed 1843, *c.* 1864; Haroldscross Road 1907; Harold's Cross Road 1936; Harolds Cross Road *c.* 2019 (OS). Harold's Cross Road/Bothar Chros Aralt 2021 (nameplate). Harold's Cross Road/ Bóthar Chrois Araild 2021 (Logainm).
Harold's Cross Cottages	See **22** Residence.

HEN AND CHICKEN LANE, 1817, BY C.M. NAIRN

Hen and Chicken Lane	See Mount Drummond Avenue.
Highway (1)	Location unknown, possibly same as Mountpleasant Avenue Lower and Upper (*q.v.*). 'High way[s] … to Colon [Cullenswood]' *c.* 1396 (*Alen's reg.*, 234).
Highway (2)	Location unknown, possibly same as Rathmines Road Lower and Upper (*q.v.*). 'High way[s] … to Milton [Milltown]' *c.* 1396 (*Alen's reg.*, 234).
Highway to Cullinswood	See Mountpleasant Avenue Lower.
Holmesville, Holmevilla, Holmeville or Homeville	(Rathmines Rd Lower E., 715640, 731812). Holmesville 1841 (*Thom*). Unnamed 1843 (OS). Holmeville 1845; Holmevilla 1846 (*Thom*). Unnamed *c.* 1864; Homeville, gate lodge 1882; Homeville, lodge 1907–8 (OS); 1913 (Electoral rolls), 1936, 1968 (OS). Demolished except for one house by *c.* 1983 (local information).

Kenelworth Square See Kenilworth Square East, Kenilworth Square North, Kenilworth Square South, Kenilworth Square West.

Kenilworth Lane or Kenilworth Lane East/Lána Kenilworth (Leinster Rd S., 714975, 731425). Unnamed *c.* 1864–1936; Kenilworth Lane 1967; Kenilworth Lane East *c.* 2019 (OS).Kenilworth Lane/Lána Kenilworth 2021 (nameplate; Logainm).

Kenilworth Lane or Kenilworth Lane South/Lána Kenilworth (Leinster Rd S., 715080, 731436). Unnamed 1876–1936; Kenilworth Lane South *c.* 2019 (OS). Kenilworth Lane/Lána Kenilworth 2021 (nameplate; Logainm).

Kenilworth Lane or Kenilworth Lane West/Lána Kenilworth (Leinster Rd S., 714802, 731321). Unnamed *c.* 1864–1936; Kenilworth Lane 1968; Kenilworth Lane West *c.* 2019 (OS). Kenilworth Lane/Lána Kenilworth 2021 (nameplate; Logainm).

Kenilworth Road/Bóthar Kenilworth (Leinster Rd S., 715029, 731361). Kenilworth Road *c.* 1864–*c.* 2019 (OS). Kenilworth Road/Bóthar Cineiln/Bóthar Cineilm/Bóthar Chineilm 2021 (nameplate). Kenilworth Road/Bóthar Kenilworth 2021 (Logainm).

Kenilworth Square East/Cearnóg Kenilworth Thoir (Harold's Cross Rd E., 714948, 731192). 40 acres to let for building houses with 7-acre square in centre 1856 (*FJ* 3.3.1856). Kenelworth Square 1856 (*Thom*). Kenilworth Square East *c.* 1864 (OS), 1874 (Thom map), 1882–*c.* 2019 (OS). Kenilworth Square East/Cearnóg Cineilm Oirthear 2021 (nameplate). Kenilworth Square East/Cearnóg Kenilworth Thoir 2021 (Logainm).

Kenilworth Square North/Cearnóg Kenilworth Thuaidh (Harold's Cross Rd E., 714841, 731273). Kenelworth Square 1856 (*Thom*). Kenilworth Square North *c.* 1864 (OS), 1874 (Thom map), 1882–*c.* 2019 (OS). Kenilworth Square North/Cearnóg Cineilm T. 2021 (nameplate). Kenilworth Square North/Cearnóg Kenilworth Thuaidh 2021 (Logainm).

Kenilworth Square South/Cearnóg Kenilworth Theas (Harold's Cross Rd E., 714923, 731058). Kenelworth Square 1856 (*Thom*). Kenilworth Square South *c.* 1864 (OS), 1874 (Thom map), 1882–*c.* 2019 (OS). Kenilworth Square South/Cearnóg Kenilworth Theas 2021 (Logainm).

Kenilworth Square or Kenilworth Square West/Cearnóg Cineilm I. (Harold's Cross Rd E., 714812, 731132). Kenelworth Square 1856 (*Thom*). Kenilworth Square West *c.* 1864 (OS), 1874 (Thom map), 1882–*c.* 2019 (OS). Kenilworth Square West/Cearnóg Cineilm I. 2021 (nameplate).

Lavaria Lane See Le Vere Terrace.

Leicester Avenue/Ascaill Leicester (Rathmines Rd Upper W., 715137, 731093). Unnamed 1843 (OS). Leicester Avenue 1850 (Val. 2), *c.* 1864–*c.* 2019 (OS). Leicester Avenue/Ascal Leicester 2021 (nameplate). Leicester Avenue/Ascaill Leicester 2021 (Logainm).

Leinster Road/Bóthar Laighean (715097, 731680). Completed in *c.* 1840 (Meyler, i, 44). Leinster Road 1842 (*Thom*), 1843 (OS), 1850 (Val. 2), *c.* 1864 (OS), 1874 (Thom map), 1876, 1882 (OS); gates to be removed from both ends 1890 (RRTM (6), 1.6.1890); 1907–*c.* 2019 (OS). Leinster Road/Bóthar Laighean 2021 (nameplate; Logainm).

Leinster Road West/Bóthar Laighean Thiar (Leinster Rd S., 714879, 731432). Leinster Road West *c.* 1864 (OS), 1874 (Thom map), 1876–*c.* 2019 (OS). Leinster Road West/Bóthar Laighean Thiar 2021 (Logainm).

Leinster Square/Cearnóg Laighean [east] (Rathmines Rd Lower W., 715484, 731765). Begun in 1830s (Lavin, 33–67). Unnamed 1843 (OS). Leinster Square *c.* 1864 (OS), 1874 (Thom map), 1882–~*c.* 2019 (OS). Leinster Square/Cearnóg Laighean 2021 (Logainm).

Leinster Square/Cearnóg Laighean [west] (Rathmines Rd Lower W., 715420, 731747). Begun in 1830s (Lavin, 33–67). Unnamed 1843 (OS). Leinster Square 1852 (*Nenagh Guardian* 24.6.1852). Leinster Square West 1856 (*Thom*). Leinster Square *c.* 1864 (OS), 1874 (Thom map), 1882–*c.* 2019 (OS). Leinster Square/Cearnóg Laighean 2021 (nameplate; Logainm).

Leinster Square West See Leinster Square.

Le Vere, LeVere or Levere Terrace/Ardán Le Vere (Harold's Cross Rd E., 714858, 732298). Lavaria Lane 1850 (Val. 2). Levere Terrace 1907–8, 1936; Le Vere Terrace *c.* 2019 (OS). LeVere Terrace/Árdán

Leiféar/Árdán Léifear 2021 (nameplate). Le Vere Terrace/Ardán Le Vere 2021 (Logainm).

Lissenfield Avenue Near Portobello Bridge (see **17** Transport), site unknown. Lissenfield Avenue 1846 (*FJ* 25.6.1846).

Maxwell Road/ Bóthar Maxwell (Rathmines Rd Upper W., 715453, 731092). Unnamed 1816 (Taylor, J.). Maxwell Road 1865 (RRTM (3), 25.3.1865). Unnamed 1874 (Thom map). Maxwell Road 1882–*c.* 2019 (OS). Maxwell Road/Bóthar Macsuel 2021 (nameplate). Maxwell Road/Bóthar Maxwell 2021 (Logainm).

Military Road/An Bóthar Míleata (Rathmines Rd Lower W., 715474, 732114). Unnamed 1821 (Duncan), 1843–1908; Military Road 1936, *c.* 2019 (OS). Military Road/An Bóthar Míleata 2021 (Logainm). See also Barrack Avenue.

Milltown Path [north] See Mountpleasant Avenue Lower, Upper.

Milltown Path/Cosán Bhaile an Mhuilinn [mid] (Rathmines Rd Upper E., 716170, 730872). Milltown Path 1760 (Rocque). Unnamed 1843, *c.* 1864 (OS). Realigned 1895–6 (RRTM (6), 4.9.1895, 1.4.1896). Milltown Path 1907–*c.* 2019 (OS). Milltown Path/Cosán Bhaile an Mhuilinn 2021 (Logainm).

Milltown Path/Cosán Bhaile an Mhuilinn [south] (Rathmines Rd Upper E., 716232, 730778). Milltown Path 1760 (Rocque). Unnamed 1843, *c.* 1864 (OS). Realigned 1895–6 (RRTM (6), 4.9.1895, 1.4.1896). Milltown Path 1907–*c.* 2019 (OS). Milltown Path/Cosán Bhaile an Mhuilinn 2021 (Logainm).

Milltown Road/ Bóthar Bhaile an Mhuilinn (Dartry Rd E., 716475, 730098). Unnamed 1843; Milltown Road *c.* 1864; unnamed 1907 (OS). Milltown Road 1913 (Electoral rolls). Unnamed 1936; Milltown Road 1968, *c.* 2019 (OS). Milltown Road/Bóthar Bhaile an Mhuilinn 2021 (nameplate; Logainm).

RATHMINES ROAD LOWER, EARLY 20TH CENT.

RELIABLE SERIES 309 / 46

Mount Drummond Avenue/Ascaill Chnocán Drummond — (Leinster Rd N., 714880, 732161). Chicken Lane 1760 (Rocque). Hen and Chicken Lane 1817 (Nairn 1), 1836 (Armstrong 4). Unnamed 1843 (OS). Hen and Chicken Lane 1850 (Val. 2), 1853 (Meath papers, box 176; Armstrong 1, 233). Mount Drummond Avenue *c.* 1864 (OS), 1874, 1898 (Thom map), 1907–*c.* 2019 (OS). Mount Drummond Avenue/Ascaill Aird Uí Dhroma/Ascal Chnoc Dhromain 2021 (nameplate). Mount Drummond Avenue/Ascaill Chnocán Drummond 2021 (Logainm).

Mount Drummond Square/Cearnóg Chnocán Drummond — (Leinster Rd N., 714915, 731949). Laid out on land purchased from Poor Clare order in *c.* 1941 (Curtis, J., 170). Mount Drummond Square 1967, *c.* 2019 (OS). Mount Drummond Square/Cearnóg Chnocán Drummond 2021 (Logainm).

Mount Pleasant or Mountpleasant Avenue Lower/Ascaill Chnocán Aoibhinn Íochtarach — (Rathmines Rd Lower E., 715743, 732334). Highway to Cullinswood 1717 (Greene). Milltown Path 1760 (Rocque). Cullenswood Road 1798 (Wilson). Old pathway from near Rathmines to Milltown 1800 (*FJ* 6.5.1800). Half Mile Road 1807 (Armstrong 1, 233). Unnamed 1816 (Taylor, J.), 1821 (Duncan). Cullens Wood Road 1830 (Sherrard and Brassington). Half Mile Road 1836 (Armstrong 4). Mount Pleasant Avenue 1834 (*Thom*). Mount Pleasant Avenue Lower 1843 (OS). Mountpleasant Avenue Lower 1850 (Val. 2), *c.* 1864–1908 (OS), 1913 (Electoral rolls). Mountpleasant Avenue 1936; Mountpleasant Avenue Lower *c.* 2019 (OS). Mountpleasant Avenue Lower/Ascal Cnocán Aoibhinn Í. 2021 (nameplate). Mountpleasant Avenue Upper/Ascaill Chnocán Aoibhinn Íochtarach 2021 (Logainm). See also Highway (1).

Mount Pleasant or
Mountpleasant
Avenue Upper/
Ascaill Chnocán
Aoibhinn
Uachtarach

(Rathmines Rd Lower E., 715855,
732041). Milltown Path 1760 (Rocque).
Pathway 1816 (Taylor, J.). Foot path 1821
(Duncan). Cullenswood Avenue Upper
1843 (OS). Mount Pleasant Avenue
Upper 1845 (*Thom*). Mountpleasant
Avenue Upper 1874 (Thom map), *c.*
1864–1907 (OS), 1913 (Electoral rolls).
Mountpleasant Avenue 1936; Mount
Pleasant Avenue Upper 1968, *c.* 2019
(OS). Mountpleasant Avenue Upper/
Ascal Cnocán Aoibhinn U. 2021
(nameplate). Mountpleasant Avenue
Upper/Ascaill Chnocán Aoibhinn
Uachtarach 2021 (Logainm). See also
Highway (1).

New Rathmines
Road

See Rathmines Road Lower.

Newington Lane

See Castlewood Terrace.

O'Hara Avenue/
Ascaill Uí Eára

(Harold's Cross Rd E., 714966, 732381).
Unnamed 1907, 1936; O'Hara Avenue
c. 2019 (OS). O'Hara Avenue/Ascaill
Ó Heára 2021 (nameplate). O'Hara
Avenue/Ascaill Uí Eára 2021 (Logainm).

Observatory Lane/
Lána na
Réadlainne

(Rathmines Rd Lower E., 715611,
732005). Lane 1807 (Armstrong 1, 233).
Unnamed 1843; Observatory Lane 1882;
unnamed 1907–8 (OS). Observatory
Lane 1909 (RRTA 1/1/73), 1936–*c.*
2019 (OS). Observatory Lane/Lána na
Réadlainne 2021 (Logainm).

Orchard Road or
Orchard Road
South/Bóthar an
Úlloird

(Dartry Rd E., 716086, 730488).
Unnamed 1874 (Thom map), 1882;
Orchard Road 1907, 1936; Orchard Road
South 1968; Orchard Road *c.* 2019 (OS).
Orchard Road/Bóthar an Úlloird 2021
(nameplate; Logainm).

Orwell Park/Páirc
Orwell

(Dartry Rd W., 715626, 730028).
Unnamed *c.* 1864; Orwell Park 1879–
c. 2019 (OS). Orwell Park/Páirc Oruel
2021 (nameplate). Orwell Park/Páirc
Orwell 2021 (Logainm).

Palmerston Court/
Cúirt Bhaile
Phámar

(Rathmines Rd Upper E., 715902,
731391). Unnamed *c.* 1864–1936;
Palmerston Court *c.* 2019 (OS).
Palmerston Court/Cúirt Palmerston
2021 (nameplate). Palmerston Court/
Cúirt Bhaile Phámar 2021 (Logainm).

RATHMINES COLLEGE, RATHMINES ROAD UPPER,
EARLY 20TH CENT.

Palmerston Gardens/
Gáirdíní Bhaile
Phámar

(Rathmines Rd Upper E.,
715935, 730829). Palmerston
Gardens 1907–*c.* 2019 (OS).
Palmerston Gardens/Gáirdíní
Baile Phámar/Gairdíní Stiguaire
2021 (nameplate). Palmerston
Gardens/Gáirdíní Bhaile Phámar
2021 (Logainm).

Palmerston Lane/
Lána Bhaile
Phámar

(Rathmines Rd Upper E., 716173,
730741). Unnamed 1882–1936;
Palmerston Lane *c.* 2019 (OS).
Palmerston Lane/Lána Bhaile
Phámar 2021 (nameplate;
Logainm).

Palmerston Park/
Páirc Bhaile
Phámar

(Rathmines Rd Upper E.,
716079, 730549). Palmerston
Park, developed on site of
former Rathmines Castle (see **22**
Residence: Rathmines Castle Old)
by 1870 (*Thom*). Unnamed 1874

(Thom map), 1882 (OS). Palmerston Park 1894 (RRTM (7), 4.4.1894), 1907–*c.* 2019 (OS). Palmerston Park/Páirc Stiguaire 2021 (nameplate). Palmerston Park/Páirc Bhaile Phámar 2021 (Logainm).

Palmerston Road/ Bóthar Bhaile Phámar (Rathmines Rd Upper E., 716012, 731074). Laid out in 1860s (Kelly, 220). Houses built from 1863 (O Brolchain) Palmerston Road *c.* 1864 (OS), 1874 (RRTM (4), 4.3.1874), 1898 (Thom map), 1907–*c.* 2019 (OS). Palmerston Road/ Bóthar Baile Phamar 2021 (nameplate). Palmerston Road/Bóthar Bhaile Phámar 2021 (Logainm).

Palmerston Villas/ Bailtíní Bhaile Phámar (Rathmines Rd Upper E., 715804, 730698). Palmerston Villas *c.* 1864 (OS), 1868 (RRTM (4), 8.1.1868), 1870 (*Thom*), 1874 (Thom map), 1882–*c.* 2019 (OS). Palmerston Villas/Bailtíní Phalmerston 2021 (nameplate). Palmerston Villas/ Bailtíní Bhaile Phámar 2021 (Logainm).

Park View Avenue See Stone Mews.

Parker Hill or Parkerhill/Cnoc Pháircéir (Rathmines Rd Lower E., 715612, 731924). Lane 1807 (Armstrong 1, 233). Unnamed 1843 (OS). Parkerhill 1850 (Val. 2). Parker Hill 1870 (*Thom*). Unnamed 1882; Parker Hill 1907–*c.* 2019 (OS). Parker Hill/Cnochán Pháircéir 2021 (nameplate). Parker Hill/Cnoc Pháircéir 2021 (Logainm).

Prince Arthur Terrace/Ardán an Phrionsa Artúr (Rathmines Rd Lower W., 715420, 731686), partly on site of former Rookville (see **22** Residence). Prince Arthur Terrace 1853 (*Thom*), 1882–*c.* 2019 (OS). Prince Arthur Terrace/Ardán an Phrionsa Artúr 2021 (Logainm).

Rathgar Avenue/ Ascaill Ráth Garbh (Rathmines Rd Upper W., 714738, 731104). Unnamed 1843, *c.* 1864; Rathgar Avenue 1882–*c.* 2019 (OS). Rathgar Avenue/Ascal Rath gCearr 2021 (nameplate). Rathgar Avenue/Ascaill Ráth Garbh 2021 (Logainm).

Rathgar Place/Plás Ráth Garbh (Rathgar Rd E., 715399, 731237). Cambridge Lane *c.* 1864–1936; Rathgar Place *c.* 2019 (OS). Rathgar Place/Plás Ráth Garbh 2021 (nameplate).

Rathgar Road/ Bóthar Ráth Garbh (715393, 731449). New road to Rathgar 1815 (*FJ* 11.9.1815). New road 1816 (Taylor, J.). Unnamed 1843 (OS). Rathgar Road 1850 (Val. 2), *c.* 1864–*c.* 2019 (OS). Rathgar Road/Bóthar Ráth gCearr 2021 (nameplate). Rathgar Road/Bóthar Ráth Garbh 2021 (Logainm).

Rathmines Avenue/ Ascaill Ráth Maoinis (Rathmines Rd Upper W., 715530, 731443). Rathmines Avenue 1847 (*FJ* 31.5.1847), 1850 (Val. 2), 1882–*c.* 2019 (OS). Rathmines Avenue/Ascal Rath Maonas 2021 (nameplate). Rathmines Avenue/Ascaill Ráth Maoinis 2021 (Logainm).

Rathmines in Court Location unknown. Rathmines in Court 1850 (*Thom*), 1867 (RRTM (3), 31.7.1867).

Rathmines Park/ Pairc Ráth Maonais (Rathgar Rd E., 715475, 731326). Rathmines Park 1869 (RRTM (4), 3.11.1869), 1881 (*FJ* 13.11.1881), 1882, 1907; unnamed 1936; Rathmines Park *c.* 2019 (OS). Rathmines Park/Pairc Ráth Maonais 2021 (nameplate; Logainm).

Rathmines, Rathmines Road or Rathmines Road Lower/Bóthar Ráth Maonais Íochtarach (715580, 732078). Highway to Rathmines 1717 (Greene). Rathmines Path, road and path depicted 1760 (Rocque). Rathmines Road 1798 (Wilson). New Rathmines Road, existing road straightened in 1800 (Archer). Old, new road unnamed *c.* 1802 (Taylor, A.). New road at Rathmines 1802 (*FLJ* 5.5.1802). 'Old road' 1810 (Armstrong 3). Rathmines 1811 (Campbell). Unnamed 1816 (Taylor, J.), 1821 (Duncan). To Ranelagh, Rathmines, Rathgar, Rathfarnham etc. 1822 (Cooke). Rathmines Road 1830 (Sherrard and Brassington). Rathmines 1834 (*Dublin almanac*). Unnamed 1843 (OS). Rathmines Road 1850 (Val. 2), *c.* 1864 (OS), 1874 (Thom map), 1882, 1907 (OS), 1913 (Electoral rolls). Rathmines Road Lower 1936–*c.* 2019 (OS). Rathmines Road/ Bóthar Rath Maonas 2021 (nameplate). Rathmines Road Lower/Bóthar Ráth Maonais Íochtarach 2021 (Logainm). See also Highway (2).

Rathmines Road, Rathmines Road Upper or Rathmines Upper/Bóthar Ráth Maonais Uachtarach (715579, 731421). Unnamed 1760 (Rocque), 1816 (Taylor, J.), 1843 (OS). Rathmines Road 1850 (Val. 2), 1874 (Thom map). Rathmines Upper 1882; Upper Rathmines 1907; Rathmines Road Upper 1936–*c.* 2019 (OS). Rathmines Road/Bóthar Rath Maonas/Bóthar Ráth

RATHMINES ROAD LOWER, LOOKING NORTH, *c.* 1910

RATHMINES ROAD LOWER, LOOKING SOUTH, *c.* 1910

Maonais Uacht. 2021 (nameplate). Rathmines Road Upper/Bóthar Ráth Maonais Uachtarach 2021 (Logainm). See also Highway (2).

Richmond Avenue or Richmond Avenue South/Ascaill Richmond Theas (Dartry Rd E., 716469, 730469). Richmond Avenue c. 1864; unnamed 1882; Richmond Avenue 1907 (OS), 1913 (Electoral rolls). Richmond Avenue South 1936–c. 2019 (OS). Richmond Avenue/Ascal Risteamain/Ascal Risteanain 2021 (nameplate). Richmond Avenue South/Ascaill Richmond Theas 2021 (Logainm).

Richmond Hill/Cnoc Richmond (Rathmines Rd Lower E., 715703, 732176). Unnamed 1816 (Taylor, J.), 1821 (Duncan). Richmond Hill 1827 (wall plaque), 1842 (*FJ* 1.9.1842), 1843 (OS), 1850 (Val. 2), c. 1864 (OS), 1874 (Thom map), 1882–c. 2019 (OS). Richmond Hill/Cnoc Risteamain 2021 (nameplate). Richmond Hill/Cnoc Richmond 2021 (Logainm).

Richmond Lane/Lána Richmond (Rathmines Rd Lower E., 715657, 732127). Unnamed 1843–c. 2019 (OS). Richmond Lane/Lána Richmond 2021 (nameplate; Logainm).

Richmond Mews/Eachlann Richmond (Rathmines Rd Lower E., 715658, 732198). Unnamed 1887–1936; Richmond Mews c. 2019 (OS). Richmond Mews/Clóis Risteamain 2021 (nameplate). Richmond Mews/Eachlann Richmond 2021 (Logainm).

Richmond Place/Plás Richmond (Rathmines Rd Lower E., 715802, 732108). Richmond Place 1843–c. 2019 (OS). Richmond Place/Plás Risteamáin 2021 (nameplate). Richmond Place/Plás Richmond 2021 (Logainm).

Richview Park/Páirc Richview (Dartry Rd N., 716337, 730591). Richview Park 1968, c. 2019 (OS). Richview Park/Páirc an Dea-Radhairc 2021 (nameplate). Richview Park/Páirc Richview 2021 (Logainm).

Saddlers Court/Cúirt an Diallatóra (Rathmines Rd Lower W., 715507, 732064). Unnamed 1936; Saddlers Court c. 2019 (OS). Saddlers Court/Cúirt an Diallatóra 2021 (Logainm).

South Hill/An Cnoc Theas (Dartry Rd E., 716085, 730176). Developed on site of former South Hill (see **22** Residence) in 1950s (*Ir. Times* 5.3.2015). South Hill 1968, c. 2019 (OS). South Hill/An Cnoc Theas 2021 (Logainm).

Spire View or Spireview Lane/Lána Radharc na Spuaice (Rathgar Rd W., 715225, 731265). Unnamed c. 1864; Spire View Lane 1907–c. 2019 (OS). Spireview Lane/Lána Radharc na Spuaice 2021 (nameplate; Logainm).

St Kevins Gardens/Gairdíní Chaoimhín [north] (Dartry Rd W., 715677, 730296). Unnamed 1907 (OS). St Kevin's Gardens 1922 (RRTM (9), 4.10.1922). Unnamed 1936; St Kevin's Gardens 1968, c. 2019 (OS). St Kevin's Gardens/Gairdíní Naomh Chaoimhín 2021 (nameplate). Saint Kevins Gardens/Gairdíní Chaoimhín 2021 (Logainm).

St Kevins Gardens/Gairdíní Chaoimhín [south] (Dartry Rd W., 715719, 730215). St Kevin's Gardens 1936; extended S. by 1968; c. 2019 (OS). St Kevin's Gardens/Gairdíní Naomh Chaoimhín 2021 (nameplate). Saint Kevins Gardens/Gairdíní Chaoimhín 2021 (Logainm).

St Kevin's Park or St Kevin's Park Terrace/Páirc Chaoimhín (Dartry Rd W., 715575, 730263). Unnamed 1882 (OS). St Kevin's Park Terrace 1900 (*Thom*). St Kevin's Park 1907–c. 2019 (OS). St Kevin's Park/Páirc Naomh Chaoimhín/Páirc Chaoimhín 2021 (nameplate). St Kevin's Park/Páirc Chaoimhín 2021 (Logainm).

Stable Lane/Lána na Stáblaí (Dartry Rd E., 715986, 730178). Unnamed c. 1864–1936 (OS). Stable Lane/Lána an Stábla 2021 (nameplate). Stable Lane/Lána na Stáblaí 2021 (Logainm).

Station Lane (Rathmines Rd Upper W., 715487, 731476). Station Lane 1907, 1936; built over by 1968 (OS).

Stone Mews/Eachlann na gCloch (Rathmines Rd Upper W., 715514, 731356). Unnamed 1843–82; Park View Avenue 1907–8, 1936; Stone Mews, closed at N. end by c. 2019 (OS). Stone Mews/Eachlann na gCloch 2021 (nameplate; Logainm).

Stream Ville or Streamville See Wynnefield Road.

Summerville Park/
Páirc Summerville

(Rathmines Rd Upper E., 715663, 731300), partly on site of former Summerville (see **22** Residence). Summerville Park 1903 (RRTM (8), 2.11.1903), 1907 (OS), 1913 (Electoral rolls), *c.* 2019 (OS). Summerville Park/Páirc Ó Somacháin 2021 (nameplate). Summerville Park/Páirc Summerville 2021 (Logainm).

Sunbury Gardens/
Gairdíní Sunbury

(Dartry Rd W., 715717, 730489). Sunbury Gardens 1882 (OS), 1890 (*Thom*), 1907–*c.* 2019 (OS). Sunbury Gardens/Garraithe na Gréine/Gáirdíní na Gréine 2021 (nameplate). Sunbury Gardens/Gairdíní Sunbury 2021 (Logainm).

Swanville Place/
Plás Bhaile na hEala

(Rathmines Rd Lower W., 715480, 731667). Swanville Place 1880 (*Thom*), 1882–*c.* 2019 (OS). Swanville Place/Plás Bhaile na hEala/Plás Suanbhaile 2021 (nameplate). Swanville Place/Plás Bhaile na hEala 2021 (Logainm).

Temple Gardens/
Gairdíní Temple

(Dartry Rd N., 716188, 730820). Temple Gardens 1888 (RRTM (6), 1.9.1888), 1890 (*Thom*), 1894 (RRTM (7), 4.4.1894), 1907 (OS), 1913 (Electoral rolls), 1936, *c.* 2019 (OS). Temple Gardens/Gairdíní Temple 2021 (nameplate; Logainm).

Temple Road/
Bóthar Temple

(Dartry Rd N., 716124, 730407). Temple Road *c.* 1864 (OS), 1864 (*Thom*), 1866 (RRTM (3), 11.4.1866), 1874 (Thom map), 1882–*c.* 2019 (OS). Temple Road/Bóthar an Teampaill/Bóthar Temple 2021 (nameplate). Temple Road/Bóthar Temple 2021 (Logainm).

William, William's, Williams or Williams' Park/
Páirc Mhic Liam

(Leinster Rd N., 715460, 731965). Wm Park 1821 (Duncan). Williams Park 1841 (*Thom*), 1843 (OS). William Park 1843 (*TH* 1.4.1843). Williams Park *c.* 1864 (OS), 1874 (Thom map). William's Park 1882 (OS). Williams Park 1891 (RRTM (6), 6.5.1891). Williams' Park 1907–8; William's 1936; Williams Park 1968, *c.* 2019 (OS). William's Park/Páirc Liam 2021 (nameplate). Williams Park/Páirc Mhic Liam 2021 (Logainm).

Wynnefield Road/
Bóthar Wynnefield

(Rathmines Rd Lower W., 715468, 731601). Streamville 1877 (OSN, 56). Stream Ville 1882 (OS). Wynnefield Road 1898 (RRTM (7), 2.11.1898); widened and extended W. by 1907–8; 1936–*c.* 2019 (OS). Wynnefield Road/Bóthar Bhán Mac Gaoithe/Bóthar Bán Mhic Gaoithe 2021 (nameplate). Wynnefield Road/Bóthar Wynnefield 2021 (Logainm).

York Avenue/
Ascaill Eabhrac

(Rathmines Rd Upper W., 715425, 731231). York Avenue 1907–*c.* 2019 (OS). York Avenue/Ascal Eabroc 2021 (nameplate). York Avenue/Ascaill Eabhrac 2021 (Logainm).

York Road/
Bóthar Eabhrac

(Rathmines Rd Upper W., 715454, 731197). York Road 1900 (*Thom*), 1907–*c.* 2019 (OS). York Road/Bóthar Eabhroc 2021 (nameplate). York Road/Bóthar Eabhrac 2021 (Logainm).

11. RELIGION

Holy Trinity Church (C. of I.), Church Ave E. (715800, 731453). Chapel of ease to united parishes of SS Peter and Kevin, erected at cost of £2,600 in 1828 (Lewis, ii, 504). Church 1843 (OS), 1874 (Thom map), 1882; Holy Trinity Church 1907–8, 1936; church (C. of I.) 1968; church *c.* 2019 (OS). See also **21** Entertainment, memorials and societies: parochial library.

St Philip's Church (C. of I.), Temple Rd S. (716104, 730377). St Philip's Church, 'built by the people of St Philip's parish by public subscription' in 1877 (OSN, 152). St Philip's Church 1882–1936; church (C. of I.) 1968; church *c.* 2019 (OS). See also **20** Education: school house; **21** Entertainment, memorials and societies: parochial hall.

Mary Immaculate Refuge of Sinners Catholic Church, Rathmines Rd Lower E. (715647, 732263). Church, Rathmines RC parish, dedicated to St Mary and St Peter 1830 (O'Carroll, 3). Dedicated in 1830 (Grimes, 105). RC chapel 1837 (Lewis, ii, 504). New Roman Catholic church 1838 (D'Alton, 777). RC chapel 1843 (OS). Demolished and rebuilt as Church of Our Lady of Refuge, first stone to be laid in 1850 (*FJ* 15.8.1850). RC chapel 1850 (Val. 2). Dedicated by Cardinal Cullen in 1856 (O'Carroll, 3). RC chapel 1874 (Thom map), 1882, 1887; RC church, extended by 1907 (OS). Burnt, rebuilt in 1922 (Kelly, 162–3). Catholic church 1936; church *c.* 2019 (OS). Mary Immaculate Refuge of Sinners Catholic Church 2021. See also **20** Education: St Mary's National School; **21** Entertainment, memorials and societies: parochial library; **22** Residence: presbytery.

Church, Grove Rd S. (715151, 732399), associated with Cathal Brugha Barracks (see **12** Defence). RC garrison church, built in 1848 (*NIAH* survey). Church 1874, 1898 (Thom map), 1907–8; Catholic church 1936; St Patrick's Military Church, statue 1936; church *c.* 2019 (OS).

HOLY TRINITY CHURCH, 1833

Church, Grosvenor Rd [south] W. (715128, 731343). Built in *c.* 1861 (RRTM (3), 9.4.1862). Improvements of £4,000 made in 1873 (*Ir. Times* 20.1.1873). Baptist chapel *c.* 1864 (OS), 1874 (Thom map). Grosvenor Hall 1882 (OS). Baptist chapel 1898 (Thom map). Grosvenor Hall 1907, 1936; church *c.* 2019 (OS).

Church of Christ, Scientist, Rathmines Park W., on site of former Rathmines Club (see **21** Entertainment, memorials and societies). Second Church of Christ, Scientist, built in 1923 (DIA). Church 1936 (OS). Refurbished, renamed Garland House in 1992 (Garland). Garland House, in use as offices 2021.

Tranquilla Convent (Carmelite), Rathmines Rd Upper E., on site of former Tranquilla (see **22** Residence). Tranquilla Convent, chapel 1850 (Val. 2), 1856, 1860 (*FJ* 17.1.1856, 13.3.1860), 1874 (Thom map); gate lodge 1882; burial ground, lodge, RC chapel, well 1907; burial ground, chapel, lodge, monument 1936 (OS). Buildings demolished, replaced by Tranquilla Park by 1987 (Gough and Quinn, 391). See also **20** Education: schools, Rathmines Rd Upper E. and W.

Convent of St Louis, Charleville Rd S., in former Charleville House (see **22** Residence). Loreto Convent 1907–8; Convent of St Louis 1936 (OS). New chapel built in 1962–4 (Archiseek). In use as convent and schools by 1968 (see **20** Education: Saint Louis Secondary School).

Gospel hall, Rathmines Rd Upper E. (715617, 730922). Protestant hall 1907, 1936; gospel hall *c.* 2019 (OS). Rathmines gospel hall 2021.

Presbyterian Mission House, Rathmines Rd Upper W., on site of former school house (see **20** Education). 1907, 1936 (OS). In commercial use *c.* 1966 (Leask, 74).

Front Elevation of a R.C. Chapel
designed for the Parish of Rathmines

RATHMINES RC CHURCH, *c.* 1830

GROSVENOR HALL, EARLY 20TH CENT.

CULLEN'S CASTLE, 1772, BY GABRIEL BERANGER

Synagogue and Jewish Congregation Hall, Grosvenor Place W. (715143, 731387). Orthodox Jewish synagogue 1936–40; Jewish Congregation Hall, moved to new premises (see next entry) in 1940 (Comerford).

Jewish Congregation Hall, Grosvenor Rd E. (715161, 731222). Moved from former premises (see previous entry) in 1940 (Comerford), 1942 (*Thom*). Congregation moved to new premises in Rathfarnham in 1948 (Comerford). Parochial Hall *c.* 2019 (OS).

Dublin Jewish Progressive Congregation Synagogue, Leicester Ave N. (715120, 731124). Synagogue opened in 1946; rebuilt in 1952 (Comerford). Dublin Jewish Progressive Congregation 1960 (*Thom*), 2021.

Sisters of Faithful Companions of Jesus convent, Kenilworth Sq. South S. (714934, 731037). 1947 (*Thom*).

Mill Hill Fathers residence, Dartry Rd W., in Dartry (see **22** Residence). 1958–2005 (local information). Saint Joseph's House *c.* 2019 (OS).

Holy Ghost Fathers residence, Rathmines Rd Lower W., in St Mary's College (see **20** Education). Established residence in 1891 (Maher, 31).

12. DEFENCE

Rathmines Castle Old. See **22** Residence.

Cullen's Castle, location unknown, probably Oakley Rd W., Ranelagh. Cullen's Castle, ruins depicted 1772 (Beranger).

Cathal Brugha (Portobello) Barracks, Rathmines Rd Lower W. (715179, 732233). Horse barracks 1816 (Taylor, J.). Barrack 1821 (Duncan). Horse barrack 1822 (Cooke). Portobello Barracks 1836 (Armstrong 4). Cavalry barracks 1838 (D'Alton, 777). Portobello Barracks, guard house, magazine, riding school 1843 (OS). Barracks 1850 (Val. 2). Portobello Barracks, flagstaff, guard house, magazine *c.* 1864 (OS). Portobello Barracks, flagstaff, magazine 1874 (Thom map). Portobello Barracks, artillery parade ground, artillery square, caponniere, flagstaff, 8 fountains, gas meter, guard room, hospital, 2 infirmary stables, manege, 2 platforms, 6 pumps, reading rooms, 2 stores, wash house, weighing machine, well 1882, 1887 (OS). Portobello Barracks, flagstaff, hospital 1898 (Thom map). Artillery parade ground, artillery square, bath, canteen, guard room, hospital, infants' school, infirmary, married soldiers, reading rooms,

sergeants' mess, stables, stores and orderlies quarters, tailor and shoe maker, wash house *c.* 1901 (Val. 3). Portobello Barracks 1907–8; Portobello Barracks, ball alley, 9 covered tanks 1936; Cathal Brugha Barracks, ball alley 1968; unnamed *c.* 2019 (OS). Cathal Brugha Barracks 2021. See also **11** Religion: church; **20** Education: infant school, school; **21** Entertainment, memorials and societies: cricket ground, ball alley.

13. ADMINISTRATION

Night watchman sentry box, Rathmines Rd Lower, site unknown. *c.* 1820 (Joyce, 169).

Police station, Rathmines Ave N. (715507, 731448). City police station 1837 (Lewis, ii, 504). Police station 1843 (OS). Police barrack 1850 (Val. 2). Moved to new premises by *c.* 1864 (see next entry).

Police station, Rathmines Ave N. (715477, 731481). Police station, moved from former premises (see previous entry) by *c.* 1864 (OS); 1874 (Thom map), 1882–1936 (OS). Moved to new premises by 1968 (see next entry).

Rathmines Garda Station, Rathgar Rd S. (715460, 731516). G.S. Station, moved from former premises (see previous entry) by 1968; *c.* 2019 (OS), 2021.

Rathmines Repeal Arbitration Courthouse, Rathmines Rd Lower E. (715623, 732286). First meeting held in Oct. 1843 (*FJ* 27.10.1843).

Town hall, Rathmines Rd Lower E. (715589, 731825). Commissioners' house, in administrative use from mid-1840s (Ó Maitiú, 159). Rathmines Township Commissioners Office 1847 (*FJ* 29.7.1847). Unnamed *c.* 1864 (OS). Commissioners' house, hall added in 1867 (Ó Maitiú, 159–63). Town hall 1874 (Thom map); weighing machine 1882 (OS). Parliamentary act obtained to rebuild in 1893 (Ó Maitiú, 159–63). Town hall 1898 (Thom map), 1907–68 (OS). Incorporated technical school (see **20** Education: Rathmines College) in 1980 (local information). Rathmines College of Further Education *c.* 2019 (OS), 2021. See also below, post office; **17** Transport: stables; **18** Utilities: telegraph office; **21** Entertainment, memorials and societies: concert hall and cinema.

TOWN HALL (OLD), 1878, BY J. O'CONNELL

TOWN HALL (NEW), *c.* 1910

Pillar letter boxes:

Rathmines Rd Lower E. (715601, 732162). 1859 (*FJ* 2.9.1859), 1882, 1907–36 (OS).

Leinster Rd N. (715084, 731684). 1876–1936 (OS).

Belgrave Rd N. (715947, 731481). 1882 (OS).

Grosvenor Rd [north] N. (715407, 731521). 1882–1936 (OS).

Kenilworth Sq. North N. (714922, 731316). 1882–1936 (OS).

Palmerston Park S. (715692, 730617). 1882–1936 (OS).

Temple Rd N. (716191, 730415). 1882 (OS), 1902 (*Thom*), 1907, 1936 (OS).

Mountpleasant Ave Upper W. (715888, 731775). Pillar letter box to be erected 1893 (RRTM (5), 7.6.1893); 1907, 1936 (OS).

Grosvenor Sq. North N. (714971, 731882). Permission for letter box granted in 1897 (RRTM (7), 7.7.1897). Pillar letter box 1902 (*Thom*); 1907, 1936 (OS).

Grosvenor Rd [south] W. (715169, 731356). 1902 (*Thom*), 1907, 1936 (OS).

Rathmines Rd Lower E. (715563, 731835). 1902 (*Thom*), 1907, 1936 (OS).

2, Church Ave N. (715602, 731383; 715753, 731458). 1907, 1936 (OS).

Cowper Rd N. (716047, 730962). 1907, 1936 (OS), 1947 (*Thom*).

Effra Rd S. (714880, 731427). 1907, 1936 (OS), 1947 (*Thom*).

Grove Park S. (715337, 732415). 1907, 1936 (OS), 1947 (*Thom*).

Temple Rd N. (716191, 730414). 1907, 1936 (OS), 1947 (*Thom*).

York Rd N. (715442, 731196). 1907 (OS), 1947 (*Thom*).

Palmerston Rd E. (715984, 731199). 1936 (OS), 1947 (*Thom*).

St Kevin's Park N. (715658, 730321). 1936 (OS), 1947 (*Thom*).

Wall letter box, Dartry Rd W. (715962, 730125). 1907, 1936 (OS), 1947 (*Thom*).

Post offices:

Rathmines Rd Lower E., in town hall (see above). Post office receiving house in Rathmines town hall opened in 1864; removed from town hall in 1870 (RRTM (4), 4.1.1864, 4.5.1870).

Rathmines Rd Lower W. (715533, 731671). 1882 (OS), *c.* 1901 (Val. 3).

Location unknown. New post office being built 1883 (RRTM (4), 4.7.1883).

Rathgar Rd E. (715262, 731079). 1907 (OS).

Rathmines Rd Lower W. (715590, 732366). 1907–8, 1936 (OS).

Wynnefield Rd N. (715489, 731615). Post office 1907–8 (OS). Closed in 1935 (*Sunday Ind.* 1.2.1935).

Rathmines Rd Upper E. (715561, 731536). Built in 1934 (datestone). Opened, transferred from Portobello District Office in 1935 (*Sunday Ind.* 17.2.1935). Post office 1936, 1968 (OS). Extended in 1989 (datestone). Post office 2021.

14. PRIMARY PRODUCTION

Arable land, manor of Colonia / St Sepulchre (see **2** Legal status), location unknown. 1288, 1326 (Murphy and Potterton, 291).

Haggard, manor of Colonia / St Sepulchre (see **2** Legal status), location unknown. Mid-13th cent. (Murphy and Potterton, 315).

Mr Boland's field, location unknown, possibly near Mountpleasant Ave Upper or Lower. 1800 (*FJ* 6.5.1800).

Mowld's farm, Rathmines Rd Lower W. (715540, 731839). 19th cent. (Kelly, 189). Old farmhouse, demolished in *c.* 1840 (Joyce, 170).

Castle Field, Upper Rathmines, site unknown. 1820 (RD 750/238/510173).

Little Paul's Hill, Upper Rathmines, site unknown. 1820 (RD 750/238/510173).

Paul's Hill, Upper Rathmines, site unknown. 1820 (RD 750/238/510173).

Sheep Field, Upper Rathmines, site unknown. 1820 (RD 750/238/510173).

The Slangs, Upper Rathmines, site unknown. 1820 (RD 750/238/510173).

Church Fields, Belgrave Sq. North S. (715882, 731676). Wasteland known as Church Fields 1848 (Kelly, 218). Built over by Belgrave Sq. in 1851 (see **10** Streets; **21** Entertainment, memorials and societies).

Meadow and aftergrass, in Belgrave Sq. (715883, 731679). Meadow and aftergrass for sale, *c.* 3½ acres 1875 (*Ir. Times* 19.6.1875).

Woodland, manor of Colonia/St Sepulchre (see **2** Legal status), location unknown. 66 acres, valued at 3½ *d.* per acre in early 14th cent. (Murphy and Potterton, 362).

Tree plantation, Williams Park E. (715491, 731902). Almost 2,000 trees 1814 (*FJ* 24.3.1814).

Gardens, 3, manor of Colonia/St Sepulchre (see **2** Legal status), locations unknown. 3 gardens, probably including orchards 1326 (Murphy and Potterton, 351).

Orchard, location unknown, associated with Rathmines Castle (see **22** Residence: Rathmines Castle Old). 1746 (RD 49/290/32027).

Orchard, Mount Drummond Ave W. (714956, 731973). Depicted 1843 (OS). Orchard *c.* 1864 (OS), 1874 (Thom map), 1876 (OS), 1898 (Thom map). Depicted 1907 (OS).

Orchard, Temple Rd N. (716040, 730476). Orchard *c.* 1864 (OS), 1874 (Thom map).

Grimwood's nursery, Rathgar Rd W. (715238, 731377). Nursery 1816 (Taylor, J.), 1821 (Duncan). Grimwood's nursery 1843; built over by residences by 1907 (OS).

Park Nursery, Rathmines Park S. (715571, 731287). Park Nursery 1875 (*Ir. Times* 13.10.1875). Nursery, fountain 1882; Park Nursery, fountain, glasshouses depicted 1907 (OS).

Hilton Nursery, Rathmines Rd, site unknown. 1886, 1892 (*FJ* 20.4.1886, 29.3.1892).

Dunlap's Nursery, Upper Rathmines, site unknown. 1893 (*Ir. Daily Ind.* 5.7.1893), 1921 (RRTM (9), 2.2.1921).

Field, market garden crops, Rathmines Rd Lower W. (715490, 731931). Market garden crops 1950s–early 1960s (local information). Unnamed 1968 (OS). Built over by 1970 (local information).

Lime kiln, Rathmines Rd Lower E. (715666, 732325). 1816 (Taylor, J.). See also next entries.

Lime kiln, Rathmines Rd, site unknown, possibly same as previous, next entry. 1816 (*FJ* 30.8.1816).

Lime kiln, Rathmines Rd Lower E. (715671, 732295), possibly same as previous entries. 1830 (Sherrard and Brassington).

Weir, R. Dodder, Orwell Park S. (715595, 729898). Unnamed 1843; weir *c.* 1864, 1879, 1882 (OS), *c.* 1901 (Val. 3), 1907 (OS).

Weir, R. Dodder, Milltown Rd S. (716118, 730081). Weir 1843, *c.* 1864 (OS), 1874 (Thom map), 1879–1968; unnamed *c.* 2019 (OS).

Granary, Rathmines Rd Upper, site unknown. 1846 (*FJ* 15.8.1846).

Lea Land, Castlewood Ave, site unknown. Oats, 2 acres 1856 (*FJ* 14.8.1856).

Dairy yards, Rathmines Rd Upper, site unknown. Dairy yards, licensed to contain 50 cows 1885 (*FJ* 12.10.1885).

15. MANUFACTURING

Mill, near R. Dodder, location unknown. In possession of De Meones family 13th cent. (Ball, ii, 100).

Mills, manor of Colonia/St Sepulchre (see **2** Legal status), location unknown. Mills worth £3 10*s.* 1326 (Murphy and Potterton, 424).

Corn mill, location unknown. Andrew Talbot, miller, demised to John Long 1729 (RD 1729/61/213/41147).

Willan's Woollen Cloth Mills, R. Dodder, Dartry Rd S. (715997, 730070). Mills 1760 (Rocque). Willan's mills 1820 (*FJ* 3.1.1820). Woollen factory, Messrs Wilans 1837 (Lewis, ii, 504). Willans' Woollen Cloth Mills 1843 (*FJ* 11.11.1843). Cloth mill 1843 (OS). Cotton factory 1850 (Val. 2). Cloth manufactory, sluice *c.* 1864 (OS), 1874 (Thom map). Cloth manufactory, chimney, 3 sluices 1879; cloth manufactory (in ruins), chimney, 3 sluices 1882 (OS). Replaced by Dartry Dye Works in 1895 (see next entry).

    Mill pond: mill dam *c.* 1864, 1843 (OS); mill pond 1874 (Thom map), 1879–1936 (OS).

    Mill race: depicted 1843, *c.* 1864 (OS); mill race 1874 (Thom map), 1879–1936 (OS).

Dartry Dye Works, R. Dodder, Dartry Rd S., on site of former cloth manufactory (see previous entry). Est. 1895 (datestone). Cloth manufactory 1898 (Thom map). Dartry Dye Works, sluices, weighing machine 1907; Dartry Dye Works 1936; factory 1968 (OS).

    Mill pond: mill pond 1898 (Thom map), 1907, 1936 (OS).

    Mill race: mill race 1907, 1936 (OS).

Dye works, Rathmines Rd Lower W. (715545, 732045). 1936 (OS).

Free Trade Bakery, Rathmines Rd, site unknown. 1850 (*FJ* 13.6.1850).

Rathmines Bakery, Rathmines Rd Upper E., site unknown. Flynn's bakery 1851 (*FJ* 1.7.1851). Rathmines Bakery, John Flynn 1888 (*FJ* 8.6.1888). Rathmines Bakery Co. 1949 (*Leinster Exp.* 10.12.1949).

Bakery, Rathmines Rd Lower E. (715563, 731708). Bakery, confectionery, William Ferguson 1933 (*Kerryman* 4.3.1933).

Slaughter house, junction Rathmines Rd Lower/Rathgar Rd, site unknown. 1853 (RRTM (2), 3.8.1853).

Slaughter house, Rathmines Rd, site unknown. 1859 (RRTM (2), 26.1.1859).

Slaughter house, location unknown. 1866 (RRTM (3), 6.8.1866).

Factory, location unknown, near R. Dodder at Milltown. Factory 1856 (RRTM (2), 30.7.1856).

Astronomical works, Observatory Lane E. (715650, 731935). Astronomical works, Thomas Grubb, moved from former

GRUBB'S ASTRONOMICAL WORKS, 1875

TAYTO CRISP FACTORY, 1958

site in Ranelagh in 1860s (Kelly, 181). Astronomical works, chimney, pump 1882; 1907–8 (OS). Replaced by waterproof factory by 1936 (see below).

Bolton and Sons steam works, Grove Park S. (715535, 732459). Steam works 1881, 1885 (*FJ* 21.6.1881, 29.8.1885). Bolton and Sons steam works 1921 (*Ir. Independent* 29.1.1921). Replaced by Brittain's motor works by 1929 (see below).

Umbrella and parasol manufactory, Rathmines Rd Lower E. (715596, 732067). 1902 (*Thom*).

Manufacturing locksmiths, Rathmines Rd Lower W. (715597, 732466). 1902 (*Thom*).

Soap works, Church Gardens W. (715585, 731529). 1907–8 (OS).

Confectionery factory, Ardee Rd E. (715509, 732081). Confectionery factory 1925 (*Munster Exp.* 20.2.1925). Mackintosh's 1932 (*Ir. Press* 31.12.1932). Confectionery factory 1936 (OS). See also below, Irish Blindcraft manufactory and shop.

Brittain's motor works, Grove Park S. (715535, 732459), on site of former steam works (see above). R.A. Brittain motor works, built in 1929; began assembly of Morris cars in 1934 (Montgomery, 127). Motor works 1936 (OS). Closed in 1977 (Montgomery, 127). See also **21** Entertainment, memorials and societies: social club.

Kodak photographic works, Rathmines Rd Lower W. (715572, 732308). Began production in 1930 (Archiseek; Kelly, 195). Moved to new premises in Dún Laoghaire by 1982 (*Ir. Independent* 28.6.1982).

Paper manufactory, Parker Hill N. (715717, 731935). Iris-Lin Factory 1936 (OS). Rathmines Paper Manufacturers 1938; Dublin Box Co. 1958 (*Ir. Press* 31.3.1938, 16.9.1958). Factory 1968 (OS). Demolished in *c.* 1980 (local information).

Waterproof factory, Rathmines Rd Lower E., on site of former astronomical works (see above). Waterproof factory 1936 (OS). Waterproof manufacturer 1945 (*Thom*). Factory 1968 (OS).

Tayto potato crisp manufactory, Mountpleasant Ave Upper W. (715812, 731851). Opened in 1956 (Curtis, M., 2019, 138). Tayto potato crisp manufactory 1958 (*Ir. Press* 21.10.1958). Factory 1968 (OS). Closed in 1981 (Curtis, M., 2019, 138).

Horse veterinary product (Reducine) manufactory, Rathmines Rd Lower W., in Mount Anthony (see **22** Residence). 1958 (*Thom*).

Rex Casting Works, Mountpleasant Ave Lower W. (715710, 732359). Rex Casting Works, aluminium, brass, bronze 1958, 1963 (*Ir. Independent* 12.2.1958, 16.3.1963).

Irish Fastener Industries, Mountpleasant Ave Upper E. (715903, 731815). 1967, 1972 (*Ir. Press* 12.2.1967, 16.11.1972).

Irish Blindcraft manufactory and shop, Ardee Rd E., in former confectionery factory (see above). Irish Blindcraft 1966 (*Ir. Press* 10.11.1966). Closed in 1990 (*Ir. Times* 12.8.2004).

Factory, Castlewood Ave N. (715638, 731693). Factory 1968 (OS).

Factory, Dartry Rd E., in former tram depot (see **17** Transport). Factory 1968 (OS). In use as offices 2021.

RATHMINES ROAD LOWER/UPPER JUNCTION, *c.* 1920

KELSO LAUNDRY, 1933

Factory, Mountpleasant Ave Upper W. (715816, 731839). Factory 1968 (OS).

Factory, Parker Hill N. (715665, 731940), partly on site of former waterproof factory (see above). Factory 1968 (OS).

Runtalrad radiator manufactory, Cambridge Rd W. (715750, 731595). 1968 (*Ir. Independent* 21.10.1968), 1969 (*Ir. Press* 25.9.1969).

Chimney, Grove Rd S. (715549, 732466). 1882, 1887 (OS).

Smithy, Observatory Lane S. (715646, 731996). *c.* 1901 (Val. 3), 1907–8 (OS).

Distillery, Church Gardens, site unknown. Donnelly's liquor whiskey 1955 (*Sunday Ind.* 18.12.1955).

Saw mills, location unknown. O'Mahony's saw mills 1955 (*Ir. Press* 21.10.1955).

16. TRADES AND SERVICES

Bank, Rathmines Rd Lower W. (715523, 731724). National Bank 1882; bank 1907–68 (OS). Bank of Ireland 2021.

Bank, Rathmines Rd Lower E. (715568, 731794). Bank 1907–68 (OS). Demolished, built over by Swan Shopping Centre by 1983 (*Ir. Independent* 2.9.1983).

Bank, Rathmines Rd Lower W. (715515, 731596). Belfast Banking Co., built in 1901 (Archiseek). Bank 1907–8, 1936 (OS). Closed in *c.* 2000 (local information).

Bank of Ireland, Rathmines Rd Lower W. (715521, 731636). Built in 1919–20 (DIA). Bank of Ireland 1958 (Thom; nameplate). Incorporated into refurbished Stella Cinema complex in 2017 (see **21** Entertainment, memorials and societies).

Kelso Laundry, Rathmines Rd Lower W. (715566, 732117). Opened in 1914 (Kelly, 195). Kelso Laundry 1936 (OS). Closed in 1994 (*Evening Herald* 15.12.1994). Sold for redevelopment in 1997 (*Ir. Independent* 27.6.1997).

Alexandra Hostel, Castlewood Ave S., in former Castlewood House (see **22** Residence). Alexandra Hostel 1915 (*Thom*); housed 26–28 working girls, run by Alexandra College Guild 1916 (*Queen* 28.10.1916). Alexandra Hostel 1936 (OS).

Bridge Hotel, Rathmines Rd Lower E. (715627, 732398). 1942 (*Ir. Independent* 18.11.1942), 1950 (*Thom*).

Laden Press printing company, Parker Hill, site unknown. 1957 (*Ir. Independent* 14.10.1957), 1960 (*Ir. Press* 11.3.1960).

17. TRANSPORT

Stable, manor of Colonia / St Sepulchre (see **2** Legal status), location unknown. Probably 14th cent. (Murphy and Potterton, 172).

Stables, Rathmines Rd Lower E., site unknown, associated with town hall (see **13** Administration). Stabling for omnibus horses 1848 (Ó Maitiú, 145–6).

PORTOBELLO BRIDGE AND THE GRAND CANAL, 1812–47, BY S.F. BROCAS

Classon's Bridge, R. Dodder, Milltown Rd S. (716325, 730046). Unnamed 1760 (Rocque). Classon's Bridge 1843, *c.* 1864 (OS); rebuilt in 1863 (*Ir. Builder* 15.12.1863); 1874 (Thom map), 1907 (OS); widened in 1928 (datestone); 1936, 1968; unnamed *c.* 2019 (OS). Classon's Bridge 2021 (nameplate).

Portobello Bridge, Grand Canal, Rathmines Rd Lower, N. end (715616, 732498). Latouche Bridge 1798 (Wilson). Portobello Bridge 1811 (*FJ* 30.8.1811). La Touche Bridge 1811 (Campbell). Latouche Bridge 1816 (Taylor, J.), 1821 (Duncan), 1822 (Cooke). La Touche Bridge 1830 (Sherrard and Brassington). Portobello Bridge 1837 (Lewis, ii, 504). Bridge 1838 (D'Alton, 777). La Touche Bridge 1843 (OS). Portobello Bridge 1846 (*FJ* 25.6.1846). La Touche bridge *c.* 1864 (OS). Widened for tramway in 1872 (RRTM (4), 8.5.1872). Latouche Bridge 1874 (Thom map), 1882–1936 (OS), 2021.

Robert Emmet Bridge, Grand Canal, Harold's Cross Rd, N. end (714869, 732435). Clanbrassil Bridge 1817 (Nairn 2), 1843, *c.* 1864; Haroldscross Bridge 1907; Robert Emmet Bridge 1936 (OS), 2021.

Mile stone, Rathmines Rd Lower, site unknown. 1818 (*FJ* 14.4.1818).

Lock house, Grand Canal, Portobello Bridge, Grove Rd S. (715593, 732469). 1830 (Sherrard and Brassington), 1850 (Val. 2), 1882, 1887 (OS).

Turnpike, junction Grove Rd/Rathmines Rd Lower (715586, 732484). Turnpike 1830 (Sherrard and Brassington). Old turnpike 1861 (*FJ* 8.4.1861).

Omnibus, Dublin city centre to Richmond Hill. Plan for omnibus system to operate between city and suburbs presented in 1848 (Ó Maitiú, 145–6). Rathmines Conveyance Co. omnibuses, every 15 minutes from Bank of Ireland (College Green) and General Post Office to Richmond Hill 1850, 1854 (*FJ* 20.5.1850, 16.9.1854). Wilson's 'Favourite' omnibus, General Post Office to Rathmines, Rathgar and Roundtown (Terenure) 1850 (*FJ* 22.5.1850).

Dublin, Wicklow and Wexford Railway. Bray–Dublin (Harcourt Rd terminus) line, opened in 1854 (*FJ* 10.7.1854). Renamed Dublin, Wicklow and Wexford Railway in 1860 (Shepherd, 35–8). Dublin Wicklow and Wexford Railway 1882 (OS). Renamed Dublin and South Eastern Railway in 1907; incorporated into Great Southern Railway in 1925; Harcourt St line closed in 1959 (Shepherd, 59, 93, 100). Luas opened in 2004 (*Ir. Times* 28.6.2004); 2021.

Milltown station, Richmond Ave South E. (716501, 730252). Opened in 1860 (Shepherd, 110). Station, 2 signal posts *c.* 1864 (OS). Milltown station, signal post 1874 (Thom map). Milltown station, level crossing, 2 signal posts 1882 (OS), 1898 (Thom map). Milltown station, foot bridge, level crossing, 2 platforms, signal post 1907; Milltown station, level crossing 1936 (OS).

Rathmines station, 0.5 km E. of township (716273, 731487). Ranelagh station, opened in 1896 (Ó Maitiú, 146–7); 1907 (OS). Rathmines station 1921 (Ó Maitiú, 146–7). Closed with closure of Harcourt St line in 1959 (Shepherd, 100). Reopened for Luas in 2004 (local information).

Car and cab company, Rathmines Rd Lower E., to rear of Largo House (see **22** Residence), site unknown. Closing 1858 (*FJ* 9.9.1858).

Stage car, Dublin city to Baltinglass via Rathmines. 1863 (*FJ* 3.4.1863).

Horse-drawn tram. Dublin Tramways Co. line, College Green (Dublin) to Garville Ave (Rathgar) via Rathmines Rd, opened in 1872 (Murphy, 3). Dublin Central Tramways Co. line, College Green (Dublin) to Rathfarnham via Harold's Cross Rd, opened in 1878 (Scannell, 7). Palmerston Park to College Green line opened in 1879 (Corcoran, 141). Dublin United Tramways Co. established in 1881 (Murphy, 3). Replaced by electrified tram by 1900 (see next entry).

Electric tram. College Green (Dublin) to Garville Ave (Rathgar). Tram electrified, replaced former horse-drawn tram (see previous entry) by 1900 (Murphy, 5). College Green (Dublin) to Garville Ave (Rathgar) via Rathmines Rd line depicted 1907–8; Dublin Central Tramways Co. line, College Green (Dublin) to Rathfarnham via Harold's Cross Rd line depicted 1907–8, 1936 (OS). Closed by 1939 (Murphy, 7).

Tram depot, Dartry Rd E. (715946, 730188). Built in 1905 (DIA). Tram depot 1907, 1936 (OS). Converted to use as factory by 1968 (see **15** Manufacturing).

Cabman's shelter, junction Rathmines Rd Lower and Rathgar Rd, site unknown. 1879 (RRTM (5), 3.12.1879).

Tow path, Grand Canal, Grove Rd (715439, 732465). Towing path 1882, 1887 (OS). Tow path *c.* 1901 (Val. 3).

Wharfage and toll bar, canal bank near Portobello Bridge (see above), site unknown. 1884 (RRTM (5), 3.9.1884).

Foot bridge, R. Dodder, Dartry Rd S. (715986, 730024). Foot bridge 1968; unnamed *c.* 2019 (OS).

18. UTILITIES

Pathway, Portobello Bridge (see **17** Transport) to village of Rathmines, site unknown. Built by Robert Wynne by 1811 (*FJ* 30.8.1811).

Watering slip, location unknown, probably Rathmines Rd Lower. 1811 (*FJ* 6.4.1811).

Street lighting. Alliance and Dublin Consumers' Gas Co. contracted to supply gas lamps in 1847; 152 lamps erected by 1852; gas lighting replaced by electric lighting in 1900 (Ó Maitiú, 103).

Pump, Wynnefield Rd N. (715523, 731606). Rathmines Pump 1853 (RRTM (2), 14.9.1853). Pump 1882 (OS).

CLANBRASSIL BRIDGE, HAROLD'S CROSS, 1817, BY C.M. NAIRN

Pump, Blackberry Lane N. (715551, 732335). 1856 (RRTM (2), 18.6.1856), 1882 (OS).

Pump yard, Upper Rathmines, site unknown. Old pump yard 1857 (RRTM (2), 5.8.1857).

Swan River culvert, Rathmines Rd Lower and Richmond Hill, R. Swan. Culverted by 1858 (RRTM (2), 3.2.1858).

Waterworks, Gallanstown, on the Grand Canal, 8 km W. of Rathmines (708312, 732246). Waterworks, constructed by Rathmines Commissioners and brought to township at 8th lock on Grand Canal in 1863 (Ó Maitiú, 88).

Telegraph office, Rathmines Rd Lower E., in town hall (see **13** Administration). Telegraph office established in 1864; closed in 1870 (RRTM (3), 15.6.1864; RRTM (4), 4.5.1870).

Gas supply, Rathmines Rd Lower, from Portobello Bridge to Roundtown (Terenure). 12-inch main gas pipe laid in 1872 (*Ir. Times* 26.9.1872).

Fountains:

Dartry Cottages E. (715971, 730014). 1879, 1882 (OS).

Castlewood Place W. (715611, 731615). 1882 (OS).

Milltown Rd S. (716249, 730093). Fountain 1882; water tap 1907, 1936 (OS).

Rathmines Ave N. (715495, 731432). Fountain 1882, 1907–8; water tap 1936 (OS).

Rathmines Rd Lower E. (715563, 731824). 1882 (OS).

Spire View Lane W. (715225, 731275). 1882; water tap 1936 (OS).

Greenfield Place N. (715008, 732139). 1907–8, 1936 (OS).

Sewage works. Begun in 1879 (40 & 41 Vict., c. 82). Completed in 1879 (Ó Maitiú, 101–2).

Fire station, Rathmines Rd Lower E. (715610, 731863). Rathmines Commissioners permitted to establish fire brigade by Rathmines and Rathgar (Milltown Extension) Act in 1880 (43 & 44 Vic. c. 108). Fire station (Rathmines UDC) 1907–8 (OS). Moved to adjacent premises in 1914 (see next entry).

Fire station, Rathmines Rd Lower E. (715588, 731866), in former public library (see **21** Entertainment, memorials and societies). Fire station, moved from adjacent premises (see previous entry) in 1914 (RRTA 1/1/103), 1936–93 (OS). Fire brigade relocated to Donnybrook, building transferred to Civil Defence Auxiliary Fire Brigade in *c.* 1982 (local information). Gallery space 2021.

Weighing machine, Rathmines Rd Lower W. (715586, 732443). Weighing machine 1882, 1887; unnamed 1907 (OS).

Weighing machine, Rathmines Rd Lower E. (715682, 731880). Weighing machine 1907, 1936 (OS).

Electricity works, Gulistan Terrace S. (715708, 731852). Board of Trade order obtained by Rathmines Commissioners to generate electricity in 1896; plant opened in Aug. 1900 (Ó Maitiú, 166). Electricity works (Rathmines UDC) *c.* 1901 (Val. 3), 1907–8; electricity station 1936; Dublin City Council *c.* 2019 (OS).

ESB transformer station, Castlewood Terrace [east] N. (715750, 731801). Electricity station 1936 (OS). ESB transformer station 1969 (*Thom*).

Latrine (underground), junction Rathmines Rd Lower/Rathmines Rd Upper (715531, 731570). Lavatory, bond for building by Rathmines Commissioners 1903 (RRTA 1/4/4). Latrine 1936; toilet 1968 (OS).

Stepping stones, R. Dodder, Milltown Rd S. (716144, 730055). 1907 (OS).

Rathmines Morgue, Castlewood Terrace [east] N. (715740, 731792). Morgue (Rathmines UDC) 1907–8 (OS). Rathmines Morgue 1932 (*Ir. Press* 24.3.1932).

Rathmines UDC service yard, Castlewood Terrace [east] N. (715673, 731835). Unnamed 1907–*c.* 2019 (OS). Dublin City Council service yard 2021.

Refuse destructor, Gulistan Terrace S. (715712, 731817). Refuse destructor (Rathmines UDC) 1907–8; unnamed 1936 (OS).

Radio Éireann studio, Rathmines Rd Lower W. (715591, 732384). Portobello Studio, opened in 1948 (*Ir. Press* 1.10.1948). Radio Éireann studio 1955 (*Thom*). Converted to RTÉ Broadcasting Museum in 1981 (*FJ* 9.6.1981). Museum closed by 1994 (*Evening Echo* 24.12.1994).

Petrol station, Rathmines Rd Upper W. (715598, 731128). 1969 (*Thom*).

19. HEALTH

Sanitary court, location unknown. Sitting by 1850 (Ó Maitiú, 82).

Dispensary, Rathmines Rd Upper W. (715545, 731460). 1882 (OS).

Dispensary, Rathmines Rd Upper E. (715591, 731451). 1907–68 (OS).

Cholera sheds, Mountpleasant Ave Upper W., at Gulistan, site unknown. Erected on commissioners' land during cholera outbreak in 1893 (Ó Maitiú, 84).

Belgrave Private Hospital, Belgrave Rd N. (715872, 731495). 1912 (*Thom*), 1915 (*BNL* 2.2.1915).

20. EDUCATION

School, Palmerston Park E., in former Rathmines Castle Old (see **22** Residence). School, Revd Charles Barry 1789 (*Gentleman's magazine*, lix); *c.* 1802 (Taylor, A.). Mansion House or Castle of Rathmines 1807 (RD 588/404/400505). School for sale, Mr Falloon 1815 (*FJ* 3.4.1815). Rathmines School 1821 (Duncan). Reverted to residential use as boarding house for invalids by 1833 (Joyce, 170). Old Rathmines Castle 1837 (Lewis, ii, 503). 'Now called the castle', formerly a school 1838 (D'Alton, 777–8). Rathmines Castle Boarding School, Mr Keily 1839 (*FJ* 3.7.1839). Rathmines Castle Old 1843 (OS). Demolished in *c.* 1844 (Palmerston papers, BR

SCHOOL IN RATHMINES CASTLE (OLD), 1789

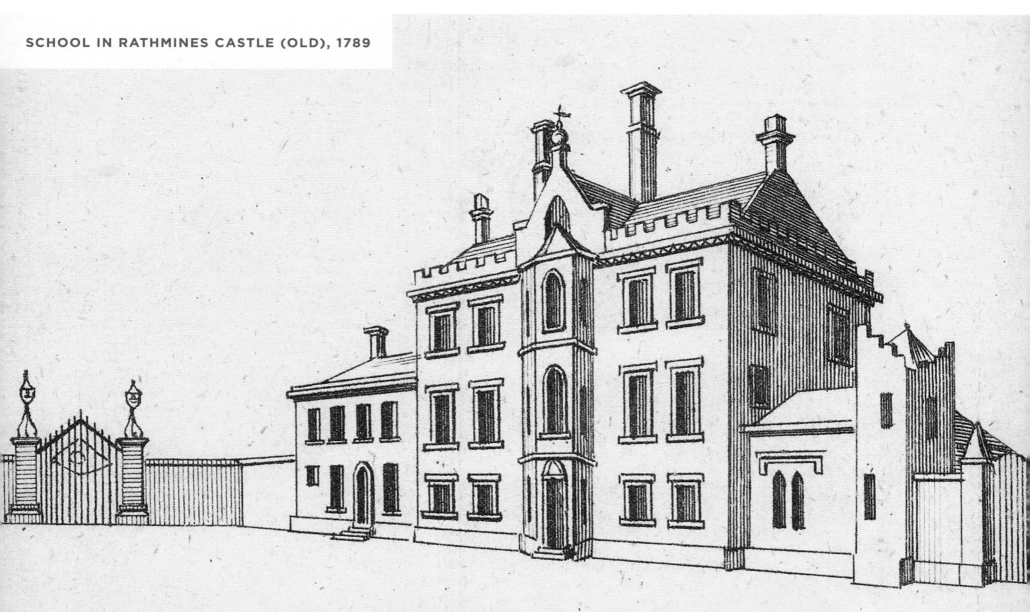

144/9/6/1–3), site laid over by Palmerston Park by 1870 (see **10** Streets; **21** Entertainment, memorials and societies).

St Mary's National School, Richmond Hill N. (715690, 732202), associated with Mary Immaculate Refuge of Sinners Catholic Church (see **11** Religion). 'School house recently erected by parishioners' 1834 (*Jesuit or Catholic Sentinel* 22.3.1834). School house 1837 (Lewis, ii, 504). Parochial school, 150 pupils, male and female 1838 (D'Alton, 778). School 1843 (OS). National school house 1850 (Val. 2). National school 1874 (Thom map), 1882 (OS). New National Schools 1886 (RRTM (6), 1.12.1886). National school, red stock brick and granite building, 6 classrooms and study halls, to accommodate 900 pupils 1886 (*Ir. Builder* 15.6.1886). National school 1887 (OS), 1898 (Thom map). School, creche 1907–8, 1936 (OS). Known as Richmond Hill School mid-20th cent.; demolished, new school built in early 1960s (local information).

Female day school, location unknown. Partly supported by subscription 1837 (Lewis, ii, 504).

Hibernian Marine School, Grove Park N., in Grove House (see **22** Residence). Grove School 1843 (OS). Hibernian Marine School *c*. 1900 (Quane, 78), 1904 (Val. 3). Demolished, built over by 1907 (OS).

School, Rathmines Rd Upper E. (715600, 731017), associated with Tranquilla Convent (see **11** Religion). School house 1843 (OS). Poor schools 1860 (*FJ* 13.3.1860). National school *c*. 1864 (OS), 1874 (Thom map), 1882 (OS), 1898 (Thom map). Moved to new premises by 1907 (see next entry).

Schools, Rathmines Rd Upper W. (715576, 731055), associated with Tranquilla Convent (see **11** Religion). Schools, moved from former premises 1907, 1936 (OS).

School house, Rathmines Rd Upper W. (715610, 731278). School house 1843 (OS). Old school, in use for evening religious services *c*. 1859; congregation moved to Rathgar in 1862 (Leask, 12, 14). Demolished, replaced by Presbyterian Mission House by 1907 (see **11** Religion).

Female free and national school, location unknown. 1846 (*Thom*).

Military, Civil Service and Collegiate Institute boarding and day school, Leinster Rd N. (715421, 731833). School for General Education, Andrew O'Callaghan principal, opened in 1850 (*FJ* 1.8.1850). Military, Civil Service and Collegiate Institute boarding and day school 1872 (*Ir. Times* 19.10.1872).

Hollymount Academy, location unknown, possibly Observatory Lane. 1852 (*FJ* 10.1.1852), 1860 (RRTM (2), 11.7.1860).

Generational and Collegiate Institute, Rathmines Rd Lower W. (715518, 731715). 1856 (*Ir. Times* 9.4.1856), 1859 (*Thom*).

Rathmines School, Rathmines Rd Lower E. (715621, 732284). Opened by Revd Charles Benson in 1858 (Moffat, 73). Rathmines School 1882, 1887 (OS). In use as library 1887–99 (see **21** Entertainment, memorials and societies). Technical school, opened by Rathmines Commissioners in 1901 (Ó Maitiú, 176). Technical school 1907–8 (OS).

ST MARY'S NATIONAL SCHOOL PLAYGROUND, EARLY 20TH CENT.

Incorporated into Rathmines College in 1913 (see below). In use as Boys' Brigade premises 1928 (see **21** Entertainment, memorials and societies). See also **21** Entertainment, memorials and societies: Fortesque Cricket Club.

Rathmines Township Schools, Rathmines Rd Upper W. (715582, 731348). School *c.* 1864 (OS). Rathmines Township Schools 1876 (Dungan, 97). School 1907, 1936 (OS). In use as rehearsal room by Rathmines and Rathgar Musical Society from 1953 (see **21** Entertainment, memorials and societies). School moved, incorporated into Kildare Place National School in 1969 (see below).

Rathmines RC Boarding and Day School, location unknown. Rathmines RC Boarding and Day School for young ladies, 'juvenile class for young gentlemen in a separate department', Misses Concanon 1868 (*FJ* 3.8.1868).

Moravian Academy, Castlewood Ave N. (715752, 731728). To be opened, with support of Moravian church 1871 (*Ir. Times* 6.4.1871). Moravain Academy 1879 (*Thom*).

Rathmines Ladies School, Rathmines Rd Upper E., in Newington Terrace, site unknown. 1874 (*Ir. Times* 21.4.1874). Moved to new premises in 1874 (see next entry).

Rathmines Ladies School, Rathmines Rd Upper E., in Newington Terrace, site unknown. Moved from former premises (see previous entry) in 1874 (*Ir. Times* 21.4.1874).

School, Grove Rd S. (715090, 732377), associated with Cathal Brugha Barracks (see **12** Defence). School 1874; school house 1898 (Thom map). School 1907–8; unnamed 1936 (OS).

Castlewood Avenue School, Castlewood Ave, site unknown. 1875 (*Ir. Times* 23.7.1875), 1881 (*Thom*).

Leinster Road School, location unknown. 1875 (*Ir. Times* 2.8.1875).

Miss Lovell's school and kindergarten, Rathmines Rd Lower, site unknown. 1875 (*Ir. Times* 28.7.1875).

Civil Service Academy, Rathmines Park, site unknown. 1881 (*FJ* 13.11.1881).

Miss Jones's school, Leinster Sq., site unknown. 1882 (*FJ* 15.9.1882).

School house, Rathmines Rd Lower W. (715508, 731686). 1882 (OS), *c.* 1901 (Val. 3).

School house, Temple Rd S. (716123, 730362), associated with St Philip's Church (see **11** Religion). School house 1882 (OS). Converted to parochial hall by 1907 (see **21** Entertainment, memorials and societies).

Ladies Collegiate School, Leinster Sq. [west] W. (715403, 731755). 1887 (*BNL* 14.6.1887), 1911 (*Thom*).

St Mary's College, Rathmines Rd Lower W., in former Lark Hill (see **22** Residence). Founded in 1890 (Maher, 28). St Mary's College *c.* 1901 (Val. 3); lodge 1907–*c.* 2019 (OS). See also **11** Religion: Holy Ghost Fathers residence.

Belgrave School, Belgrave Rd S. (715843, 731423). 1902 (*Thom*).

Miss Moore's day and boarding school for girls and small boys, Castlewood Ave N. (715719, 731717). 1902 (*Thom*).

Rathmines College, Rathmines Road Upper E. (715637, 731330). Rathmines College 1907 (OS).

School, Stone Mews E. (715528, 731330). 1907, 1936 (OS).

Infant school, Grove Rd S. (715095, 732357), associated with Cathal Brugha Barracks (see **12** Defence). School (infants) 1907–8; unnamed 1936 (OS).

Rathmines Municipal School of Domestic Economy, Rathmines Rd Upper E., in Carleton Terrace, site unknown. Established by UDC in 1908 (Duff et al., 9). Moved to Rathmines College in 1913 (see next entry).

Rathmines College/Dublin Institute of Technology, Conservatory of Music and Drama, Rathmines Rd Lower W. (715518, 731865). New building, incorporating former technical school (see above: Rathmines School) and Rathmines Municipal School of Domestic Economy (see previous entry) opened in 1913 (Duff et al., 9); 1924 (*Sunday Ind.* 21.12.1924). Technical school 1936 (OS). Extended in 1944; renamed Rathmines College of Commerce *c.* 1950; designated High School of Commerce by Co. Dublin VEC in 1955 (Duff et al., 157–8). Technical school, vocational school 1968 (OS). Technical school (second level school), moved to town hall (see **13** Administration) in 1980 (local information). College of Commerce, moved to Aungier Street in 1995–6 (Duff et al., 157–8). Conservatory of Music and Drama *c.* 2019 (OS). Dublin Institute of Technology, Conservatory of Music and Drama 2021.

Emerald Standard Commercial School, Rathmines Rd Lower E. (715627, 732386). 1913 (*FJ* 26.8.1913), 1915 (*Thom*). Converted to Portobello Nurses Home by 1945 (see **22** Residence).

Saint Louis Secondary School, Charleville Rd S., in former Loreto Convent (see **11** Religion). St Louis Secondary School, opened in 1913 (Ní Thiarnaigh, 50). St Louis Senior School, chapel opened in 1964 (*Ir. Press* 17.7.1964). Convent and schools 1968; Saint Louis Secondary School *c.* 2019 (OS). See also **21** Entertainment, memorials and societies: basket ball ground.

Rathgar Junior School, Grosvenor Rd [south] E. (715199, 731309). Founded by Society of Friends in 1919 (RJS website). Rathgar Junior School 2021.

Castlewood School, Cambridge Rd E. (715814, 731620). Founded by Frances Winifred Forbes in 1928; closed in 1958 (Levistone Cooney, 42, 54).

Mount Temple Preparatory School for boys and girls, Palmerston Park N. (715911, 730669). 1935 (*Thom*).

Commercial College, Leinster Rd N. (715136, 731742). O'Donnell's Commercial College 1952 (*Ir. Independent* 14.4.1952). Commercial College, Miss O'Donnell 1965 (*Thom*). The O'Donnell Commercial College 1981 (*Evening Herald* 11.6.1981).

Saint Louis Infant and Senior Primary School, Williams Park E. (715366, 731880). St Louis National School, extended in 1958 (*Ir. Press* 22.10.1958). School 1968; Saint Louis Infant and Senior Primary School *c.* 2019 (OS).

Church of Ireland College of Education, Rathmines Rd Upper E., on site of former Rathmines Castle (new) (see **22** Residence). Church of Ireland College of Education, moved from former Kildare Place premises in 1963 (Parkes, 182). New chapel, lecture halls, residential accommodation erected in 1968–9; incorporated into Dublin City University in 2016 (Walsh, 273, 455). College *c.* 2019 (OS). See also below, Kildare Place National School.

Saint Michael's House Special School, Grosvenor Rd [south] W. (715122, 731314). School, Association of Parents and Friends of Handicapped Children 1963 (*Ir. Press* 10.7.1963). Saint Michael's House Special School *c.* 2019 (OS).

École d'été de Dublin, Palmerston Park N. (716005, 730679). 1965 (*Thom*), 1971 (*Ir. Independent* 4.2.1971).

Trinity College Dublin botanic garden, Palmerston Park S. (715826, 730599). Moved from former premises at Ballsbridge in 1966–7 (Wyse Jackson, 309). Trinity College Dublin botanic garden 2021.

School, Palmerston Park N. (715913, 730666). 1968 (OS).

Kildare Place National School, Rathmines Rd Upper E. (715691, 731214), associated with Church of Ireland College of Education (see above). Moved from former site in Dublin city centre incorporating former Rathmines Township Schools in 1969 (Parkes, 182, 189). Kildare Place National School *c.* 2019 (OS).

21. ENTERTAINMENT, MEMORIALS AND SOCIETIES

Parochial library, Church Ave E., in vestry of Holy Trinity Church (see **11** Religion). 1837 (Lewis, ii, 504).

Parochial library, Rathmines Rd Lower E., in Mary Immaculate Refuge of Sinners Catholic Church (see **11** Religion). Library of parochial church (RC) 1865 (*FJ* 9.9.1865).

Public library, Rathmines Rd Lower E., in former Rathmines School (see **20** Education). Rathmines Commissioners adopted Public Libraries (Ireland) Act 1855 in 1887; library opened in 1887 (Ó Maitiú, 183–4). Moved to new premises in 1899 (see next entry).

Public library, Rathmines Rd Lower E. (715588, 731866). Moved from former premises (see previous entry) in 1899 (Ó Maitiú, 183). Public library 1907–8 (OS). Moved to new premises in 1913 (see next entry). Converted to fire station in 1914 (see **18** Utilities).

Public library, Rathmines Rd Lower W. (715540, 731839). New library built on site of former skating rink (see below)

PALACE SKATING RINK, 1909–13

and Leinster Lodge (see **22** Residence), to replace former library (see previous entry), in 1913 (Ó Maitiú, 183–4). Public library 1936; library 1968, *c.* 2019 (OS). Dublin City Library Rathmines 2021.

Day and Co. circulating library, Rathmines Rd, site unknown. 1872 (*Ir. Times* 27.6.1872).

Precursor Society premises, location unknown. Established in 1838 (*FJ* 11.11.1838).

Grattan's Spa, Grove Rd S. (715533, 732456). Unnamed 1843 (OS). Grattan's Spa 1874 (Thom map).

Rathmines Relief Committee soup depot, Rathmines Ave, site unknown. 1846 (*FJ* 28.12.1846).

Belgrave Square, Belgrave Sq. North S., on site of former Church Fields (see **14** Primary production). Belgrave Square, residential square constructed on wasteland known as Church Fields in 1851 (Kelly, 218). Sports grounds, The High School *c.* 1890–1961 (Smith, 17–29). Belgrave Square 1907, 1936 (OS). Acquired by Dublin Corporation for development as public park in *c.* 1975 (Smith, 17–29). Belgrave Square 2021.

Grosvenor Square, Leinster Rd N. (715008, 731838). Grosvenor Square 1874 (Thom map), 1876, 1907–8; 3 pavilions 1936; bowling green, 3 pavilions, tennis grounds 1967; Grosvenor Square *c.* 2019 (OS). See also below, Kenilworth Bowling Club, Stratford Lawn Tennis Club.

Kenilworth Square, Kenilworth Sq. North S. (714879, 731167). 1874 (Thom map), 1882–1936; Kenilworth Square, sports ground 1968; unnamed *c.* 2019 (OS).

Pavilion: unnamed 1907, 1936; pavilion 1968; unnamed *c.* 2019 (OS).

Palmerston Park, Palmerston Park S. (716075, 730600), on site of former Rathmines Castle (see **20** Education: school; **22** Residence: Rathmines Castle Old). Pleasure grounds laid out and planted in *c.* 1844 (Palmerston papers). Gardens depicted 1874 (Thom map). Ground gifted to Rathmines Commissioners by Lady Mount Temple for use as public park in 1893 (Ó Maitiú, 173). Opened to public in 1895 (RRTM (7), 6.3.1895). Palmerston Park, fountain 1907; 1936–*c.* 2019 (OS).

Leinster Cricket Club, in Grosvenor Sq. (715008, 731838). Established in 1852 (McDevitt, 15). Moved to new premises in 1865 (see next entry).

Leinster Sports Complex, Rathmines Rd Lower E. (715758, 732004). Leinster Cricket Club, moved from former premises (see previous entry) in 1865 (McDevitt, 15). Cricket ground 1874 (Thom map). Leinster Cricket Ground, flagstaff 1882; cricket ground 1907–8; Leinster Cricket Ground, 1936, 1968; Leinster Sports Complex *c.* 2019 (OS). See also below: Leinster Bowling Club, Leinster Squash Club, Leinster Table Tennis Club, Leinster Tennis Club.

Pavilion: 1907–8, 1936 (OS).

Pavilion: 1936 (OS); demolished, replaced by new clubhouse in 1995 (McDevitt, 46).

Charleville Cricket Club premises, location unknown. 1857 (*Leinster Exp.* 18.7.1857).

KENILWORTH BOWLING CLUB, EARLY 20TH CENT.

Emerald Cricket Club ground, Rathmines Rd Upper, site unknown. 1857 (*FJ* 27.6.1857).

Kenilworth Cricket Club premises, location unknown, possibly in Kenilworth Square (see above). 1861 (*Leinster Exp.* 8.6.1861).

Rathmines Cricket Club premises, location unknown. 1861 (*Leinster Exp.* 8.6.1861).

Fortesque Cricket Club premises, location unknown, associated with Rathmines School (see **20** Education). 1863 (*FJ* 13.7.1863).

Cricket ground, Rathmines Rd Lower W. (715420, 732280), associated with Cathal Brugha Barracks (see **12** Defence). Cricket ground 1882 (OS), *c.* 1901 (Val. 3). Unnamed 1907–8, 1936 (OS).

Conference of St Vincent de Paul Rathmines premises, location unknown. 1856 (*Nation* 20.12.1856).

Loton's billiard rooms, location unknown. 1859 (*BNL* 2.5.1859).

Billiard rooms, Rathmines Rd Lower E. (715584, 732008). 1902 (*Thom*).

Billiard saloon, Rathmines Rd Lower E. (715604, 732110). 1945 (*Thom*).

Rathmines Oriental Baths, Rathmines Rd Upper E., site unknown. 1860 (*FJ* 6.9.1860).

Skating rink, Rathmines Park S. (715490, 731266). Rathmines skating rink 1876, 1880 (*FJ* 5.10.1876, 5.1.1880). Skating rink 1882; demolished by 1907 (OS).

Skating rink, Rathmines Rd Lower W. (715540, 731839). Palace Roller Rink, 12,000–15,000 sq. ft, opened in 1909 (*FJ* 15.6.1909). Demolished, replaced by public library by 1913 (see above).

Hall, Kenilworth Lane N. (714701, 731309). Built in 1882 (datestone). Unnamed 1878; parochial hall 1907; hall 1936, 1968; Century House *c.* 2019 (OS).

Hollymount Room, Observatory Lane S. (715629, 731999). 1882 (OS), *c.* 1901 (Val. 3). Unnamed 1907–8 (OS).

Concert hall and cinema, Rathmines Rd Lower E., in town hall (see **13** Administration). Concert hall to accommodate 2,000, opened in 1897 (Ó Maitiú, 162).

O'Donovan Rossa Hall (Gaelic League), Observatory Lane S. (715594, 732003). Gaelic League, Rathmines branch 1900 (*Ir. Monthly*, Apr. 1900). O'Donovan Rossa Hall (Gaelic League) 1930 (*Thom*). Craobh Liam Bulfin, Conradh na Gaeilge 1960 (local information). O'Donovan Rossa Hall 1965 (*Ir. Press* 16.6.1965). Demolished and built over by apartments in *c.* 1993 (local information).

Ormond Rooms, Rathmines Rd Lower W. (715529, 731680). Ormond Rooms, Young Men's Services and Christian Association, South Dublin Loyal Registration Association 1902 (*Thom*). Young Men's Christian Association, moved to new premises in 1911 (see below: hall).

Parochial hall, Temple Rd S., in former school house (see **20** Education), associated with St Philip's Church (see **11** Religion). Parochial hall 1907, 1936 (OS). Parish hall 2021.

Hall, Belgrave Ave E. (715998, 731591). Parochial hall 1907–8; hall 1936 (OS). Demolished, built over by apartments in *c.* 1991 (*Ir. Independent* 22.2.1991).

Hall, Rathmines Rd Lower W. (715588, 732412). Rathmines YMCA, moved from former premises in Ormond Rooms (see above), erected in 1911 (datestone). Hall 1936 (OS). In use as St Mel's guest house by 1969 (*Thom*).

Stella Rooms meeting rooms, location unknown, possibly in Stella Theatre (see below). 1933 (*Leitrim Obs.* 11.3.1933).

Bernadette Hall, Richmond Hill N. (715741, 732203). Bernadette Hall 1937 (*Sunday Ind.* 17.1.1937). Building sold in 1989 (*Ir. Press* 15.12.1989). Bernadette Hall apartments 2021.

Annunciation House, Rathmines Rd Lower E. (715630, 732455). De Montford Youth Centre 1945; Annunciation House 1958 (*Thom*).

Legion of Mary Hall, Rathmines Rd Lower W. (715511, 731907). Opened in 1958 (*Ir. Press* 20.6.1958). In residential use *c.* 1960 (local information). See also next entry.

St Joseph's Catholic Youth Centre, Rathmines Rd Lower W. (715539, 731902), associated with Legion of Mary Hall (see previous entry). 1958 (*Ir. Press* 20.6.1958). Closed in *c.* 1975 (local information).

National League Rathmines branch, location unknown. 1886 (*RRTM* (6), 3.2.1886).

Rathmines Choral Society premises, location unknown. 1892 (*Musical Times* June 1892).

Rathmines Club premises, Rathmines Park W. (715463, 731269). 1907 (OS). Demolished, replaced by church in 1923 (see **11** Religion: Church of Christ, Scientist).

Catholic Young Men's Society football field, Richmond Hill, site unknown. 1912 (Meath papers C3/31/157).

Rathmines Athletic (Association Football Club), location unknown. Established in 1922 (*Sunday Ind.* 1.10.1922).

Princess Cinema, Rathmines Rd Lower W. (715551, 731954). Princess Cinema 1913 (*Evening Herald* 16.4.1913). Cinema 1936 (OS). Closed in 1968 (Archiseek). Sold for redevelopment in 1981 (*Ir. Independent* 24.7.1981).

Stella Theatre, Rathmines Rd Lower W. (715530, 731638), partly in former Bank of Ireland (see **16** Trades and services). Stella, opened in 1923 (Zimmerman, 160–1). Cinema 1936, 1968 (OS). Closed in 2004; refurbished, reopened in 2017 (Zimmerman, 160–1). Stella Theatre 2021.

Leinster Bowling Club premises, Rathmines Rd Lower E., in Leinster Sports Complex (see above). Founded in 1913 (McDevitt, 70). Leinster Bowling Club 2021.

Kenilworth Bowling Club premises, in Grosvenor Sq. (see above). Kenilworth Bowling Green 1936–7; bowling green 1967; Kenilworth Bowling Club *c.* 2019 (OS).

Rathmines and Rathgar Musical Society premises, Rathmines Rd Lower, site unknown. Founded in 1913 (Dungan, 6). Moved to new premises in 1953 (see next entry).

Rathmines and Rathgar Musical Society premises, Rathmines Rd Upper W., in former Rathmines Township Schools (see **20** Education). Moved from former premises (see previous entry) in 1953 (Dungan, 97). Rathmines and Rathgar Musical Society premises 2021.

Catholic Boy Scouts of Ireland, 20th Dublin Troop premises, Richmond Hill N. (715648, 732186). 1950s–60s (local information).

Leinster Tennis Club premises, Rathmines Rd Lower E., in Leinster Sports Complex (see above). Founded in 1925 (McDevitt, 87). LCC Tennis Club 2021.

Ashbrook Tennis Club premises, Bushes Lane E. (715051, 731246). Moved from Kimmage in 1927 (Curtis, M., 2015, 154). Ashbrook Tennis Ground, pavilion 1936; tennis ground, pavilion 1968; Ashbrook Lawn Tennis Club *c.* 2019 (OS).

Brookfield Tennis Club premises, Palmerston Park N. (715830, 730666). Established in 1906 (Curtis, M., 2015, 154). Brookfield Tennis Ground, pavilion 1936; tennis ground, pavilion 1968; Brookfield Tennis Club *c.* 2019 (OS).

Mount Temple Tennis Ground, Dartry Rd W. (715654, 730450). 1936 (OS). Closed in 1961 (Curtis, M., 2015, 154).

Stratford Lawn Tennis Club premises, in Grosvenor Sq. (see above). Leinster Tennis Courts 1936; 2 tennis grounds 1967; Stafford Lawn Tennis Club *c.* 2019 (OS).

Boys' Brigade premises, Rathmines Rd E., in former Rathmines School (see **20** Education). Boys' Brigade, 1st Dublin Company 'Old Corps Club' 1928 (*Thom*).

Young Women's Christian Association premises, Rathmines Rd Lower E. (715564, 731724). 1940 (*Thom*).

Leinster Table Tennis Club premises, Rathmines Rd Lower E., in Leinster Sports Complex (see above). Founded in 1940s (McDevitt, 93). LCC Table Tennis Club 2021.

Labour Party Rathmines Branch premises, Rathmines Rd Lower W. (715527, 731661). 1945 (*Thom*).

Rathmines Camogie Club premises, location unknown. 1948 (*Ir. Press* 7.4.1948).

Social club premises, Rathmines Rd Lower E. (715629, 732384), associated with Brittain's motor works (see **15** Manufacturing). 1965 (*Thom*).

Basketball ground, Charleville Rd S. (715363, 731567), associated with Saint Louis Secondary School (see **20** Education). 1968 (OS). Basketball court 2021.

Leinster Squash Club premises, Rathmines Rd Lower E., in Leinster Sports Complex (see above). Founded in 1969 (McDevitt, 91). LCC Squash Club 2021.

22. RESIDENCE

Single and paired houses

Rathmines Castle Old, Palmerston Park E. (715988, 730570). Built by Sir George Radcliffe, valued at £7,000 in *c.* 1633–9; burnt in 1642; 6 hearths 1649–60 (Ball, ii, 101, 105); on 259 acres 1654–6 (*CS*, vii, 302). Lord Chief Justice Yorks 1760 (Rocque). In use as school by 1789 (see **20** Education). See also **14** Primary production: orchard.

Barmeen, Dartry Rd E. (715984, 730149). Built as hunting lodge in *c.* 1750 (*Ir. Times* 4.6.2004). Unnamed 1760 (Rocque). Barmeen 1843 (OS), 1850 (Val. 2), 1874 (Thom map), 1882, 1907 (OS), 1913 (Electoral rolls), 1936 (OS), 2021 (nameplate).

Grove House, Grove Park N. (715436, 732419). Depicted 1809 (Snagg). In use as school by 1843 (see **20** Education: Hibernian Marine School). Grove House *c.* 1864 (OS), 1874 (Thom map); fountain 1882, 1887 (OS); 1898 (Thom map). Reverted to educational use in *c.* 1900 (see **20** Education: Hibernian Marine School).

    Gate lodge: *c.* 1864 (OS), 1874 (Thom map).

Mount Anthony, Rathmines Rd Lower W. (715434, 732003). Mt Anthony 1816 (Taylor, J.), 1821 (Duncan). Mount Anthony 1843 (OS), 1850 (Val. 2), 1874 (Thom map), 1882–1936 (OS). Rathmines Mansions 1941 (*Ir. Press* 28.2.1941). Demolished, replaced by Mount Anthony Flats in 1962 (see below). See also **15** Manufacturing: horse veterinary product (Reducine) manufactory.

    Lodge: gate lodge *c.* 1864, 1882; lodge 1907–8 (OS).

Parker Hill, Rathmines Rd Lower E. (715590, 731944). Parker Hill 1816 (Taylor, J.), 1843, 1882; unnamed 1907–8 (OS).

Rathmines Castle (new), Rathmines Rd Upper E. (715773, 731148). Castle 1816 (Taylor, J.). Rathmines Castle 1821 (Duncan), 1837 (Lewis, ii, 504), 1843 (OS), 1850 (Val. 2), 1874 (Thom map), 1882–1936 (OS). Demolished, built over by Church of Ireland College of Education in 1963 (see **20** Education).

    Lodge: unnamed 1843 (OS); gate lodge 1874 (Thom map), 1882; lodge 1907, 1936 (OS).

    Summer house: 1843, 1907 (OS).

Tour Ville, Rathmines Rd Lower W. (715515, 731958). Tourville 1816 (Taylor, J.). Tournville 1819 (*FJ* 1.9.1819). Tourville 1843 (OS), 1850 (Val. 2). Tour Ville 1874 (Thom map), 1882, 1907–8; demolished by 1936 (OS).

    Gate lodge: 1882 (OS).

Gulistan, Gulistan Terrace N. (715743, 731928). Gulistan 1833 (Applotment bk), 1843 (OS), 1850 (Val. 2), 1874 (Thom map), 1882 (OS), 1898 (Thom map). Demolished, built over by Gulistan Cottages by 1894 (see below).

The Lodge, Castlewood Ave N. (715601, 731692). Castlewood Lodge 1833 (Applotment bk), 1843 (OS), 1850 (Val. 2). The Lodge 1907–8 (OS), 1913 (Electoral rolls). Castlewood Lodge 1936; unnamed 1968 (OS). Demolished, built over by Swan Shopping Centre by 1983 (*Ir. Independent* 2.9.1983).

Tranquilla, Rathmines Rd Upper E. (715622, 731013). Tranquilla 1833 (Applotment bk), 1843 (OS). Demolished, rebuilt as Tranquilla Convent by 1854 (see **11** Religion).

Swan Brook, Leinster Rd S. (714910, 731548). Swan Brook 1836 (OSN). Swanbrook 1870 (*Thom*). Swan Brook 1876 (OS), 1877 (OSN, 19). Unnamed 1907–8, 1936 (OS).

Ashgrove Cottage, Dartry Rd W. (715739, 730612). Ashgrove 1837 (Lewis, ii, 504), 1843 (OS). Ashgrove Cottage *c.* 1864 (OS), 1874 (Thom map), 1882 (OS), 1898 (Thom map). Unnamed 1907 (OS).

GROVE HOUSE (IN TREES ON LEFT), PORTOBELLO, 1809, BY THOMAS SNAGG

Clareville, Dartry Rd E. (715921, 730346). Campobello 1837 (Lewis, ii, 504), 1843 (OS), 1850 (Val. 2). Clareville 1852 (*FJ* 25.5.1852). Clare Ville 1874 (Thom map), 1882; Clareville 1907, 1936 (OS).

Lodge: gate lodge 1882; lodge 1907 (OS).

Fortfield House, Cowper Rd S. (715809, 730879). Fortfield 1837 (Lewis, ii, 504), 1843 (OS), 1874 (Thom map), 1882; Fortfield House 1907, 1936 (OS). Fortfield House 2021 (nameplate).

Lodge: unnamed 1843 (OS); gate lodge 1874 (Thom map); lodge 1907 (OS).

Woodpark, Dartry Rd E. (715987, 730291). Wood Park 1837 (Lewis, ii, 504). Woodpark 1843 (OS), 1850 (Val. 2), 1874 (Thom map), 1882–1936 (OS). Demolished, built over by Dartry Park by 1968 (see **10** Streets).

Lodge: gate lodge 1843 (OS); 2 gate lodges 1874 (Thom map); gate lodge 1882; lodge 1907 (OS).

Arbuth, Rathmines Rd Lower W. (715390, 732059). Unnamed 1843 (OS). Arbuth *c.* 1864 (OS), 1874 (Thom map), 1882–1936 (OS). Demolished, built over by Saddlers Court apartments by 1991 (*Ir. Independent* 1.2.1991).

Lodge: unnamed 1843–87; lodge 1907–8 (OS).

Arley, Leinster Rd S. (715082, 731625). Arley Cottage 1843 (OS). Arley 1850 (Val. 2). Unnamed 1907, *c.* 2019 (OS).

Summer house: 1876 (OS).

Aspenville, Rathmines Rd Upper W. (715571, 731025). Aspen Ville 1843 (OS). Aspenville 1849 (*Thom*). Demolished by 1907 (OS).

Aubrey Cottage, Gulistan Terrace S. (715852, 731917). Aubrey Cottage 1843 (OS), 1850 (Val. 2). Unnamed 1907–8, 1936 (OS). Aubrey Cottage 2021 (nameplate).

Batesville, Rathmines Rd Upper W. (715573, 731022). Bates Ville 1843 (OS). Batesville 1850 (Val. 2). Bates Ville 1882; unnamed 1907, 1936 (OS).

Beddyville, Dartry Rd W. (715795, 730308). Beddyville 1843 (OS), 1849; demolished by 1855 (*Thom*).

Beechlawn Cottage, Rathgar Rd E. (715335, 731124). Beechlawn Cottage 1843 (OS), 1850 (Val. 2). Unnamed 1907, *c.* 2019 (OS).

Belfield House, Rathmines Rd Upper W. (715497, 731519). 1843 (OS), 1850 (Val. 2), 1882; unnamed 1907–8 (OS).

Brookfield, Richmond Ave South W. (716400, 730563). Brookfield 1843 (OS), 1850 (Val. 2), 1874 (Thom map), 1882–1968 (OS). Built over by Brookfield apartments by *c.* 2019 (OS).

Dartry, Dartry Rd W. (715814, 730013). Dartry 1843 (OS), 1850 (Val. 2), 1874 (Thom map). Dartry, fountain 1879, 1882; Dartry 1907, 1936 (OS). Converted to Mill Hill Fathers residence in 1958 (see **11** Religion). Saint Joseph's House *c.* 2019 (OS).

Lodge: gate lodge 1843; lodge 1907, 1936 (OS).

Elm Mount, Rathmines Rd Lower W. (715413, 732002). Elm Mount 1843 (OS). Built over by Beverston by 1845 (see below).

Green Field, Grove Rd S. (714910, 732366). 1843 (OS).

Green Lodge, Stone Mews E. (715519, 731354). 1843 (OS), 1850 (Val. 2).

RATHMINES CASTLE (NEW), 1833

Hilton, Rathmines Rd Lower W. (715424, 732111). Unnamed 1843 (OS). Hilton Lodge 1850 (Val. 2), 1874 (Thom map); pump 1882, 1887 (OS), c. 1901 (Val. 3). Hilton 1907–8, 1936 (OS).

Gate lodge: c. 1864 (OS), 1874 (Thom map), 1882, 1887 (OS).

Hilton Ville, Rathmines Rd Lower W. (715410, 732088). Hilton Lodge 1843 (OS). Hilton Ville c. 1864 (OS), 1874 (Thom map), 1882, 1887 (OS), c. 1901 (Val. 3), 1907–8, 1936 (OS).

Lodge: unnamed 1843 (OS); gate lodge 1874 (Thom map), 1882, 1887; lodge 1907–8 (OS).

Lark Hill, Rathmines Rd Lower W. (715452, 732194). Unnamed 1843 (OS). Lark Hill c. 1864 (OS), 1874 (Thom map); pump 1882, 1887 (OS), 1898 (Thom map). Converted to St Mary's College by c. 1901 (see 20 Education).

Gate lodge: c. 1864 (OS), 1874 (Thom map), 1882, 1887 (OS), 1898 (Thom map).

Leinster Cottage, Leinster Rd S. (715095, 731633). Leinster Cottage 1843; unnamed 1876–c. 2019 (OS).

Leinster Ville, Leinster Rd N. (715421, 731833). Leinster Villa 1843 (OS), 1850 (Val. 2). Leinster Ville 1882; unnamed 1907–8, c. 2019 (OS).

Lissonfield House, Rathmines Rd Lower W. (715511, 732290). Lissenfield 1843 (OS). Lissonfield 1850 (Val. 2). Lissenfield c. 1864 (OS), 1874 (Thom map); pump 1882, 1887 (OS). Lissenfield 1898 (Thom map). Lissonfield House 1907–8, 1936 (OS). Demolished by 1988 (Ir. Independent 28.1.1989).

Gate lodge: gate lodge c. 1864, 1882, 1887; lodge 1907–8, 1936 (OS).

Melrose Villa, Rathgar Rd E. (715369, 731306). Melrose Villa 1843 (OS), 1850 (Val. 2), 1882; unnamed 1907–c. 2019 (OS).

Noursdale Park, Richmond Ave South W. (716296, 730258). Richmond Park 1843 (OS), 1850 (Val. 2). Richmond Lodge c. 1864 (OS), 1874 (Thom map), 1882, 1907; Noursdale 1936; Noursdale Park 1968 (OS). Spiritan Provincialate 2021.

Nullamore House, Milltown Rd N. (716378, 730201). Nullamore 1843 (OS), 1850 (Val. 2), 1874 (Thom map), 1882–1936 (OS). In use as Opus Dei university residence in 1954 (Noonan, 226). Nullamore 1968; Nullamore House c. 2019 (OS). Nullamore 2021 (nameplate).

Lodge: unnamed 1843; gate lodge 1874 (Thom map), 1882; lodge 1907 (OS).

Plantation House, Mount Drummond Ave N. (714827, 732258). Jessamine Cottage 1843 (OS), 1850 (Val. 2), 1874 (Thom map), 1907–8; Plantation House 1936 (OS).

Rathfarnham House, Rathmines Park S. (715542, 731286). Rathfarnham House 1843 (OS), 1850 (Val. 2). Unnamed 1907 (OS).

Richview House, Palmerston Park E. (716276, 730619). Richview 1843 (OS), 1850 (Val. 2), 1874 (Thom map), 1882, 1907, 1936; Richview House 1968; unnamed c. 2019 (OS). Richview House 2021 (nameplate).

Rookville, Rathmines Rd Lower W. (715394, 731669). Rookville 1843 (OS). Demolished, built over by Prince Arthur Terrace by 1853 (see 10 Streets).

Salem House, Rathmines Rd Upper W. (715517, 731156). 1843 (OS), 1850 (Val. 2), 1874 (Thom map), 1882–c. 2019 (OS).

South Hill, Milltown Rd N. (716148, 730159). South Hill 1843 (OS), 1850 (Val. 2), 1860 (BNL 4.2.1860), 1874 (Thom map); glasshouses unnamed 1882–1936 (OS). Built over by South Hill estate in 1950s (see 10 Streets).

Lodge: gate lodge c. 1864 (OS), 1874 (Thom map), 1882; lodge 1907 (OS).

St Bernard's, Rathmines Rd Lower W. (715419, 731903). Bernard Ville 1843 (OS). Bernardville 1850 (Val. 2). St Bernard's 1882–1936; Carlton Court c. 2019 (OS).

Lodge: unnamed 1843; gate lodge 1882; lodge 1907–8 (OS).

Summerville, Rathmines Rd Upper E. (715650, 731286). Summerville 1843 (OS), 1850 (Val. 2). Summerville House 1854 (FJ 4.11.1854). Summerville 1874 (Thom map). Summer Ville 1882 (OS). Summerville 1898 (Thom map). Incorporated into Summerville Park (see 10 Streets) by 1907 (OS).

Auburn Lodge, Rathmines Rd Upper W. (715604, 731230). 1850 (Val. 2), 1874 (Thom map), 1882 (OS), 1898 (Thom map).

Beverston, Rathmines Rd Lower W., on site of former Elm Mount (see above). 1850 (Val. 2), 1860 (FJ 3.3.1860), 1874 (Thom map), 1882–1936 (OS).

Emmet House, Mount Drummond Ave N. (714843, 732240). Grenfield House 1850 (Val. 2). Green Field House c. 1864 (OS). Greenfield House 1874, 1898 (Thom map), 1907–8; Emmet House 1936 (OS).

Greenville, York Rd N. (715552, 731247). Greenville 1837 (Lewis, ii, 504), 1843 (OS). Green Ville 1850 (Val. 2). Greenville 1874 (Thom map), 1882 (OS), 1898 (Thom map). Unnamed 1907 (OS).

Grosvenor House, Grosvenor Rd N. (715373, 731518). Grosvenor House 1850 (Val. 2), 1882; unnamed 1907–8 (OS).

Hazelwood, Rathmines Rd Upper W. (715608, 731217). Hazelwood 1850 (Val. 2), 1882; unnamed 1907 (OS).

Lota, Rathmines Rd Upper W. (715612, 731201). Lota 1850 (Val. 2), 1882; unnamed 1907 (OS).

Melrose, Leinster Rd N. (715433, 731835). Melrose 1850 (Val. 2), 1882 (OS), c. 1901 (Val. 3). Unnamed 1907–8 (OS).

Merton Lodge, Rathgar Rd E. (715390, 731357). Merton Lodge 1850 (Val. 2), 1882; unnamed 1907, 1936 (OS).

St Alban's, Rathgar Rd E. (715312, 731167). St Alban's 1850 (Val. 2), 1882; unnamed 1907, 1936 (OS).

Surrey Lodge, Rathgar Rd E. (715369, 731304). Surrey Lodge 1850 (Val. 2), 1882; unnamed 1907, 1936 (OS).

St Kevin's, Dartry Rd W. (715561, 730235). St Kevin's 1853 (FJ 25.5.1853), 1874 (Thom map), 1882 (OS), 1898 (Thom map), 1907, 1936 (OS).

Gate lodge: c. 1864, 1882 (OS), 1898 (Thom map).

Presbytery, Rathmines Rd Lower E. (715622, 732245), associated with Mary Immaculate Refuge of Sinners Catholic Church (see 11 Religion). Presbytery 1858 (FJ 22.11.1858), 1907–8, 1936 (OS).

St Brendan's, Grosvenor Place E. (715191, 731395). St Brendan's 1860 (FJ 3.3.1860), 1876; unnamed 1907–8 (OS).

Ardgowan, Grosvenor Rd N. (715322, 731488). Ardgowan c. 1864 (OS), 1874 (Thom map), 1882 (OS), 1898 (Thom map). Unnamed 1907–8 (OS).

Brighton Ville, Rathmines Rd Upper E. (715640, 731318). Brighton Ville *c.* 1864 (OS), 1874 (Thom map). Brighton Villa 1882 (OS). Brighton Ville 1898 (Thom map). Unnamed 1907 (OS).

Charleville House, Charleville Rd S. (715261, 731539). Charleville House *c.* 1864 (OS), 1874 (Thom map), 1882 (OS), 1898 (Thom map), *c.* 1901 (Val. 3). In use as Loreto Convent by 1907–8 (see **11** Religion).

Churchville, Church Ave S. (715749, 731340). Church Villa *c.* 1864 (OS), 1874 (Thom map), 1882, 1907; Churchville 1936 (OS).

Eglinton House, Rathgar Rd W. (715356, 731443). Eglinton House *c.* 1864 (OS), 1874 (Thom map), 1882 (OS), 1898 (Thom map). Unnamed 1907–8, 1936; demolished, built over by Rathgar Court Residence by *c.* 2019 (OS).

Esker House, Rathmines Rd Upper E. (715653, 731217). Esker House *c.* 1864 (OS), 1874 (Thom map), 1882 (OS), 1898 (Thom map). Unnamed 1907 (OS).

Gate lodge: *c.* 1864, 1882 (OS).

Grosvenor Park, Leinster Rd S. (714989, 732559). Grosvenor Park 1874 (Thom map); flagstaff, pump 1876; 1907–8, 1936; demolished, replaced by Grosvenor Park by *c.* 2019 (OS).

Palmerston House, Palmerston Park N. (715748, 730651). Palmerston House *c.* 1864 (OS), 1874 (Thom map), 1882, 1907 (OS). Incorporated, with Glen-na-Smoil (see below), into Trinity Hall by 1936 (see below).

Gate lodge: gate lodge *c.* 1864 (OS), 1874 (Thom map), 1882; lodge 1907 (OS).

Palmerston Lodge, Milltown Rd N. (716025, 730171). Palmerston Cottage *c.* 1864 (OS), 1874 (Thom map), 1882 (OS). Palmerston Lodge 1898 (Thom map), 1907–68 (OS), 2021 (nameplate).

Rathmines House, Rathmines Park S. (715540, 731286). Rathmines House *c.* 1864 (OS), 1874 (Thom map), 1882; unnamed 1907 (OS).

Richmond Cottage, Richmond Ave E. (716338, 730683). Richmond Cottage *c.* 1864 (OS), 1874 (Thom map), 1882 (OS), 1898 (Thom map). Demolished by 1907 (OS).

Richmond Villa, Richmond Ave E. (716296, 730714). Richmond Villa *c.* 1864 (OS), 1874 (Thom map). Richmond Ville 1882 (OS). Richmond Villa 1898 (Thom map). Demolished by 1907 (OS).

Richview Lodge, Richmond Ave E. (716260, 730729). Richview Lodge *c.* 1864, 1882; demolished by 1907 (OS).

Rosetta, Grosvenor Rd [south] W. (715084, 731166). Rosetta *c.* 1864 (OS), 1874 (Thom map), 1882; unnamed 1907 (OS).

Temple House, Temple Rd N. (716166, 730448). Temple House *c.* 1864 (OS), 1874 (Thom map), 1882 (OS), 1898 (Thom map). Unnamed 1907 (OS).

Templeton, Temple Rd N. (716119, 730449). Temple Villa *c.* 1864 (OS), 1874 (Thom map). Templeton 1882 (OS). Temple Villa 1898 (Thom map). Unnamed 1907–*c.* 2019 (OS).

Thorn Ville, Grosvenor Rd [north] W. (715137, 731324). *c.* 1864 (OS), 1874 (Thom map), 1882 (OS).

Woburn, Grosvenor Rd [south] N. (715196, 731137). 1874 (Thom map).

Kenilworth Villa, Grosvenor Place W. (715120, 731425). 1876 (OS), *c.* 1901 (Val. 3), 2021 (nameplate).

Wynnefield House, Charleville Rd W. (715168, 731600). Wynnefield House, summer house 1876; 1907–8, 1936 (OS).

Alma House, Grosvenor Rd [south] W. (715124, 731283). 1882 (OS), 2021 (nameplate).

Alston, Temple Rd N. (716246, 730448). Alston 1882; unnamed 1907–*c.* 2019 (OS). Alston 2021 (nameplate).

Alton Lodge, Rathgar Rd E. (715381, 731338). Alton Lodge 1882; unnamed 1907, 1936 (OS).

Arborfield, Grosvenor Rd [south] W. (715081, 731155). Arborfield 1882; unnamed 1907 (OS).

Arbutus House, Rathgar Rd E. (715358, 731278). Arbutus House 1882; unnamed 1907, 1936 (OS).

Ardeen, Palmerston Rd N. (716035, 730677). Ardeen 1882; unnamed 1907 (OS). Ardeen 2021 (nameplate).

Atherston, Temple Rd S. (716247, 730448). Atherstone 1882; unnamed 1907–*c.* 2019 (OS). Atherston 2021 (nameplate).

Balnagowan, Palmerston Park S. (716171, 730539). Balnagowan House 1882; Balnagowan 1907, 1936 (OS). In use by Benedictine Order as student hostel 1950 (*Thom*). Balnagowan 2021 (nameplate).

Beech Lawn, Rathgar Rd E. (715335, 731125). Beech Lawn 1882; unnamed 1907, 1936 (OS).

Bloomfield, Grosvenor Rd [south] N. (715220, 731127). Bloomfield 1882; unnamed 1907, 1936 (OS).

Bushley, Grosvenor Rd [south] W. (715131, 731311). 1882 (OS).

Cambridge House, Cambridge Rd E. (715793, 731600). Cambridge House 1882–1936; unnamed *c.* 2019 (OS).

Castlewood Cottage, Castlewood Ave N. (715648, 731693). 1882 (OS), *c.* 1901 (Val. 3).

Castlewood House, Castlewood Ave S. (715637, 731644). Castlewood House 1882 (OS), *c.* 1901 (Val. 3), 1907–8 (OS). Converted to Alexandra Hostel by 1915 (see **16** Trades and services).

The Chalet, Temple Rd S. (716032, 730378). Unnamed 1882; The Chalet 1907, 1936 (OS).

Chetwode, Grosvenor Rd [south] N. (715202, 731134). 1882 (OS).

Church View, Castlewood Ave N. (715768, 731733). 1882 (OS), *c.* 1901 (Val. 3).

Clevedon House, Temple Rd. N. (716380, 730462). Clevedon House 1882; unnamed 1907–*c.* 2019 (OS).

Clifden, Grosvenor Rd [south] N. (715179, 731143). Clifden 1882; unnamed 1907, 1936 (OS).

Clonbrone, Temple Rd S. (716243, 730375). Clonbrone 1882; unnamed 1907–*c.* 2019 (OS). Clonbrone 2021 (nameplate).

Cora Linn, Dartry Rd W. (715744, 730448). Cora Linn 1882; unnamed 1907 (OS).

Drayton, Cambridge Rd W. (715748, 731596). 1882–1936 (OS).

Eastwell, Palmerston Park N. (716044, 730680). Eastwell 1882 (OS), 1887 (RRTA 1/1/91). Unnamed 1907 (OS). Eastwell 2021 (nameplate).

Elderslie, Rathgar Rd E. (715326, 731101). 1882 (OS).

Ellerslie, Temple Rd S. (716372, 730386). Ellerslie 1882; unnamed 1907–*c.* 2019 (OS). Ellerslie 2021 (nameplate).

Everton Lodge, Cambridge Rd E. (715795, 731573). 1882 (OS).

Garmento, Grosvenor Rd [south] E. (715207, 731320). 1882 (OS).

Grosvenor Cottage, Grosvenor Rd [north] S. (715376, 731465). Grosvenor Cottage 1882; unnamed 1907, 1936 (OS).

Hatherton, Richmond Ave South W. (716455, 730311). 1882–1968 (OS), 2021 (nameplate).

Havelock House, Grosvenor Rd [north] N. (715400, 731529). Havelock House 1882 (OS), *c.* 1901 (Val. 3). Unnamed 1907 (OS).

Holywood House, Palmerston Rd N. (716004, 730674). Holywood House 1882; unnamed 1907 (OS).

Kenilworth Cottage, Kenilworth Rd S. (715004, 731323). 1882 (OS).

Kensington Lodge, Grove Park S. (715565, 732389). Kensington Lodge 1882 (*Ir. Builder* 18.8.1882). Unnamed 1907–*c.* 2019 (OS). Kensington Lodge 2021 (nameplate).

Kingston Lodge, Rathgar Rd W. (715328, 731340). Kingston Lodge 1882; unnamed 1907, 1936 (OS).

Knockdomney, Grosvenor Rd [south] S. (715137, 731113). 1882 (OS).

Lachoza, Rathgar Rd E. (715308, 731156). Lachoza 1882; unnamed 1907, 1936 (OS).

Laranda, Grosvenor Rd [north] E. (715200, 731311). 1882 (OS).

Largo House, Rathmines Rd Lower E. (715590, 731917). 1882 (OS).

Leicester Cottage, Leicester Ave N. (715113, 731122). 1882 (OS).

Leicester House, Kenilworth Sq. East E. (714979, 731169). 1882 (OS).

Leinster Lodge, Rathmines Rd Lower W. (715527, 731850). 1882, 1907–8 (OS). Demolished, replaced by public library by 1913 (see **21** Entertainment, memorials and societies).
  Lodge: unnamed 1882; lodge 1907–8 (OS).

Lisanore, Kenilworth Rd S. (715079, 731358). 1882 (OS).

Lisnoe, Orwell Park S. (715594, 729980). Lisnoe 1882; unnamed 1907 (OS).

Lonsdale, Temple Rd N. (716286, 730449). Lonsdale 1882; unnamed 1907–*c.* 2019 (OS). Lonsdale 2021 (nameplate).

Mantua Cottage, Castlewood Ave S. (715659, 731653). 1882 (OS), *c.* 1901 (Val. 3), 1907–8, 1936 (OS).

Melcomb, Leinster Sq. N. (715540, 731811). Unnamed 1882–*c.* 2019 (OS). Melcomb 2021 (nameplate).

Milverton, Temple Rd S. (716320, 730381). Milverton 1882; unnamed 1907–*c.* 2019 (OS).

Ontario Lodge, Rathgar Rd W. (715332, 731348). Ontario Lodge 1882; unnamed 1907, 1936 (OS).

The Orchards, Palmerston Park S. (716008, 730501). Ham Ville 1882 (OS). Ham Villa 1898 (Thom map). The Orchards 1907, 1936 (OS).
  Gate lodge: gate lodge 1882; 2 lodges 1907, 1936 (OS).

Oxford House, Leicester Ave N. (715184, 731095). 1882 (OS).

Rathgar Cottage, Rathmines Rd Upper S. (715677, 730611). Rathgar Cottage 1882; demolished by 1907 (OS).

Rathlin, Temple Rd S. (716179, 730373). 1882–1936 (OS).

Rathmore, Grosvenor Rd [south] W. (715119, 731270). 1882 (OS), 1898 (Thom map), 2021 (nameplate).

Redan Lodge, Rathgar Rd E. (715417, 731448). Redan Lodge 1882; unnamed 1907–8, 1936 (OS).

Richmond House, Rathgar Rd W. (715290, 731261). Richmond House 1882; unnamed 1907, 1936 (OS).

Rostellan, Temple Rd N. (716413, 730464). Rostellan 1882; unnamed 1907–*c.* 2019 (OS). Rostellan 2021 (nameplate).

Shamrock Lodge, Grosvenor Rd [south] N. (715171, 731146). Shamrock Lodge 1882; unnamed 1907, 1936 (OS).

Somerset House, Temple Rd S. (716296, 730379). Somerset House 1882; unnamed 1907–*c.* 2019 (OS).

Spring Ville, Temple Rd S. (716344, 730383). Spring Ville 1882; unnamed 1907–*c.* 2019 (OS).

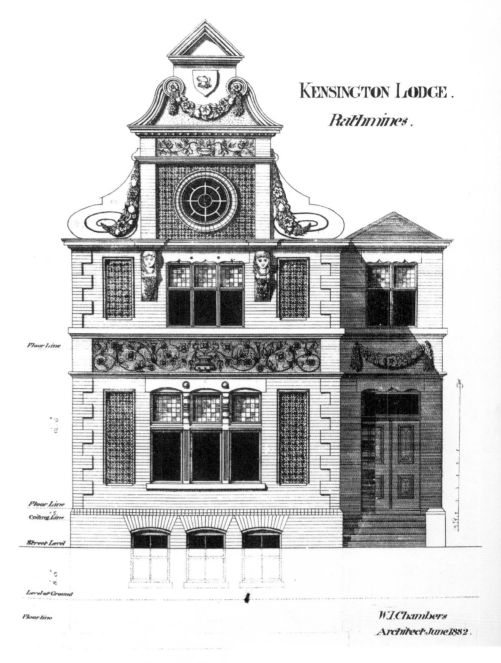

KENSINGTON LODGE, 1882

St Andrew's, Richmond Ave South W. (716419, 730382). 1882–1968 (OS).
  Lodge: gate lodge 1882; lodge 1907, 1936 (OS).
St Anne's, Grosvenor Rd [north] E. (715199, 731303). 1882 (OS).
St Helen's, Rathgar Rd W. (715351, 731438). St Helen's 1882; unnamed 1907–8, 1936; demolished, built over by Rathgar Court Residence by c. 2019 (OS).
St Kevin's Park, Dartry Rd W. (715718, 730177). Unnamed 1882; St Kevin's Park 1907; St Kevin's 1936; unnamed c. 2019 (OS).
  Gate lodge: 1907 (OS).
St Mary's, Temple Rd N. (716219, 730449). St Mary's 1882; unnamed 1907–c. 2019 (OS).
Stradford Lodge, Grosvenor Rd [north] N. (715333, 731494). Stradford Lodge 1882; unnamed 1907–8 (OS).
Tavistock, Grosvenor Rd [south] N. (715191, 731137). Tavistock 1882; unnamed 1907, 1936 (OS).
Thorndale, Temple Rd N. (716439, 730467). Thorndale 1882; unnamed 1907–c. 2019 (OS). Thorndale 2021 (nameplate).
Toronto Lodge, Rathgar Rd W. (715336, 731360). Toronto Lodge 1882; unnamed 1907, 1936 (OS).
The Turret, Rathmines Rd Upper E. (715664, 731261). The Turret 1882; unnamed 1907, 1936 (OS).
Valentia Lodge, Rathgar Rd W. (715339, 731368). Valentia Lodge 1882; unnamed 1907, 1936 (OS).
Walnut Lodge, Rathgar Rd E. (715377, 731328). Walnut Lodge 1882; unnamed 1907, 1936 (OS).
Warwick House, Kenilworth Sq. West W. (714771, 731150). Warwick House 1882; unnamed 1907, 1936 (OS).
Weston, Rathgar Rd W. (715305, 731310). Weston 1882; unnamed 1907, 1936 (OS).
Williamston, Grosvenor Rd [north] E. (715208, 731328). Williamston 1882; unnamed 1907, 1936 (OS).
Wilton Lodge, Rathgar Rd E. (715286, 731098). Wilton Lodge 1882; unnamed 1907, 1936 (OS).
Winstead, Temple Rd N. (716289, 730451). Winstead 1882; unnamed 1907–c. 2019 (OS). Winstead 2021 (nameplate).
Wynnefield Park, Charleville Rd E. (715400, 731642). 1882 (OS), c. 1901 (Val. 3), 1907–68 (OS). Demolished, built over by Wynnefield Park apartments by 1982 (Ir. Independent 15.3.1982).
Eversden, Rathmines Rd Lower E. (715596, 732121). Eversden 1887 (OS), c. 1901 (Val. 3). Unnamed 1907–8, 1936 (OS).
Palmerston Park, Temple Rd N. (715961, 730517). 1898 (Thom map). Divided into 2 dwellings by 1907 (see below: Esterel, Greenane).
Ann's Cottage, Castlewood Ave N. (715782, 731740). Ann's Cottage c. 1901 (Val. 3). Unnamed 1907, 1936 (OS).
Brighton Cottage, Belgrave Sq. North N. (715808, 731751). Brighton Cottage c. 1901 (Val. 3). Unnamed 1907, 1936 (OS).
Clonlee, Grove Park S. (715481, 732380). c. 1901 (Val. 3).
Cozy Lodge, Castlewood Ave N. (715794, 731739). Cozy Lodge c. 1901 (Val. 3). Unnamed 1907, 1936 (OS).
The Grange, Grove Park N. (715359, 732431). c. 1901 (Val. 3).
Grove Villas, Grove Park N. (715387, 732382). c. 1901 (Val. 3).
Roseair, Grove Park S. (715427, 732375). c. 1901 (Val. 3).

Sunnybank, Grosvenor Place E. (715147, 731473). c. 1901 (Val. 3).
Esterel, Temple Rd N., in part of Palmerston Park (see above). 1907, 1936; unnamed c. 2019 (OS).
Glen-na-Smoil, Palmerston Park N. (715889, 730479). Glen-na-Smoil 1907 (OS). Incorporated, with Palmerston House (see above) into Trinity Hall by 1936 (see below).
  Lodge: 1907 (OS).
Greenlands, Dartry Rd W. (715747, 730447). Unnamed 1907; Comeragh 1968; Greenlands c. 2019 (OS).
Greenane, Temple Rd N., in part of Palmerston Park (see above). 1907, 1936; unnamed c. 2019 (OS).
Santon, Dartry Rd W. (715749, 730420). Unnamed 1907, 1936; Santon 1968 (OS).
Trinity Hall, Dartry Rd E. (715906, 730522). Built, incorporating former Palmerston House and Glen-na-Smoil (see above), by 1936; Trinity Hall 1968 (OS), 2021.
  Gate lodges, 2: 1936 (OS).
Portobello Nurses Home, Rathmines Rd Lower E., in former Emerald Standard Commercial School (see **20** Education). 1945 (Thom).
Ardmore, Richmond Ave South W. (716422, 730239). 1968 (OS), 2021 (nameplate).
Glenart, Richmond Ave South W. (716465, 730280). 1968 (OS), 2021 (nameplate).
Hilton House, Dartry Rd N. (716011, 730157). Altadore 1968 (OS). Hilton House 2021 (nameplate).
Nutgrove, Richmond Ave South W. (716468, 730257). 1968 (OS), 2021 (nameplate).
Richmond Lodge, Richmond Ave South W. (716409, 730242). 1968 (OS), 2021 (nameplate).

Almshouses and private asylums

Methodists widows' home, Palmerston Park N. (716044, 730680). 1940 (Thom).
Cortona Nursing Home, Belgrave Sq. West W. (715860, 731588). 1950 (Thom).
Nursing home, Belgrave Rd S. (715900, 731445). 1950 (Thom).
Home for White Russian refugees, Temple Rd S. (715932, 730379). 1960 (Thom).

Rows and terraces

Rathmines Mall, Rathmines Rd Lower E. (715631, 732062). Rathmines Mall 1812 (FJ 16.3.1812), 1836, 1839 (Thom), 1843 (OS), 1847 (FJ 12.6.1847), 1860 (BNL 26.6.1860).
Newington Terrace, Rathmines Rd Upper E. (715601, 731743). Unnamed 1821 (Duncan). Newington Terrace 1850 (Val. 2), 1860 (FJ 3.3.1860), 1874 (Thom map), 1882 (OS), 1898 (Thom map). Unnamed 1907–8, 1936 (OS). Demolished, built over by Swan Shopping Centre by 1983 (Ir. Independent 2.9.1983).
Rathmines Terrace, Rathmines Rd Upper E. (715553, 731554). 1835 (Kerry Evening Post 11.2.1835), 1843 (OS), 1850 (Val. 2), 1882 (OS), c. 1901 (Val. 3), 1907–8 (OS), 1913 (Electoral rolls), 1936; unnamed 1968–c. 2019 (OS).

Berry's Buildings, Rathmines Rd Lower E. (715615, 732223). Barry's Buildings, Berry's Buildings 1836 (*FJ* 13.6.1836). Berry's Buildings 1843 (OS), 1845 (*Thom*), 1850 (Val. 2). Unnamed 1907–8, 1936 (OS).

Ulster Terrace, Leinster Sq. [east] S. (715507, 731743). Ulster Terrace 1842 (*Thom*), 1843 (OS), 1850 (Val. 2). Unnamed 1907–*c*. 2019 (OS).

Belfield Terrace, Rathmines Rd Upper W. (715525, 731493). Barry's Terrace 1843 (OS), 1850 (Val. 2). Belfield Terrace *c*. 1864, 1882; unnamed 1907–8, 1936 (OS). Demolished, built over by supermarket in 1988 (*Ir. Times* 4.2.2015).

Berry Terrace, Rathmines Rd Upper W. (715587, 731329). Berry Terrace 1843 (OS), 1846 (*Thom*). Berry Terrace 1848 (*FJ* 24.3.1848). Berry's Terrace 1850 (Val. 2). Unnamed 1882–*c*. 2019 (OS).

De Vesci Terrace, Leinster Rd N. (715110, 731716). De Vesci Terrace 1843 (OS), 1850 (Val. 2), 1876; unnamed 1907–*c*. 2019 (OS).

Cambridge Terrace, Rathgar Rd E. (715274, 731231). 1843 (OS), 1850 (Val. 2), 1874 (Thom map), 1882 (OS), 1898 (Thom map), 1913 (Electoral rolls). Unnamed 1907–*c*. 2019 (OS).

Carlton Terrace, Rathmines Rd Upper E. (715609, 731408). Carleton Terrace 1843 (*Thom*). Carlton Terrace 1882, 1907–8 (OS). Carleton Terrace 1913 (Electoral rolls). Carlton Terrace 1936; unnamed *c*. 2019 (OS).

Connaught Terrace, Leinster Sq. [east] N. (715511, 731799). Connaught Terrace 1843; unnamed 1882, 1907 (OS).

Diamond Terrace, Dartry Rd E. (715953, 730170). Diamond Place 1843 (OS), 1849 (*Thom*), 1850 (Val. 2). Diamond Terrace 1856 (*Thom*), 1874 (Thom map), 1882, 1907 (OS), 1913 (Electoral rolls), 1936; unnamed *c*. 2019 (OS).

Duggan Place, Rathmines Rd Lower W. (715524, 731640). 1843 (*Thom*), 1850 (Val. 2), 1867 (RRTM (3), 28.8.1867), 1882–1936; unnamed *c*. 2019 (OS).

Elm Grove, Rathmines Rd Lower W. (715542, 731891). 1843 (OS), 1847 (*Leinster Exp.* 15.5.1847), 1861 (*Thom*), 1882, 1907–8 (OS), 1913 (Electoral rolls), 1936; unnamed 1968, *c*. 2019 (OS).

Fortescue Terrace, Rathmines Rd Lower E. (715627, 732370). Unnamed 1843 (OS). Fortesque Terrace 1845 (*Thom*), 1847 (*FJ* 11.9.1847). Fortescue Terrace *c*. 1864 (OS), 1874, 1898 (Thom map). Unnamed 1936–*c*. 2019 (OS).

Leinster Terrace, Leinster Sq. [west] W. (715405, 731747). Leinster Terrace 1843 (OS), 1841 (*Nenagh Guardian* 12.5.1841), 1850 (Val. 2), 1874 (Thom map), 1882 (OS), 1898 (Thom map). Unnamed 1907–*c*. 2019 (OS).

Spire View, Rathgar Rd W. (715252, 731175). Spire View 1843 (OS), 1850 (Val. 2), 1874 (Thom map), 1882 (OS), 1898 (Thom map). Unnamed 1907–*c*. 2019 (OS).

Union Place, Grove Rd S. (715024, 732385). Holbrook Cottages 1843 (OS). Holbrook Cottages, Union Place 1850 (Val. 2), 1853 (RRTM (2), 7.12.1853) 1874, 1898 (Thom map), 1907–8, 1936 (OS). Demolished, built over by Grove Road Flats in 1963 (see below).

Kensington Terrace, Belgrave Sq. North N. (751851, 731780). 1845 (*FJ* 18.12.1845), *c*. 1901 (Val. 3), 1913 (Electoral rolls), 2021 (nameplate).

Wynnefield Place, Rathmines Rd Upper W. (715579, 731103). Wynnfield Place 1845 (*Thom*). Wynnfield Terrace 1846 (*FJ* 16.6.1846). Wynnfield Place 1850 (Val. 2). Wynnfield Terrace 1856 (*Thom*). Wynnefield Terrace 1874 (Thom map). Wynnefield Place 1882 (OS). Wynnefield Terrace 1898 (Thom map). Unnamed 1907, 1936 (OS).

Cornish Terrace, Castlewood Ave N. (715706, 731712). Cornish Terrace 1846 (*Nation* 22.8.1846), 1850 (Val. 2), 1882, 1907–8 (OS), 1913 (Electoral rolls), 1936; unnamed *c*. 2019 (OS).

Hollyfield, Rathmines Rd Upper W. (715513, 731025). Hawleyfield 1847; Hawley's Field 1849 (*Thom*). Hollysfield 1850 (Val. 2). Hollyfield *c*. 1864 (OS), 1874 (Thom map). Demolished, built over by Hollyfield Buildings by 1903 (see below).

Wynnefield Parade, Maxwell Rd S. (715498, 731090). Wynnfield Parade 1847 (*Thom*). Wynnfield Parade 1850 (Val. 2), 1874, 1898 (Thom map). Unnamed 1907–*c*. 2019 (OS).

Kensington Villas, Mountpleasant Ave Upper W. (715868, 731877). Kensingtonville 1849 (*Thom*). Kensington Villa 1850 (Val. 2). Kensington Terrace 1882; Kensington Villas 1907–8, 1936 (OS), 2021 (nameplate).

Erin Terrace, Leinster Rd N. (715149, 731737). Erin Terrace 1850 (Val. 2), 1846 (*Thom*), 1874 (Thom map), 1876, 1882 (OS), 1898 (Thom map). Unnamed 1907–8, 1936 (OS). Erin Terrace 2021 (nameplate).

Ormond Terrace, Rathmines Rd Lower W. (715521, 731704). Ormond Terrace 1850 (Val. 2), 1882 (OS), *c*. 1901 (Val. 3), 1907–8, 1936; unnamed *c*. 2019 (OS).

Wharton Terrace, Harold's Cross Rd E. (714872, 732353). Wharton Terrace 1850 (Val. 2). Wharten Terrace 1907–8, 1936 (OS). Wharton Terrace / Ardán Wharton 2021 (nameplate).

Westbourne Terrace, Leinster Rd N. (714990, 731657). Westbourne Terrace 1852 (*Thom*), 1876; unnamed 1907–*c*. 2019 (OS).

Richmond Terrace, Richmond Hill N. (715764, 732200). Richmond Terrace 1853 (RRTM (2), 2.7.1853), 1882, 1887 (OS), *c*. 1901 (Val. 3), 1907–8 (OS), 1913 (Electoral rolls), 1936 (OS). Demolished, built over by Richmond Manor apartments by 1990 (*Evening Press* 9.7.1990).

Mount Temple Terrace, Dartry Rd W. (715809, 730256). Upper Terrace (late Beddyville) 1855 (*Thom*). Upper Terrace 1856 (*Nation* 1.11.1856), 1874 (Thom map), 1882 (OS), 1898 (Thom map). Extended, Mount Temple Terrace 1907, 1936 (OS).

Arbutus Terrace, Leinster Rd S. (714929, 731557). Arbutus Terrace 1857 (*Anglo-Celt* 5.3.1857), 1861 (*Thom*), 1876; unnamed 1907–*c*. 2019 (OS).

Grosvenor Terrace, Rathgar Rd W. (715244, 731149). Grosvenor Terrace 1858 (*Thom*), 1882; unnamed 1907–*c*. 2019 (OS).

Delhi Terrace, Rathgar Rd S. (715445, 731509). Delhi Terrace 1860 (*FJ* 3.3.1860), 1882; unnamed 1907–*c*. 2019 (OS).

Fife Terrace, Belgrave Sq. South S. (715912, 731568). Fife Terrace 1861 (RRTM (3), 31.7.1861), 1863 (*Thom*), 1874, 1898 (Thom map). Unnamed 1907–8 (OS). Fife Terrace 1913 (Electoral rolls). Unnamed 1936, *c*. 2019 (OS).

Wickham Terrace, Leinster Rd S. (715279, 731737). Wickham Terrace 1861 (*Thom*), 1874 (Thom map), 1882 (OS), 1898 (Thom map), *c*. 1901 (Val. 3). Unnamed 1907–*c*. 2019 (OS).

BELFIELD TERRACE (RIGHT), *c.* 1910

FORTESCUE TERRACE, *c.* 1910

Annesley Terrace, Rathgar Rd W. (715299, 731285). Annesley Terrace c. 1864 (OS), 1874 (Thom map), 1882 (OS), 1898 (Thom map). Unnamed 1907–c. 2019 (OS).

Malakoff Terrace, Rathgar Rd E. (715405, 731405). Malakoff Terrace c. 1864 (OS), 1874 (Thom map), 1882 (OS), 1898 (Thom map). Unnamed 1907–c. 2019 (OS).

Rydalmount Villas, Richmond Ave South E. (716545, 730218). Ridalmount Villas c. 1864 (OS), 1874 (Thom map), 1882; Rydalmount Villas 1907, 1936; unnamed c. 2019 (OS).

Wilton Terrace, Grosvenor Place W. (715137, 731377). Wilton Terrace 1870 (Thom), 1876 (OS), c. 1901 (Val. 3). Unnamed 1907–c. 2019 (OS).

Effra Villas, Leinster Rd West S. (714889, 731413). Effra Villa 1876 (OS). Effra Villas 1880 (Thom). Unnamed 1907–c. 2019 (OS).

Dartry Cottages, Dartry Rd S. (715956, 729999). 1879–c. 2019 (OS).

Belgrave Villas, Belgrave Ave E. (715975, 731542). 1880 (Thom), 1882, 1907–8 (OS), 1913 (Electoral rolls), 1968, c. 2019 (OS).

Waverley Terrace [north], Kenilworth Sq. North N. (714706, 731241). Waverley Terrace 1880 (RRTM (6), 6.10.1880), 1882 (OS), 1898 (Thom map), 1907; unnamed 1936, c. 2019 (OS).

Waverley Terrace [south], Kenilworth Sq. North S. (714692, 731190). Waverley Terrace 1880 (RRTM (6), 6.10.1880), 1882 (OS), 1898 (Thom map), 1907, 1936; unnamed c. 2019 (OS). Waverley Terrace 2021 (nameplate).

Temple Villas, Palmerston Rd W. (716023, 730842). Begun in 1880s (Kelly, 229); 1890 (Thom), 1907 (OS), 1913 (Electoral rolls), 1936 (OS), 2021 (nameplate).

Alma Villas, Rathgar Rd E. (715426, 731475). Alma Villas 1882; unnamed 1907–c. 2019 (OS).

Annefield Terrace, Kenilworth Sq. N. (714797, 731283). Annefield Terrace 1882; unnamed 1907–c. 2019 (OS).

Belgrave Terrace, Mountpleasant Ave Upper W. (715869, 731846). 1882, 1907–8 (OS), 1913 (Electoral rolls), 1936 (OS), 2021 (nameplate).

Kenilworth Terrace, Kenilworth Rd N. (714986, 731368). Kenilworth Terrace 1882 (OS), 1886 (RRTM (6), 3.2.1886), 1895 (RRTM (7), 6.3.1895), c. 1901 (Val. 3). Unnamed 1907–c. 2019 (OS).

Moylurg Terrace, Grosvenor Rd [south] E. (715148, 731183). Moylurg Terrace 1882; unnamed 1907–c. 2019 (OS).

Palmerstown Terrace, Rathmines Rd Upper E. (715609, 730952). Palmerstown Terrace 1882; unnamed 1907–c. 2019 (OS).

Stanley Terrace, Rathgar Rd E. (715393, 731379). Stanley Terrace 1882; unnamed 1907–c. 2019 (OS).

Aylwards Cottages, Castlewood Lane N. (715692, 731763). Castlewood Cottages c. 1901 (Val. 3). Aylwards Cottages 1907–8, 1936; unnamed c. 2019 (OS).

Grattan Terrace, Grove Park S. (715364, 732392). c. 1901 (Val. 3).

Grove Park Terrace, Grove Park N. (715444, 732411). c. 1901 (Val. 3).

Coffey's Cottages, Church Gardens W. (715582, 731545). Coffey's Cottages, built by Rathmines and Rathgar UDC by 1907–8 (OS).

Cowper Villas, Cowper Rd N. (715913, 730972). Cowper Villas 1907, 1936; unnamed c. 2019 (OS).

Davis's Cottages, Church Gardens E. (715647, 731521). Davis's Cottages, built by Rathmines and Rathgar UDC by 1907–8 (OS); 1913 (Electoral rolls), 1936 (OS).

Flynn's Cottages, Church Gardens W. (715611, 731512). Flynn's Cottages, built by Rathmines and Rathgar UDC by 1907–8 (OS).

Fortfield Villas, Rathmines Rd Upper E. (715657, 730806). Fortfield Villas 1907, 1936; unnamed 1970, c. 2019 (OS).

Winfield Cottages, Rathmines Rd Upper W. (715473, 731056). 1907, 1936 (OS).

Coughlan's Cottages, Grove Rd S. (715074, 732375). Unnamed 1907–8; Coughlan's Cottages 1936 (OS).

Holmes Cottages, Castlewood Place E., (715654, 731580). 1907–8 (OS), 1913 (Electoral rolls), 1936 (OS), 2021 (nameplate).

Mallon's Terrace, Grove Ave E. (714996, 732364). Unnamed 1907–8; Mallon's Terrace 1936; unnamed c. 2019 (OS).

Rathmines Park Terrace, Rathmines Ave E. (715454, 731375). 1907–8; unnamed 1936, c. 2019 (OS).

St Clare Terrace, Mount Drummond Ave N. (714991, 732096). 1907–8, 1936 (OS), 2021 (nameplate).

Housing estates and flat complexes

Gulistan Cottages, Mountpleasant Ave Upper W. (715737, 731910), partly on site of former Gulistan (see above). Tender accepted to build 28 artisans' dwellings at cost of £3,250 in 1894 (Ir. Builder 1.8.1894). 30 more cottages built by Rathmines and Rathgar UDC in 1898 (Ó Maitiú, 156). Township Cottages 1901 (Census). Gulistan Cottages c. 1901 (Val. 3), 1907–c. 2019 (OS). Gulistan Cottages / Iostáin Gulistan 2021 (nameplate; Logainm).

Harold's Cross Cottages, Harold's Cross Rd E. (714923, 732356). 120 cottages built by Dublin Artisans' Dwelling Co., in 1884–5 (Hofman, 59–70). Harold's Cross 1899 (RRTM (7), 3.4.1899). Harold's Cross Cottages 1907–8 (OS). Artisans Dwellings Co.'s buildings 1920 (Thom). Harold's Cross Cottages 1936, c. 2019 (OS). Harold's Cross Cottages / Iostáin Cros Aralt 2021 (nameplate). Harold's Cross Cottages / Iostáin Chrois Araild 2021 (Logainm).

Hollyfield Buildings, Rathmines Rd Upper W. (715521, 731026), partly on site of former Hollyfield (see above). Built by Rathmines and Rathgar UDC by 1903 (Ó Maitiú, 157); 1907, 1936 (OS). Demolished in early 1980s (local information).

Church Gardens, Church Gardens W. (715637, 731490). Church Place, built by Rathmines and Rathgar UDC in 1928 (RRTA 1/C/555). Renamed Church Gardens by 1936 (OS).

Mount Anthony Flats, Williams Park N. (715395, 731994), partly on site of former Mount Anthony (see above). Mount Anthony Flats, 40 homes built by the Iveagh Trust, opened in 1962 (Iveagh Trust website); 1968, c. 2019 (OS).

Rathmines Avenue Flats, Rathmines Ave W. (715462, 731432). Built by Dublin Corporation in 1962 (DCC flat schemes). Rathmines Avenue Flats 2021.

Grove Road Flats, Grove Rd S., on site of former Union Place (see above). Built by Dublin Corporation in 1963 (DCC flat schemes). Grove Road Flats 2021 (nameplate).

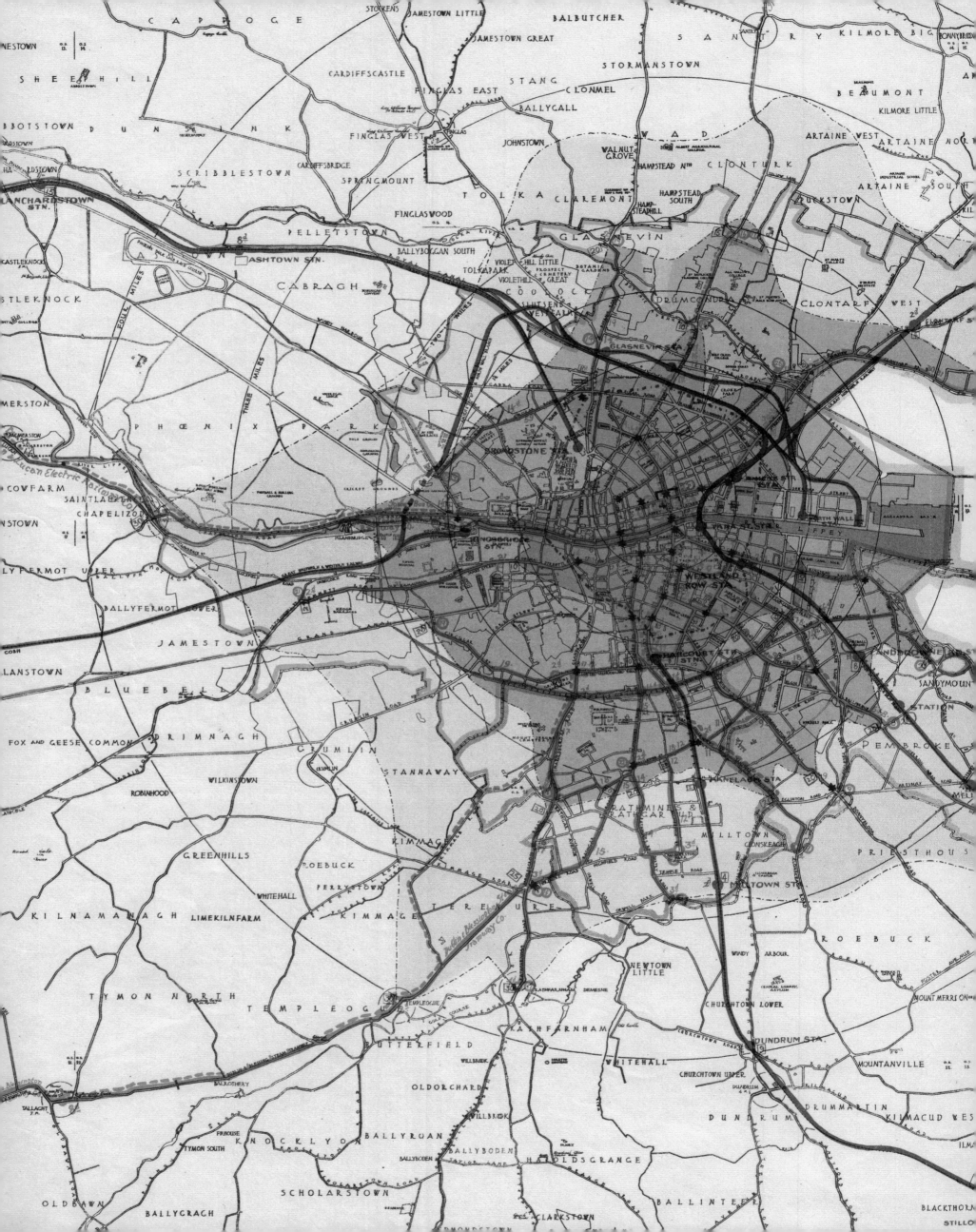

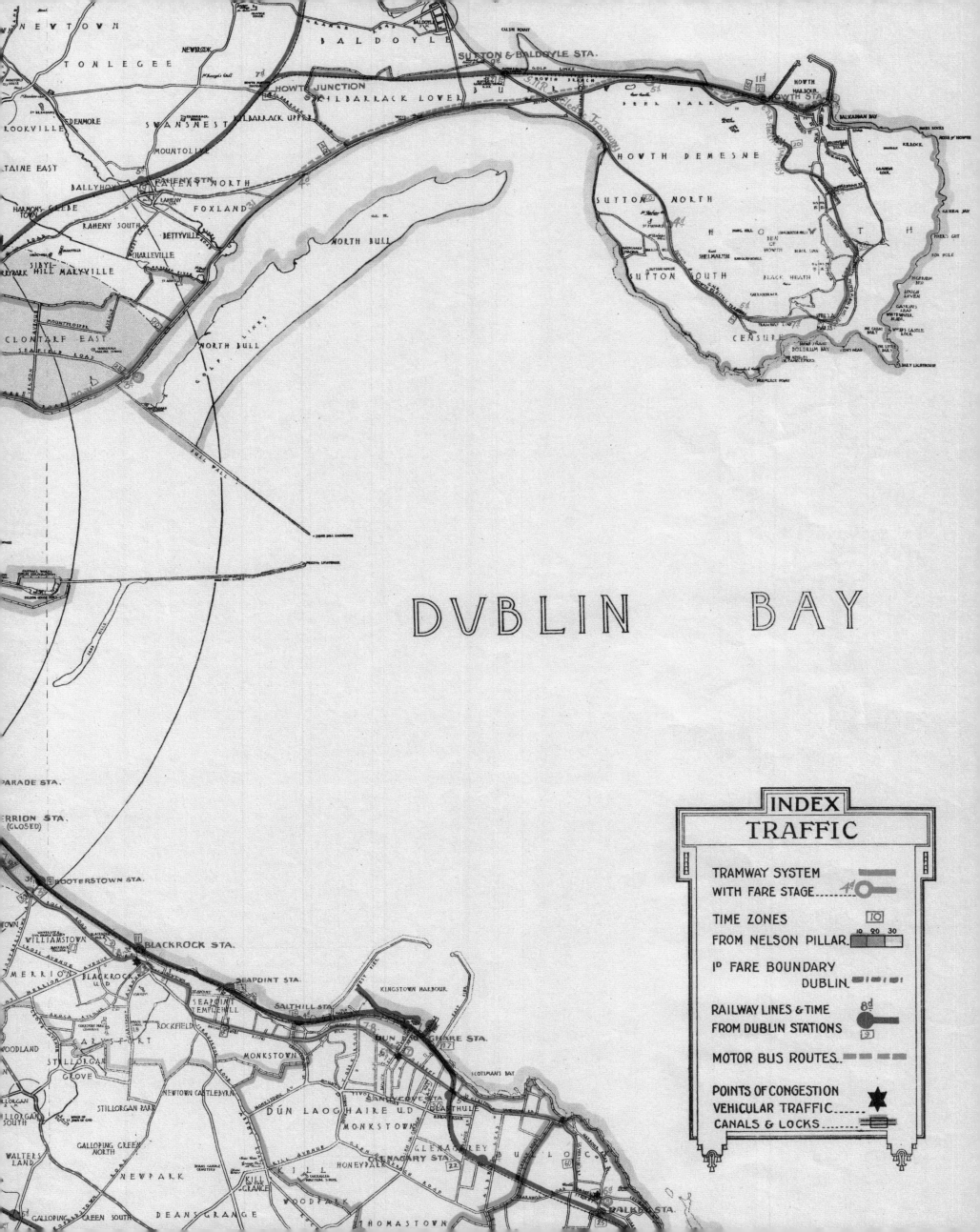

DUBLIN BAY

INDEX
TRAFFIC

TRAMWAY SYSTEM
WITH FARE STAGE

TIME ZONES
FROM NELSON PILLAR

10 20 30

1D FARE BOUNDARY
DUBLIN

RAILWAY LINES & TIME
FROM DUBLIN STATIONS

MOTOR BUS ROUTES

POINTS OF CONGESTION
VEHICULAR TRAFFIC

CANALS & LOCKS

Maps

Changes to the topography of Rathmines are vividly recorded in maps and views. Some of these early views have been used alongside period reconstructions and thematic maps to illustrate the text. The following section, included across the suburbs series, is dedicated to the cartographic record. Maps and plates are presented in a style based on that of the main Irish Historic Towns Atlas series, allowing links to be made between the city of Dublin and its suburbs.

The section begins with the presentation of core maps that follow the guidelines for the European Historic Towns Atlas and allow comparative study. Map 1 shows the suburb in its mid-nineteenth-century setting at 1:50,000 and has been prepared from the first edition of the one-inch to the mile (1:63,360) Ordnance Survey map of Dublin (1860). Map 2, considered the principal map for each atlas, is a large-scale representation of the suburb in the nineteenth century. For this series, this is a reproduction of the original twenty-five-inch (1:2500) Ordnance Survey parish map for Co. Dublin (surveyed 1863–7) at the reduced scale of 1:5000 with an extract at 1:2500 also included. The third core map (Map 3) is a modern Ordnance Survey town plan at 1:5000, which includes contours (3 m intervals) and grid co-ordinates (100 m intervals, Irish Transverse Mercator). Maps 4 and 5, also at 1:5000, depict the urban area in the early to mid-twentieth century and have been compiled using the twenty-five-inch (1:2500) Ordnance Survey plans (1906–9) and subsequent revision of 1935–8. Map 6 is an extract from Ordnance Survey Ireland's Discovery series (1:50,000). Finally, a modern air photograph is included as Plate 1 at 1:5000.

Following these are reproductions of historic maps (facsimiles) in chronological order from the eighteenth century onwards. Some of these, such as maps by John Rocque (1760) and the Ordnance Survey (from 1843) cover the city as a whole and comparative extracts may be expected across the Dublin suburbs atlases.

Unlike the towns series, which is loose leaf with some folded pages, large maps are spread over multiple pages with an index on p. 84. Pages have perforated edges to allow users to disassemble their atlas, to join and compare the maps, should they so wish. Captions are kept to a minimum, with full details being given on the introductory list on pp 85–6.

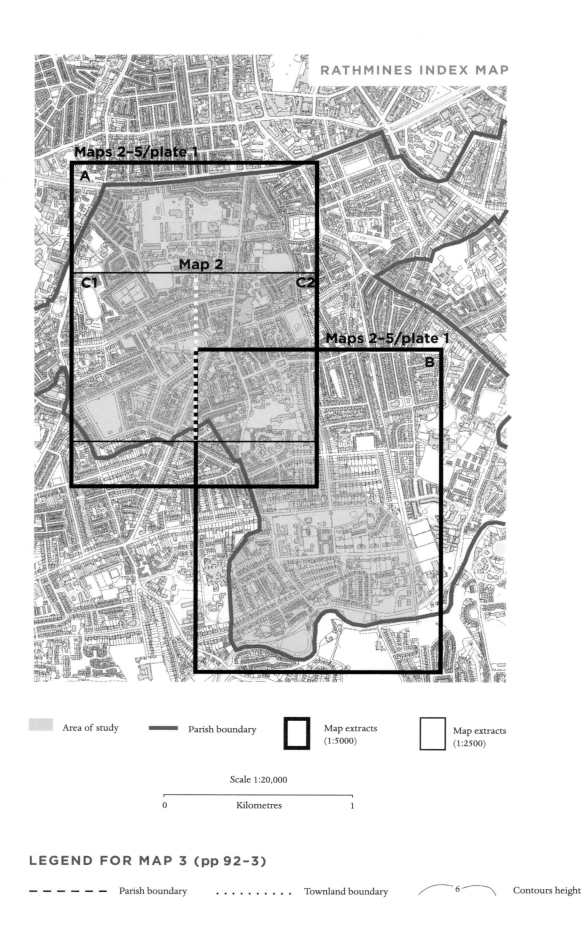

Maps 2–5/plate 1

A

Map 2

C1 C2

Maps 2–5/plate 1

B

Area of study	Parish boundary	Map extracts (1:5000)	Map extracts (1:2500)

Scale 1:20,000

0   Kilometres   1

LEGEND FOR MAP 3 (pp 92–3)

– – – – – Parish boundary   · · · · · · · · · · Townland boundary   ⌣6⌣ Contours height

Maps

Map 1   **Dublin city and suburbs, 1860**   87
Ordnance Survey of Ireland, scale 1:50,000
Reproduced courtesy of the National Library of Ireland.
© Ordnance Survey Ireland/Government of Ireland.

Map 2   **Parish of St Peter, *c.* 1864**   88
Ordnance Survey of Ireland, scale 1:5000 (A–B), 1:2500 (C)
Reproduced courtesy of Andrew Bonar Law.
© Ordnance Survey Ireland/Government of Ireland.

Map 3   **Rathmines, *c.* 2019**   92
Ordnance Survey Ireland, scale 1:5000
© Ordnance Survey Ireland/Government of Ireland.

Map 4   **Rathmines, 1907–8**   94
Ordnance Survey of Ireland, scale 1:5000
© Ordnance Survey Ireland/Government of Ireland.

Map 5   **Rathmines, 1936**   96
Ordnance Survey of Ireland, scale 1:5000
© Ordnance Survey Ireland/Government of Ireland.

Plate 1   **Aerial view of Rathmines, 2017**   98
Ordnance Survey Ireland, Scale 1:5000
© Ordnance Survey Ireland/Government of Ireland.

Map 6   **Dublin city and suburbs, 2015**   100
Ordnance Survey Ireland, Discovery series, scale 1:50,000
© Ordnance Survey Ireland/Government of Ireland.

Map 7   **Farm of St Sepulchre, 1717, Greene**   101
'A survey of part of the farme of St Sepulchers lyeing in the barony of Newcastle and
county of Dublin belonging to … William lord archbishop of Dublin', 1717,
by John Greene. Reproduced courtesy of the Representative Church Body Library.

Map 8   **Farm of St Sepulchre, 1782, Brownrigg**   102
'A survey of part of the farm of St Sepulchers in the county of Dublin let by his grace
Robert, lord archbishop of Dublin to Mrs Frances Usher', 1782, by John Brownrigg.
Reproduced courtesy of the Representative Church Body Library.

Map 9   **Rathmines, 1760, Rocque**   103
An actual survey of the county of Dublin, by John Rocque (Dublin, 1760;
reprinted London, 1802), extract. Reproduced courtesy of the Royal Irish Academy,
RR/MC/6/12.

Map 10   **Rathmines, *c.* 1802, A. Taylor**   103
'A sketch of the environs of Dublin', *c.* 1802, by Alexander Taylor, extract.
Reproduced courtesy of the British Library, Add MS 32451D.

Map 11   **Cullinswood, 1810, Armstrong (3)**   104
'A map of part of the lands of Cullinswood in the county of Dublin now let to
Major Taylor being part of the estate of the earl of Meath', 1810, by W.A. Armstrong.
Reproduced courtesy of the Meath Estate, Meath papers, box 158.

Map 12   **Rathmines, 1816, J. Taylor**   105
Taylor's map of the environs of Dublin, by John Taylor, scale two inches to one mile
(Dublin, 1816), extract. Reproduced courtesy of the Royal Irish Academy, RR/31/2/B/1.

Map 13   **Rathmines, 1821, Duncan**   105
Map of the county of Dublin, by William Duncan (Dublin, 1821), extract.
Reproduced courtesy of Andrew Bonar Law.

Map 14   **Farm of St Sepulchre, 1826, Sherrard, Brassington and Greene**   **106**
'Survey of part of the farm of Saint Sepulchre in the county of Dublin, belonging to the
Very Reverend Richard Hastings Graves', 1826, by Sherrard, Brassington and Greene.
Reproduced courtesy of the National Archives of Ireland, MS M 2574.

Map 15   **Meath estate, Rathmines, 1836, Armstrong (4)**   **107**
'Part of the estate of the Right Hon. the earl of Meath in the south suburbs of the
city of Dublin', 1836, by W.A. Armstrong. Reproduced courtesy of Survey and Mapping
Department, Dublin City Council. With redrawing and transcribed reference table.

Map 16   **Lower Rathmines, 1843, OS**   **112**
Ordnance Survey, manuscript town plan, Dublin city, 1843, sheet 42, extract,
reproduced to scale, five feet to one mile (1:1056). Reproduced courtesy of the National
Archives of Ireland, OS 140. © Ordnance Survey Ireland/Government of Ireland.

Map 17   **Upper Rathmines, 1843, OS**   **113**
Ordnance Survey, manuscript town plan, Dublin city, 1843, sheet 46, extract,
reproduced to scale, five feet to one mile (1:1056). Reproduced courtesy of the
National Archives of Ireland, OS 140.

Map 18   **Rathmines, 1843, OS**   **114**
Ordnance Survey six-inch map of Co. Dublin, 1843, sheets 18 and 22, extract,
reproduced to scale (1:10,560). © Ordnance Survey Ireland/Government of Ireland.

Map 19   **Rathmines, 1869–75, OS**   **115**
Ordnance Survey six-inch map of Co. Dublin, 1869–75, sheets 18 and 22, extract,
reproduced to scale (1:10,560). © Ordnance Survey Ireland/Government of Ireland.

Map 20   **Kenilworth Square and Swan River, 1857**   **116**
Map of Kenilworth Square and Swan River, 1857. Reproduced courtesy of
Dublin City Library and Archive, RRTM (2), 11.2.1857.

Map 21   **Belgrave Square, 1872–97**   **117**
Map of 'Belgrave Square, also ground to be let for building in the neighbourhood,
J. Holmes, Architect', 1872–97. Reproduced courtesy of Erasmus Smith Trust Archive,
Dublin, EE/1369 (2).

Map 22   **The Chains, Rathmines, 1889**   **118**
Map of the Chains, Rathmines Road, 1889. Reproduced courtesy of Dublin City Library
and Archive, RRTM (6), 6.7.1889.

Map 23   **Township of Rathmines, 1898, Thom map**   **119**
'Map of the city of Dublin and its environs', 1898, from *Thom's Irish Almanac and
official directory*, extract. Reproduced courtesy of University College Dublin Digital Library.

Map 24   **Traffic, 1925, Dublin civic survey**   **120**
Traffic map from *The Dublin civic survey report* (Liverpool, 1925), extract.
Reproduced courtesy of Arnold Horner.

Map 25   **Rathmines, 1948, OS**   **121**
Ordnance Survey, Dublin, popular edition, scale 1:25,000, 1948.
© Ordnance Survey Ireland/Government of Ireland.

Map 26   **Rathmines, 1959, OS**   **121**
Ordnance Survey, Dublin, popular edition, scale 1:25,000, 1959.
© Ordnance Survey Ireland/Government of Ireland.

Map 27   **Rathmines, 1971, OS**   **121**
Ordnance Survey, Dublin City South, 8th popular edition, scale 1:18,000, 1971.
© Ordnance Survey Ireland/Government of Ireland.

Map 28   **Further study, 1907–8**   **122**
Rathmines base map, redrawn from Ordnance Survey, 1907–8. Scale 1:10,000.

Map 29   **Further study, c. 2019**   **123**
Rathmines base map, Ordnance Survey Ireland, *c.* 2019. Scale 1:10,000.
© Ordnance Survey Ireland/Government of Ireland.

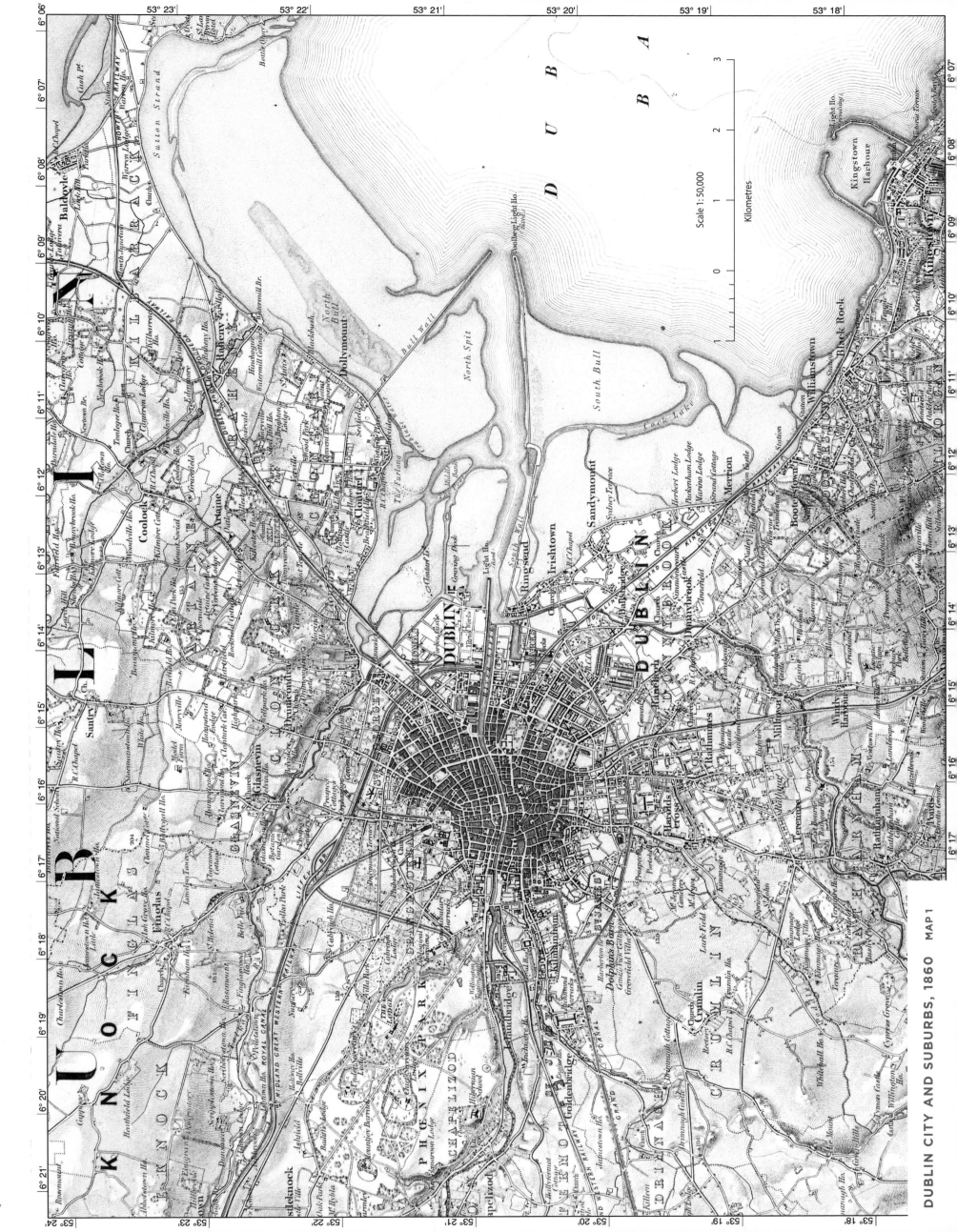

DUBLIN CITY AND SUBURBS, 1860 MAP 1

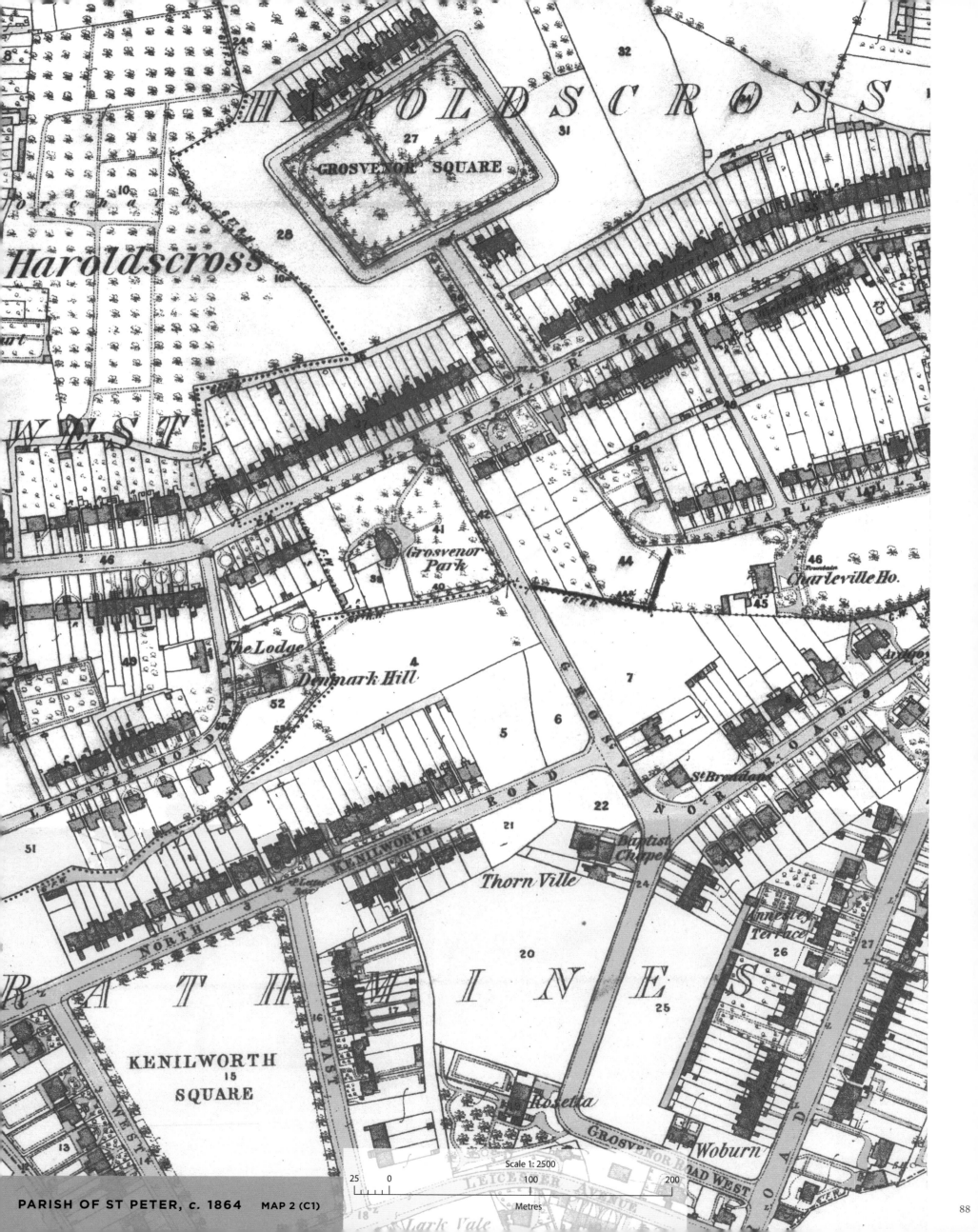

HAROLDS CROSS

GROSVENOR SQUARE

Haroldscross

WEST

Grosvenor
Park

The Lodge

Denmark Hill

Charleville Ho.

Charleville

St Brendan

Baptist
Chapel

Thorn Ville

Annesley
Terrace

Rosetta

Woburn

R A T H M I N E S

KENILWORTH
SQUARE

GROSVENOR ROAD WEST

LEICESTER AVENUE

Lark Vale

Scale 1 : 2500

25   0   100   200

Metres

PARISH OF ST PETER, c. 1864   MAP 2 (C1)

88

PARISH OF ST PETER, c. 1864 MAP 2 (C2)

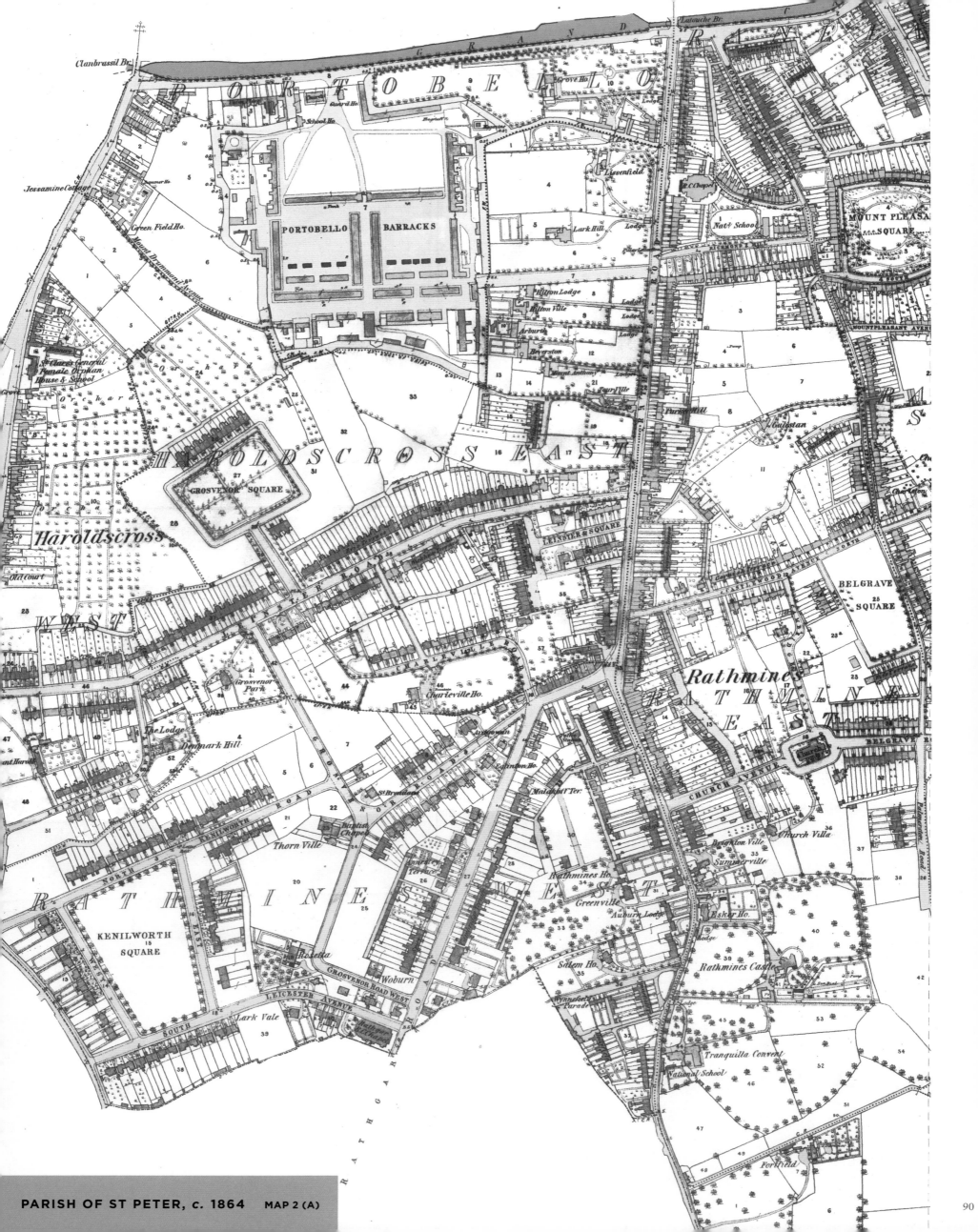

PARISH OF ST PETER, c. 1864   MAP 2 (B)

Scale 1 : 5000

100   50   0   100   200   300

Metres

91

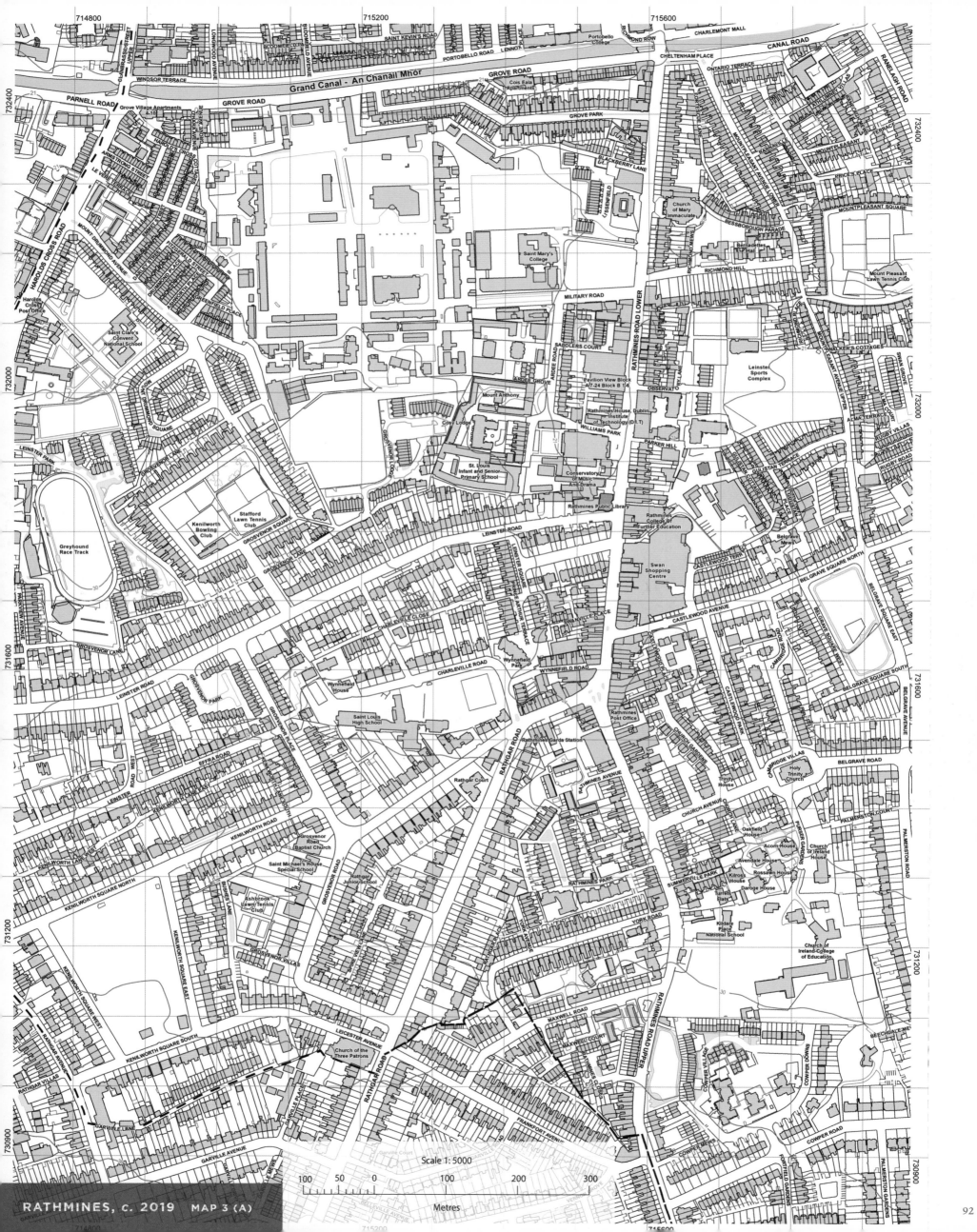

Scale 1: 5000

100   50   0   100   200   300

Metres

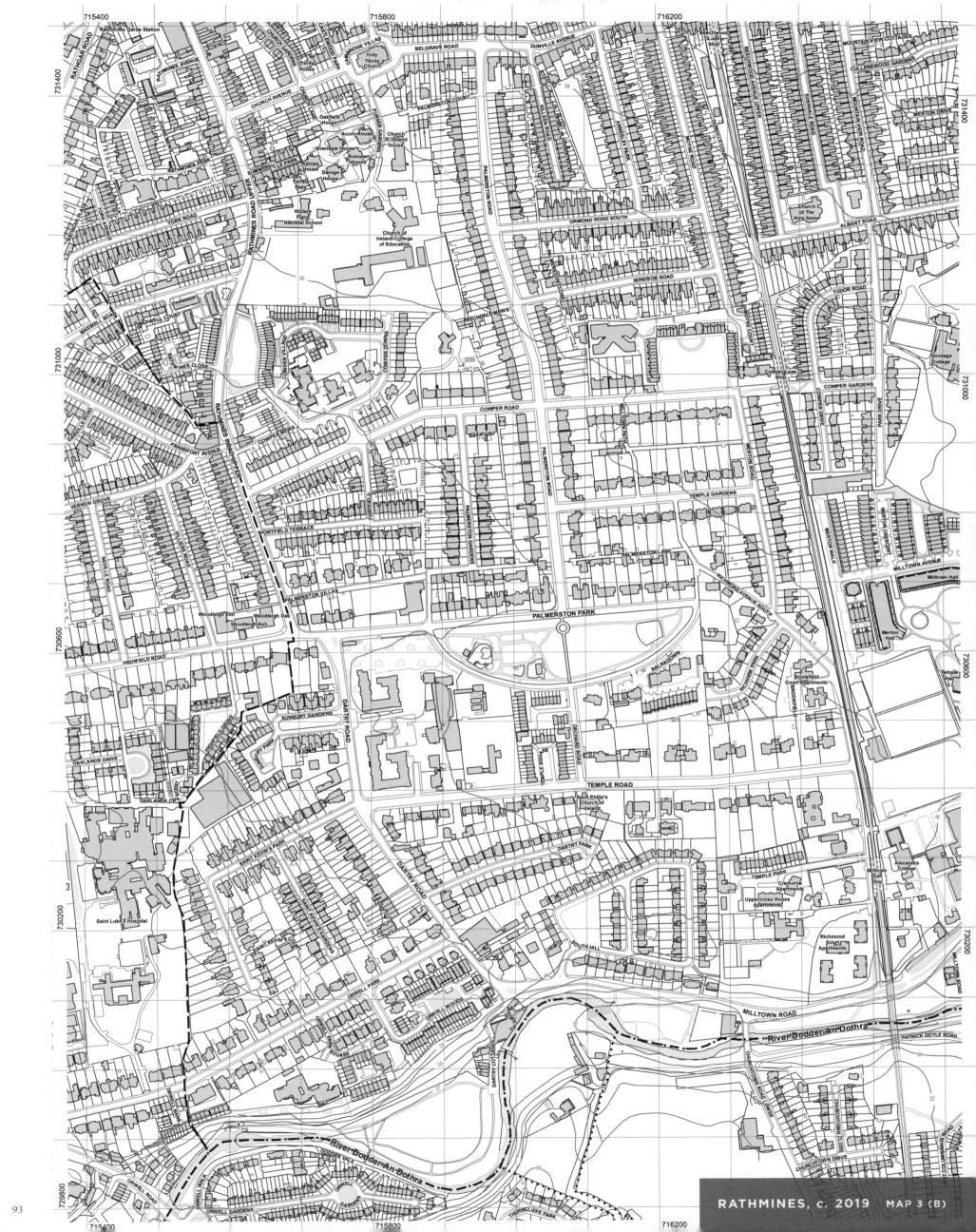

RATHMINES, c. 2019   MAP 3 (B)

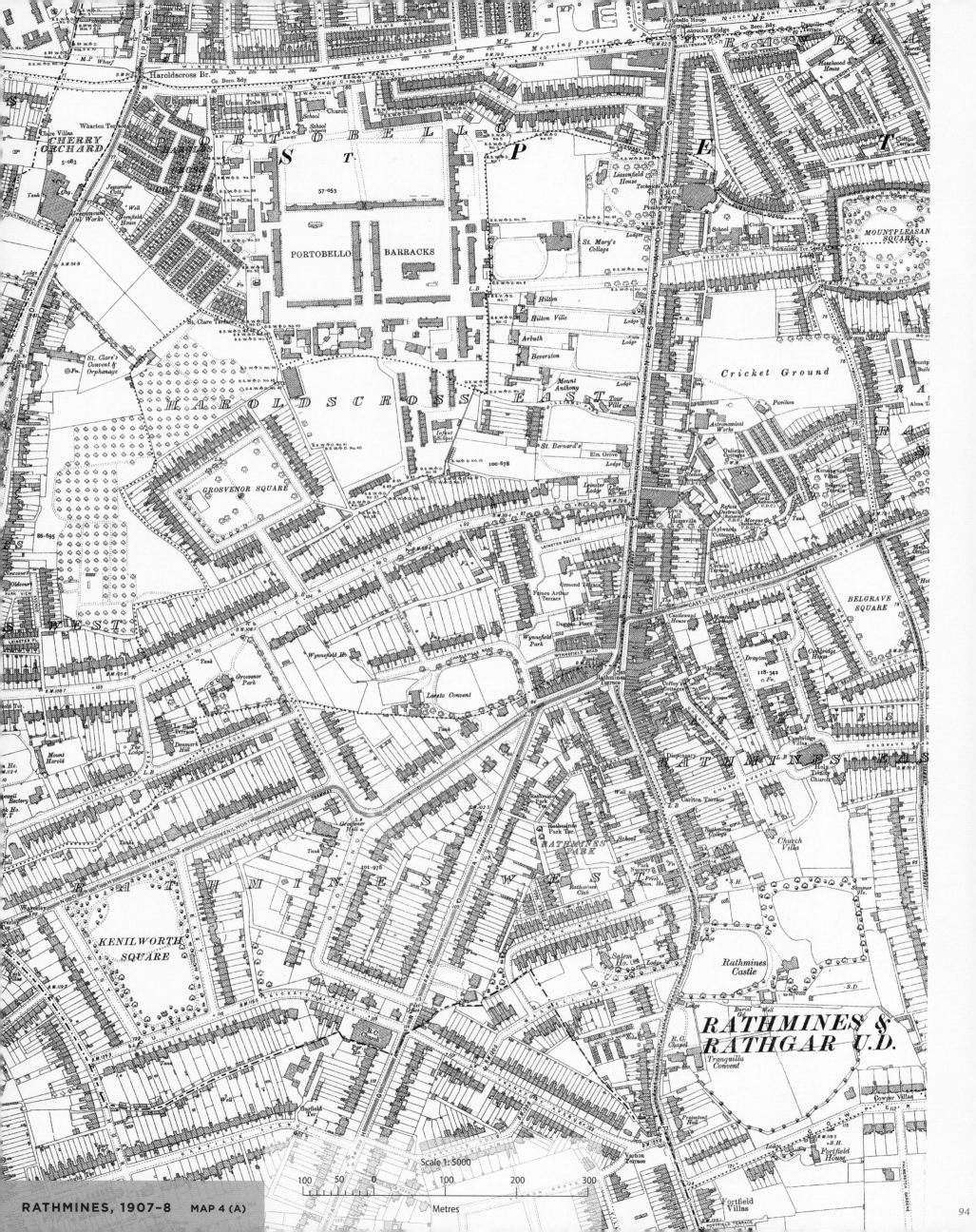

Scale 1:5000

100 50 0   100   200   300

Metres

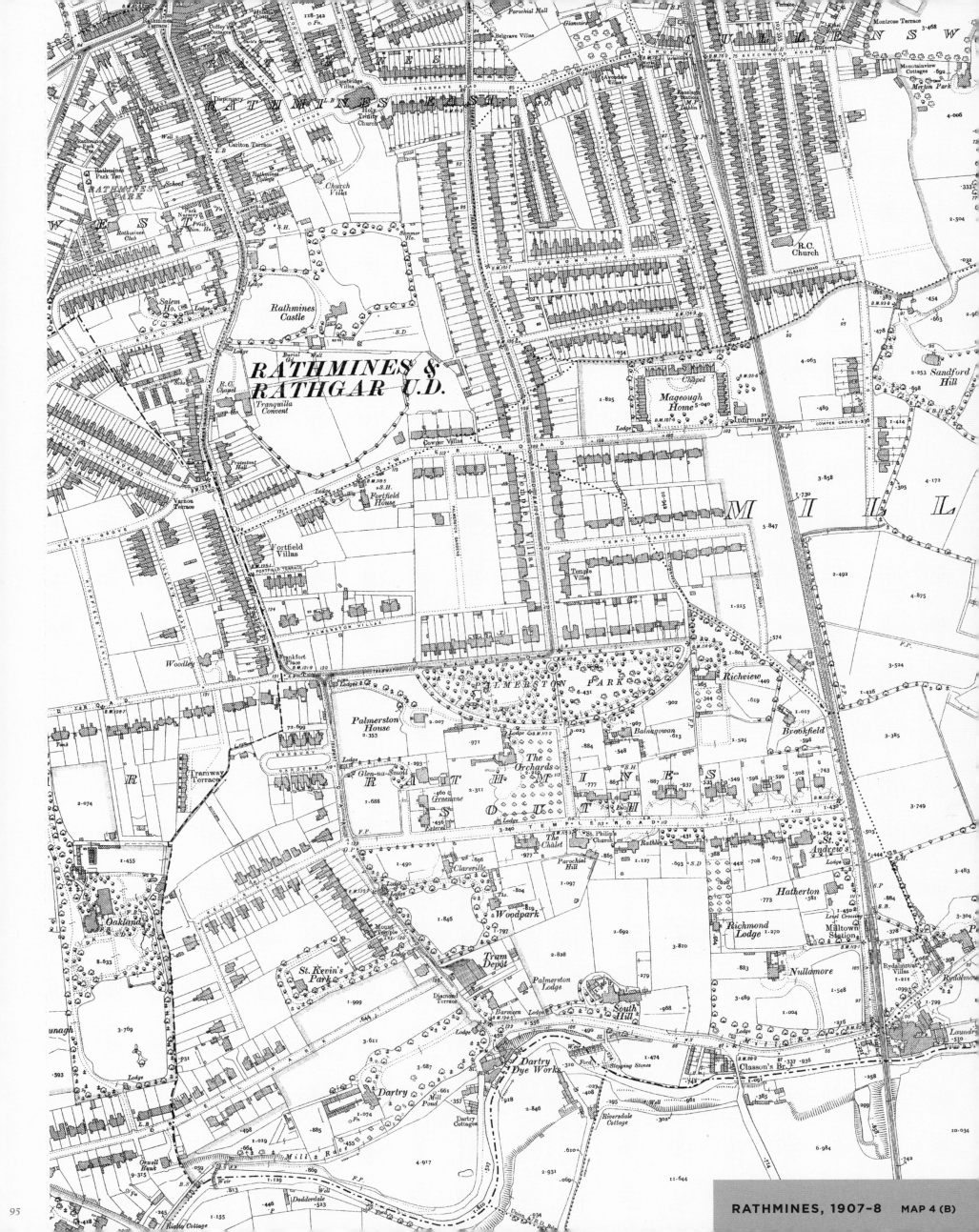

RATHMINES, 1907–8   MAP 4 (B)

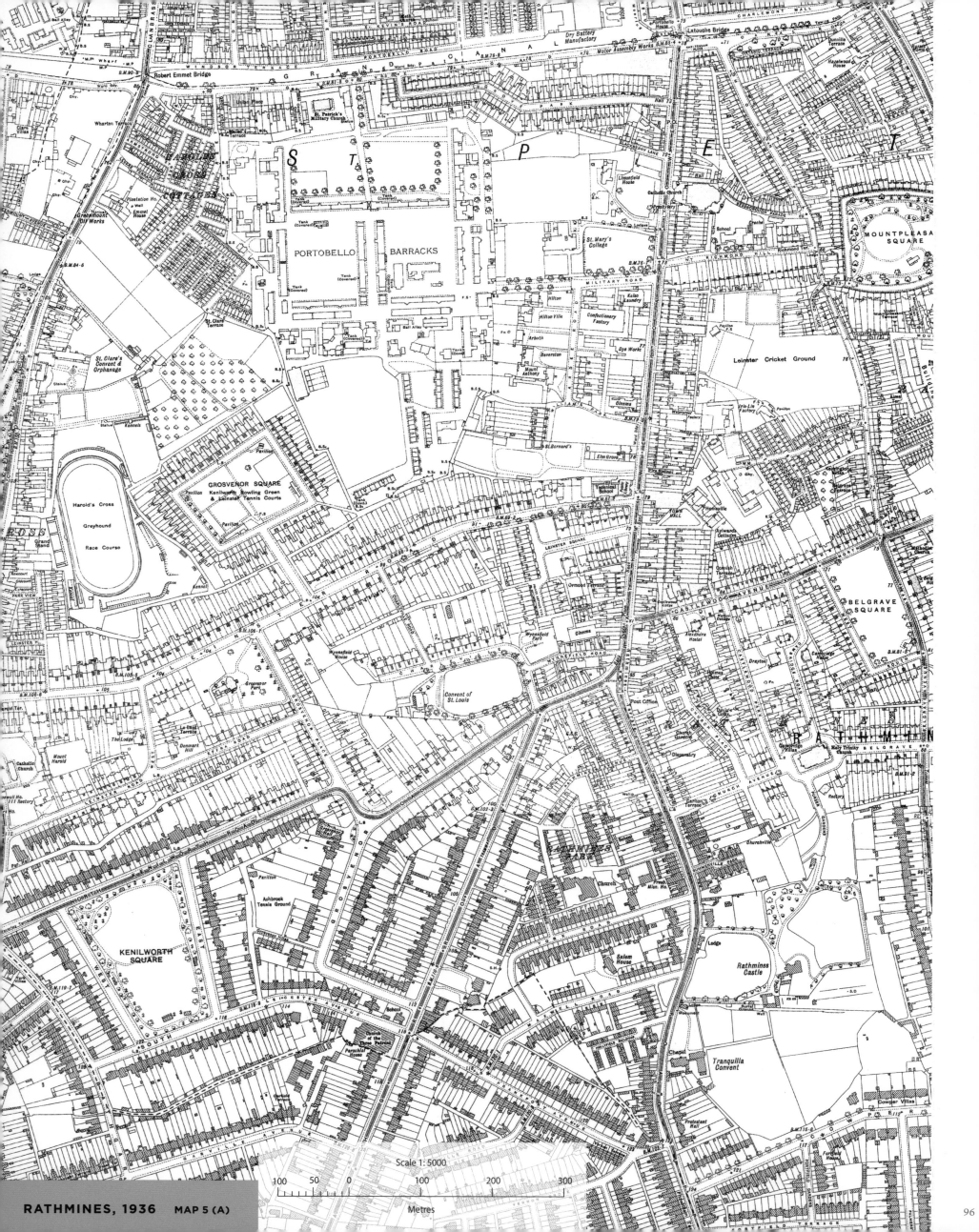

RATHMINES, 1936 MAP 5 (A)

Scale 1:5000

Metres

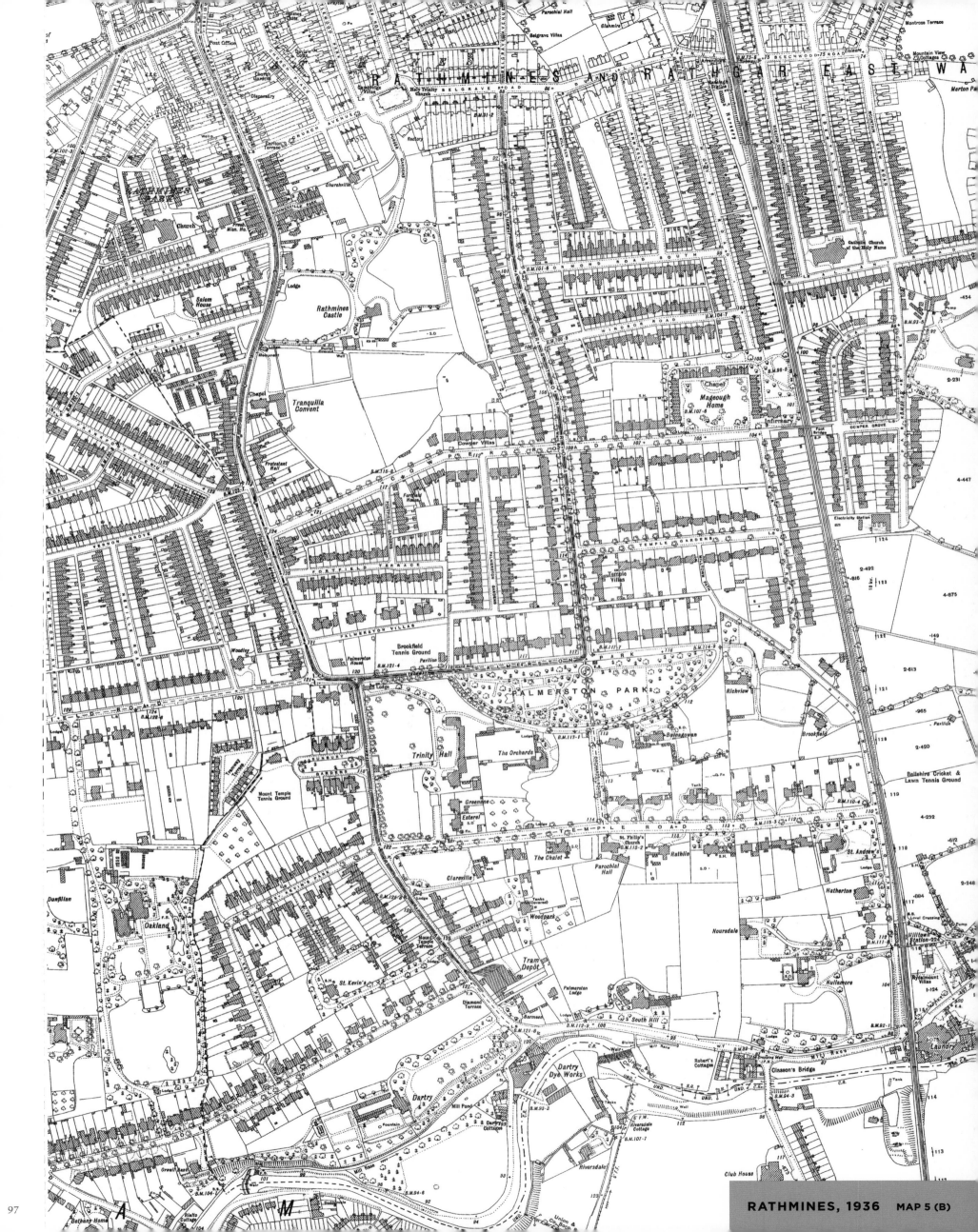

RATHMINES, 1936   MAP 5 (B)

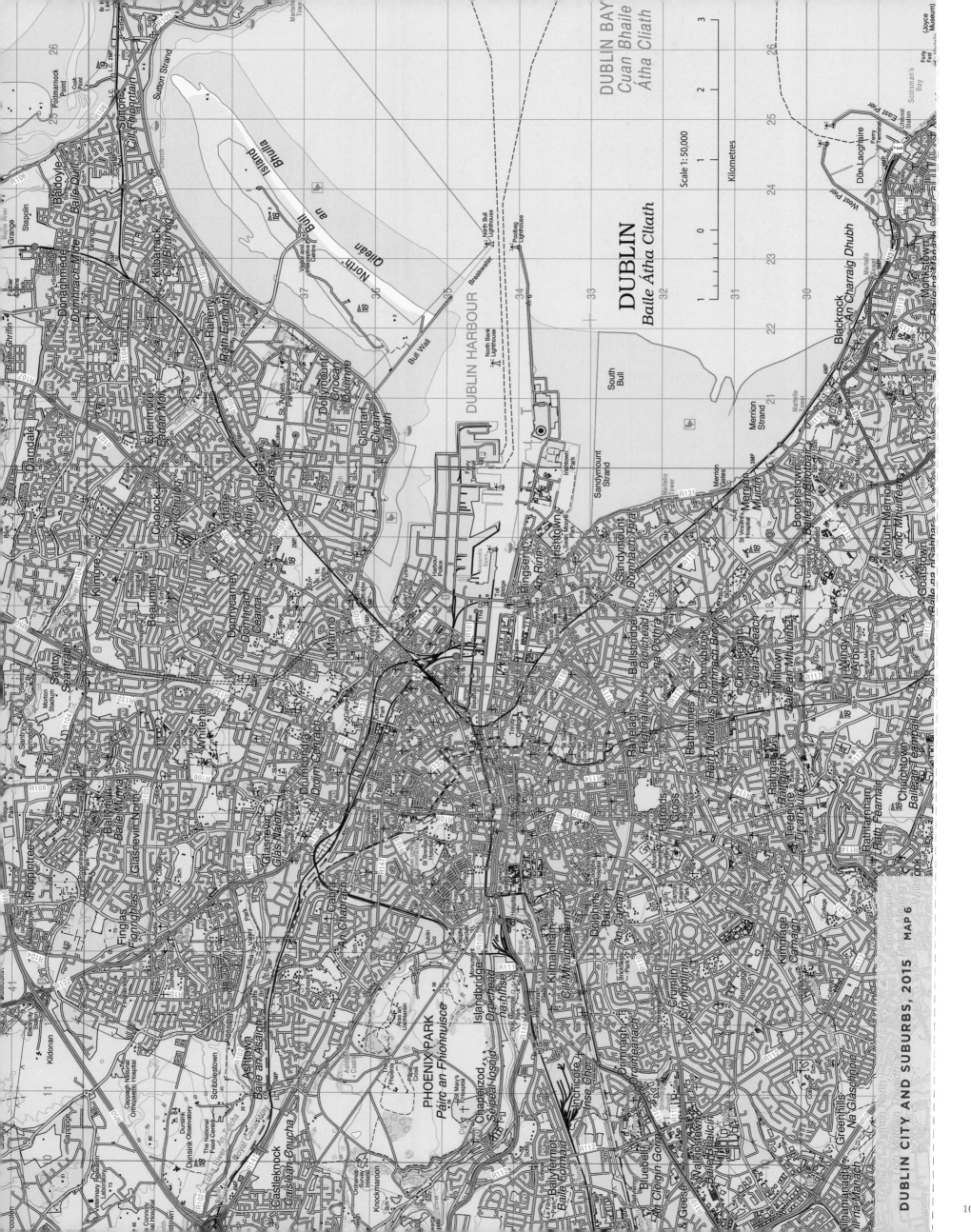

DUBLIN CITY AND SUBURBS, 2015   MAP 6

110

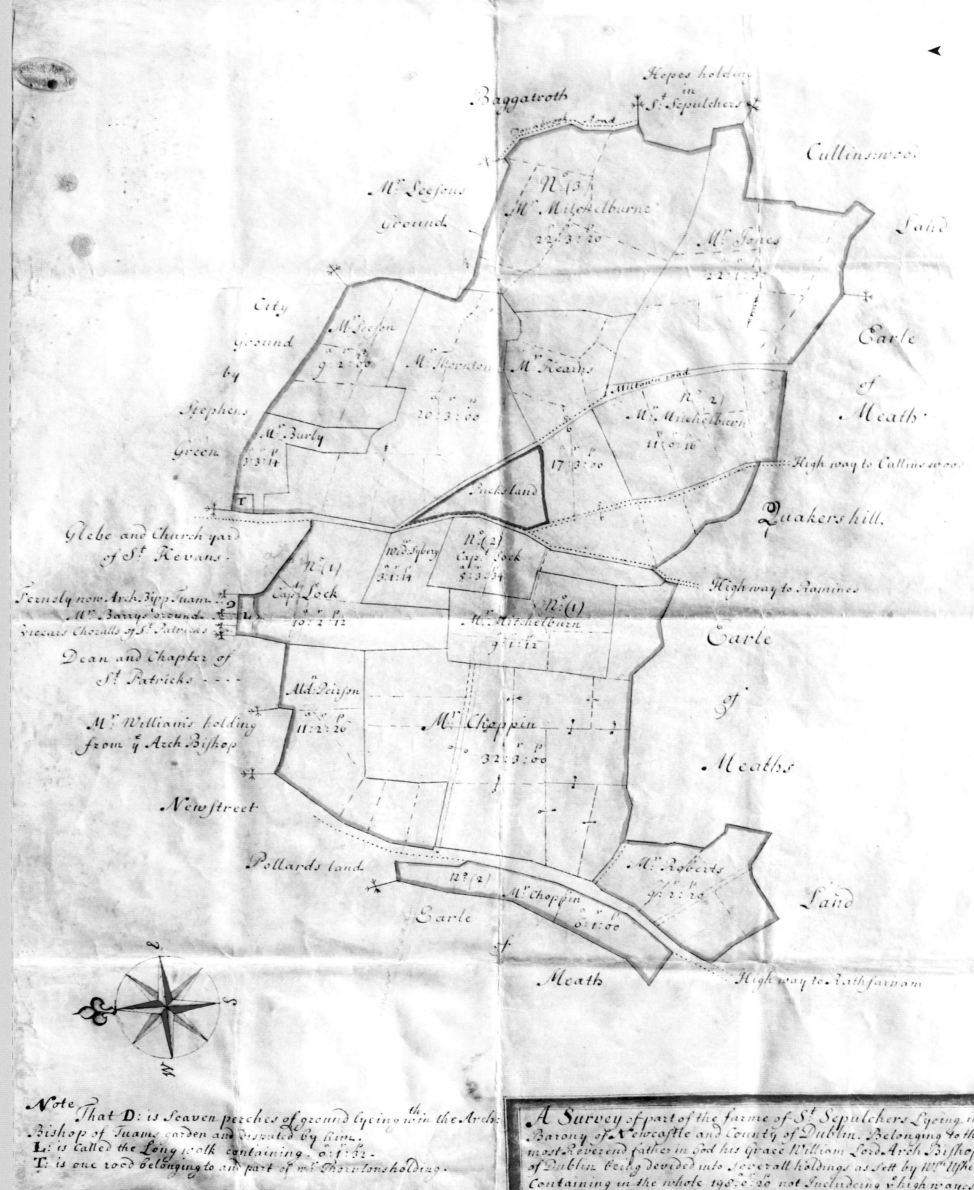

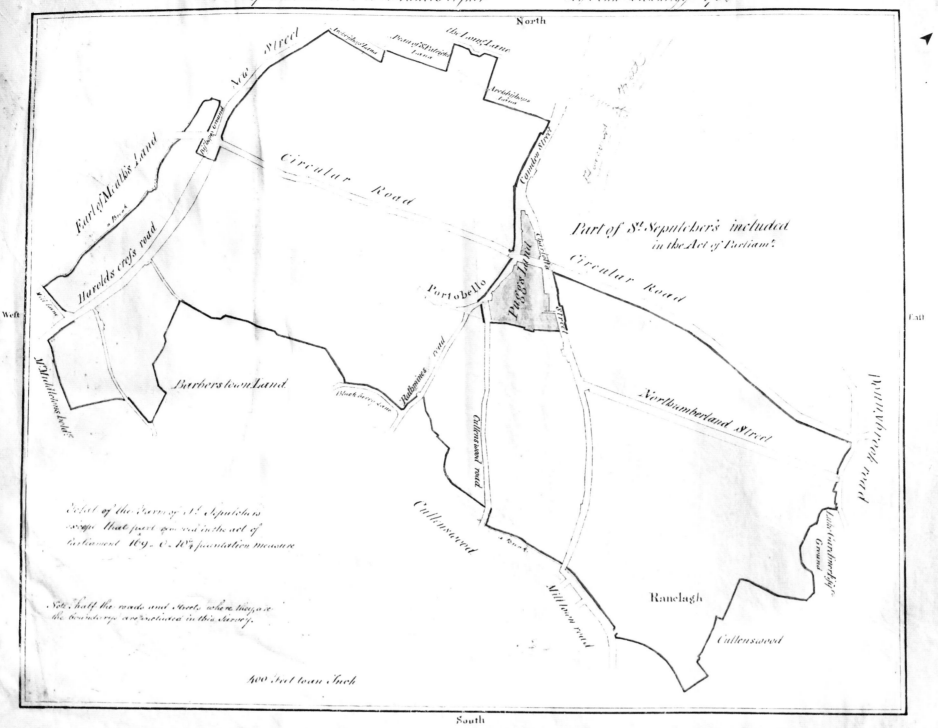

FARM OF ST SEPULCHRE, 1782, BROWNRIGG MAP 8

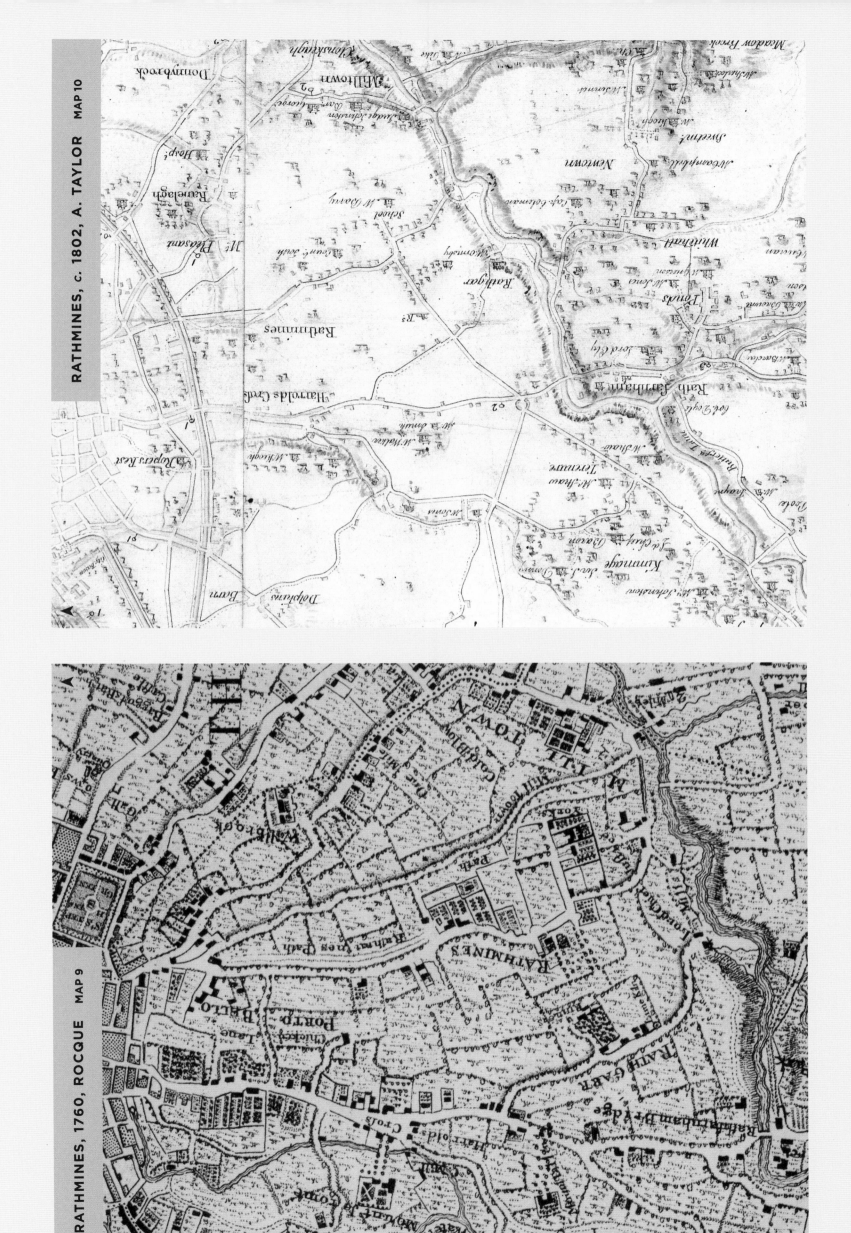

RATHMINES, c. 1802, A. TAYLOR MAP 10

RATHMINES, 1760, ROCQUE MAP 9

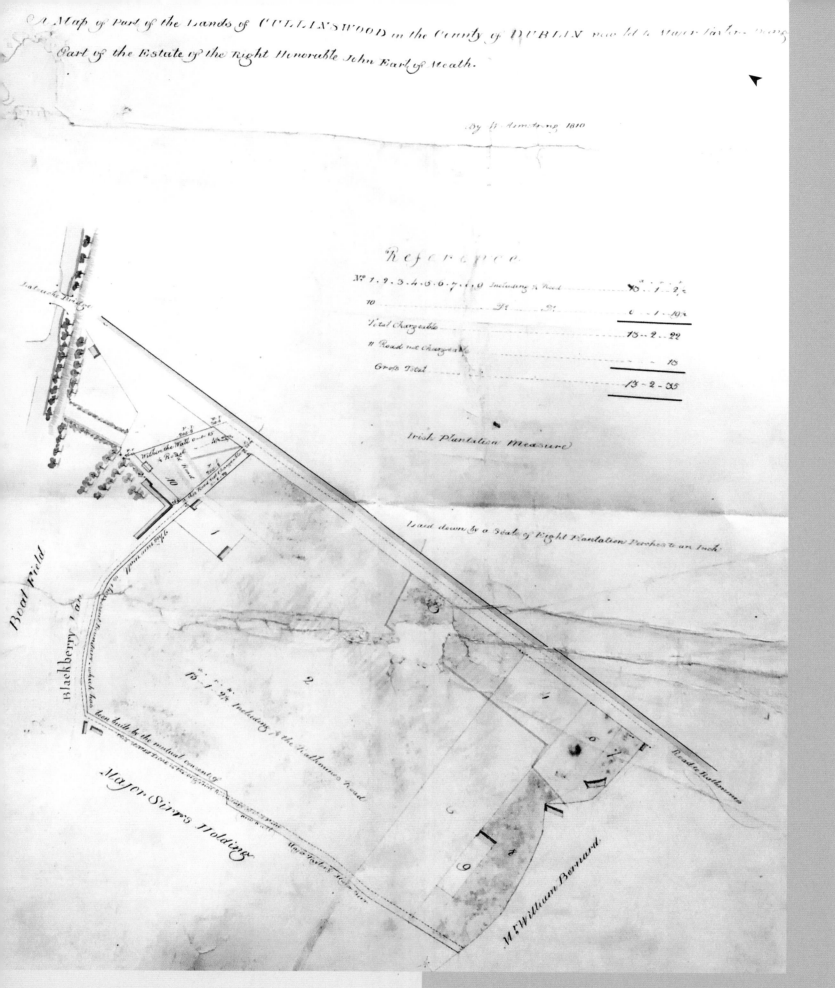

A Map of Part of the Lands of *CULLINSWOOD* in the County of *DUBLIN* now let to Major Taylor 18—

Part of the Estate of the Right Honorable John Earl of Meath.

By B. Armstrong 1810

Reference.

No 1. 2. 3. 4. 5. 6. 7. 8. 9 Including ye Road		10 . 1 . 2 ½
10	D° D°	0 . 1 . 10 ½
Total Chargeable		13 . 2 . 22
11 Road not Chargeable		— . 13
Gross Total		13 . 2 . 35

Irish Plantation Measure

Is laid down by a Scale of Eight Plantation Perches to an Inch.

Boat Field

Blackberry Lane

Major Sirr's Holding

Mr William Bernard

Road to Rathmines

CULLINSWOOD, 1810, ARMSTRONG (3)   MAP 11

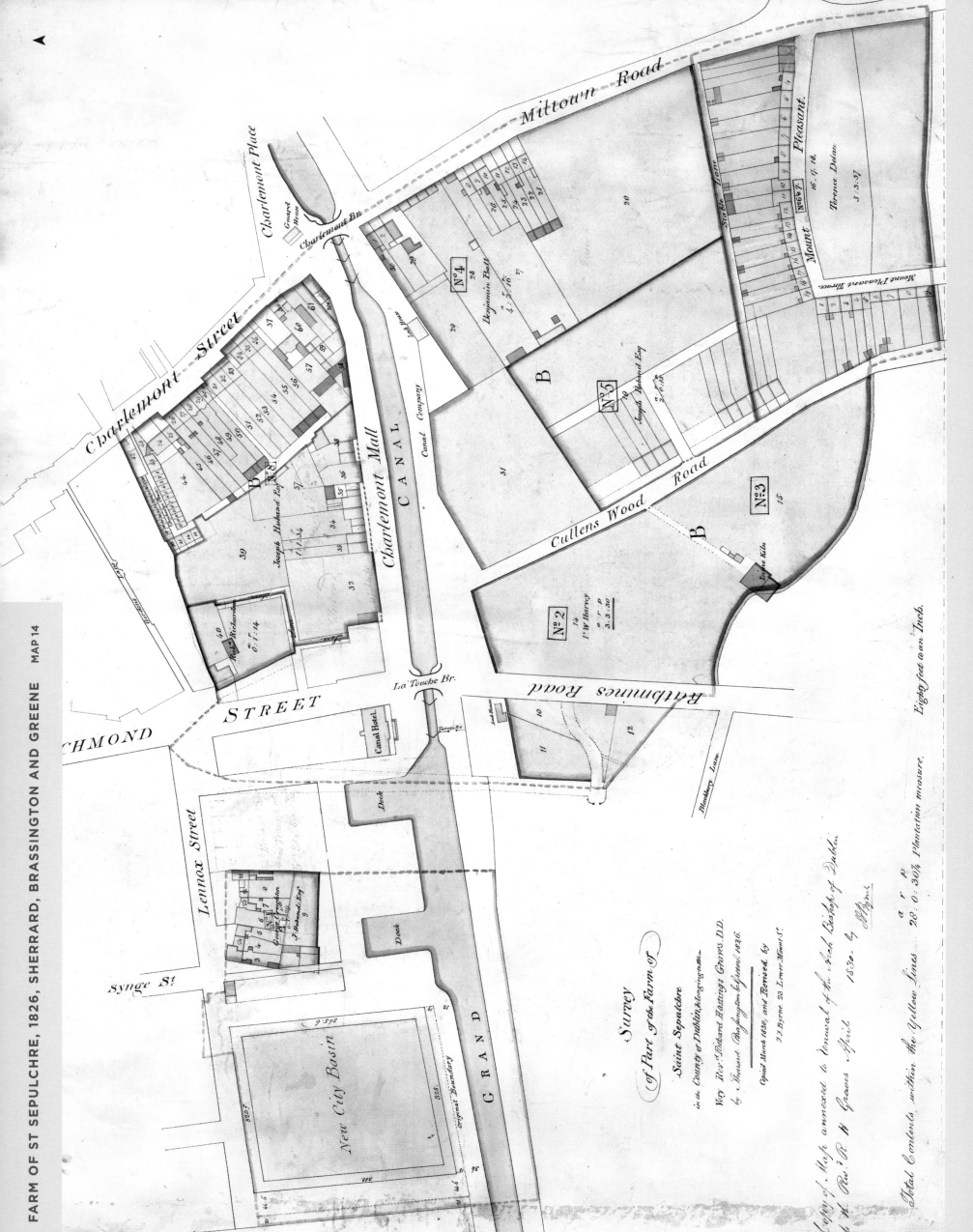

Charlemont Place

Gospel House

Charlemont Br.

Charlemont Street

Mittoun Road

Mount Pleasant.

16. 17. 18.
Terence Dolan
3 : 3 : 37

No 6 7

Mount Pleasant Terrace

Stable Lane

N.º 4
28
Benjamin Buff

B
N.º 5
Joseph Hubbard Esq
a. r. p.
2 : 0 : 15

Charlemont Mall

CANAL

Canal Company

Lock House

B   N.º 8
Joseph Hubband Esq
1 : 1 : 34

Ro.º Richardson
0 : 1 : 14

Cullens Wood   Road

N.º 3
15

B
E
Lime Kiln

N.º 2
P. W. Harvey
a. r. p.
3 : 3 : 30

La' Touche Br.

Rathmines Road

Lock House

10
12
11

Blackberry Lane

RICHMOND   STREET

Canal Hotel.

Turnpike

GRAND

Lennox Street

George Creighton
F. Hubband Esq.
9

Synge St.

CANAL

Dock

Dock

New City Basin

Original Boundary

Survey
of Part of the Farm of
Saint Sepulchre
in the County of Dublin, belonging to the
Very Rev.ᵈ Richard Hastings Graves, D.D.

Copied March 1830, and Revised by
Sherrard Brassington & Greene 1826.
J. J. Byrne 23 Lower Mount St.

a. r. p.
Copy of Map annexed to Renewal of the Lish Bishop of Dublin
to the Rev.ᵈ R. H. Graves April   1830. by Hynes

Total Contents within the Yellow Lines .... 28 : 0 : 30¾ Plantation measure.   Eighty feet to an Inch.

118

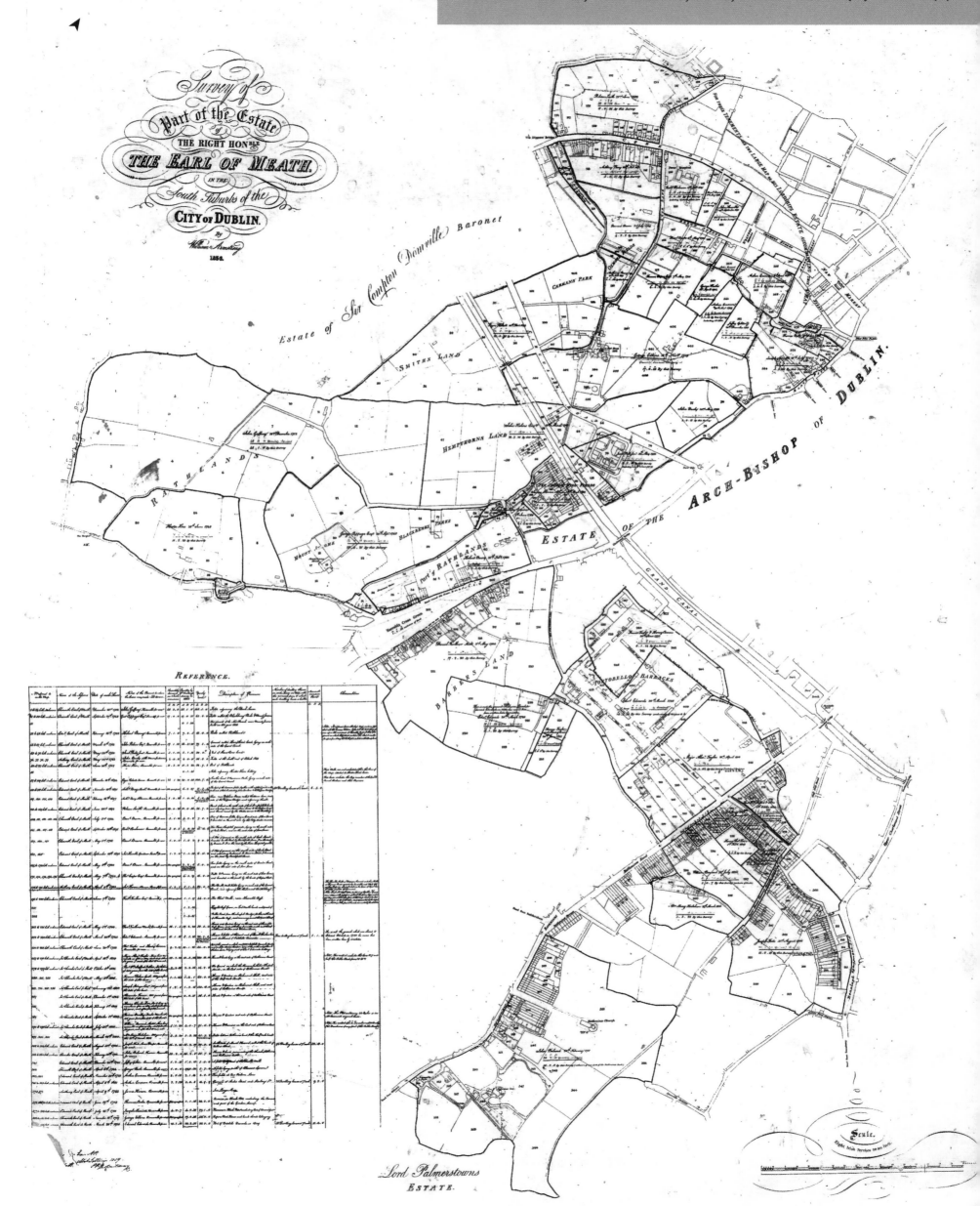

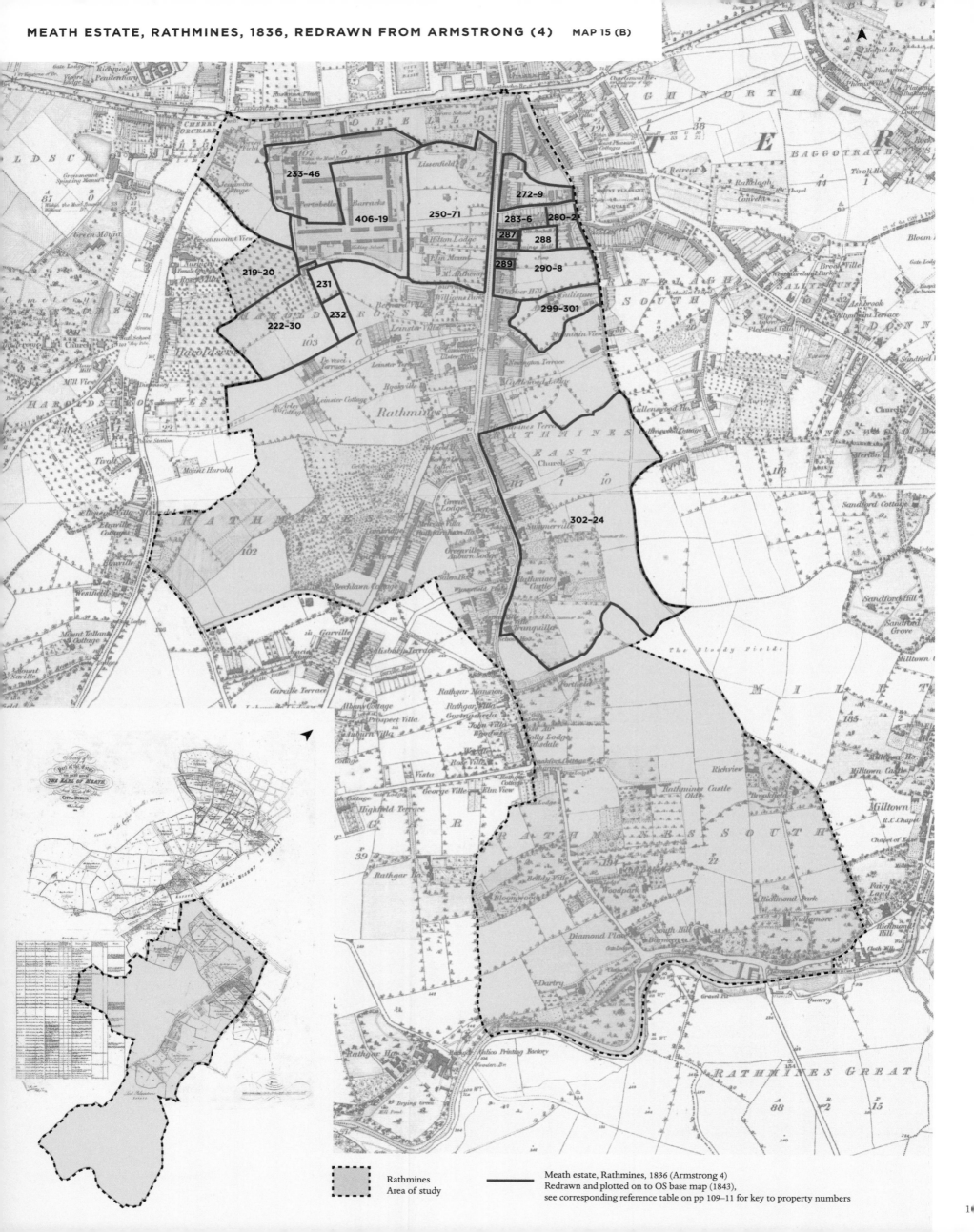

233–46

406–19

250–71

272–9

283–6   280–2

287   288

289   290–8

299–301

219–20

231

232

222–30

302–24

Rathmines
Area of study

Meath estate, Rathmines, 1836 (Armstrong 4)
Redrawn and plotted on to OS base map (1843),
see corresponding reference table on pp 109–11 for key to property numbers

REFERENCE TO SURVEY OF THE ESTATE OF THE EARL OF MEATH, 1836

Properties within the Rathmines study area are highlighted and included on reference map on p. 108

included on reference map on p. 108

No.	Date of lease	Lessee	Area (Armstrong's survey of 1835)			Yearly rent			Description of premises	No. of houses 1837	Observations
			A	R	P	£	s.	d.			
1–14	23 Dec. 1752	John Gaffney	48	1	11	146	5	0	Fields adjoining the Dark Lane		
15–30	27 Sept. 1749	George Cuppage Esq.	19	0	21	63	6	0	Fields called the Blackberry Parks & Mount Jerome		
31			0	1	30				The ground of the New Church near Mount Jerome built on the year 1836		
32–45	16 Feb. 1703	Hobart Barry	7	2	5	18	0	0	Parks called Rathland		Note. It appears from [–] mark on 1771 that all the houses between letter a & the R.C. Chapel [–] the commons of Harolds Cross: that the ground on which they stand remains 30 perches. And it would also appear from May that the chapel is included in [–].
46–67	15 Mar. 1763	John Robins Esq.	18	3	10	79	5	0	Ground called Hempthorn's land, lying on each side of the Grand Canal		
68–75	30 May 1750	Jacob Powle jnr	5	1	16	30	0	-	East of Hempthorns land		
76–9	22 May 1783	John Busty, silk manufacturer	4	0	15	36	8	0	Fields at the south end of Black Pitts		
80–7	28 Jun. 1749	Hester Kerr	11	2	22	32	9	3	Part of Rathlands		
88			0	1	35				Mills adjoining Hester Kerr's holding		These mills are not included within the lines of the map attached to Hester Kerr's lease.
89–109	10 Dec. 1694	Roger Roberts, farmer	23	0	38	100	7	0	Smiths Land & Carmans Park, lying on each side of the Grand Canal		This lease includes the Bog meadow at the Grand Canal Harbour and other premises.
110–18	10 Nov. 1691	Anthony Percy	6	2	27	11	3	4	The last of the Oxmore fields, together with a plot of ground on the south side of Cork Street including from Love Lane to the Dippers Bridge	50 at 2s. 6d. each	
119–22	16 Feb. 1697	Anthony Percy	1	0	14	5	0	0	Close, near Dolphins Barn called Chittons [–] Lane, west side of the Dippers Bridge, and adjoining thereto		
123–49	22 Jun. 1692	Rebecca Smith	11	0	36	36	7	0	Parcel of land on the north side of Cork Street called Halls Land, and extending from Marrowbone Lane to the Dippers Bridge and thence round by the water course to the distillery		
150–4	2 Jul. 1724	Bernard Brown	4	2	2	7	0	0	Five of Oxmore fields, lying on the west side of Love Lane & bounded on the west side by the City Water course		

No.	Date of lease	Lessee	Area (Armstrong's survey of 1835)			Yearly rent			Description of premises	No. of houses 1837	Observations
			A	R	P	£	s.	d.			
155–8	10 Sept. 1695	Richard Ruckman	3	0	30	13	16	6	The Fever Hospital grounds, lying on the south side of Cork Street, and on the east side of Love Lane		
159–61	3 May 1718	Bernard Brown	1	0	2	9	0	0	A plot of ground on the south side of Cork Street, bounded on the east by Brickfield Lane & on the south by Brown Street, & on the west by the Fever Hospital ground		
162–3	10 Sept. 1695	John Humble, gardiner	1	1	38	6	15	0	A plot of ground on the south side of Cork Street extending backward to Brown Street & bounded on the west by Brickfield Lane		
165–70	8 May 1700	Bernard Brown	2	2	6	5	0	0	Five fields lying on the south side of Brown Street and on the east side of Love Lane		
171–5	7 May 1740	Thomas Cooper Esq.	4	3	29	16	0	0	Fields & premises lying on the east side of Love Lane and bounded on the south by the lands of Ropers Rest		
176–94	9 Apr. 1783	James Horan	5	1	4	80	0	0	The Double Mill Fields lying on each side of the Grand Canal, and adjoining the Richmond Penitentiary		The Double Mills and Warren Mount and the Mills of Thomas Brush [–] appear to be over the road and 176 to 196 on this map are all included on the lease of April the 9th 1783 at £80 per annum.
195–200	9 Jun. 1760	Frederick Faulkner Esq.	1	1	17	44	0	0	The Wood Mills, near Harrolds Cross		Note. That nos 199 & 200, containing together 17 acres now (1837) on the [–] of Frederick Faulkners Representation yet the are section the [–] of the May 6 related to said Love Lane of May 9th 1723 and represented by the letter [–] on the [–] by the [–].
201			1	2	32				Harrolds Cross Green on Lord Meath's lands undisposed of		
202			2	3	21				Public road from Clanbrassil Bridge to the south end of Harrolds Cross, and running round the green through		
203–21	3 May 1700	Daniel Faulkner	19	2	20	32	0	0	Houses & gardens lying on the east side of Harrolds Cross Green, and returning from the south and thereof [–] to Hen and Chicken Lane		
222–30	20 Mar. 1720	Edward Edwards	8	1	23	20	7	0	Houses & fields at the east end of Hen & Chicken Lane and southwest of Portobello Barracks	3 at 7d. each	This is not the ground which was leased to Edward Edwards in 1720 his name has been written here by mistake.
231–46	20 Jun. 1753	Thomas Taylor and Harry Carman	10	1	26	34	0	0	Part of the grounds on which now (1837) Portobello Barracks stands and the fields situated there from lying at the south end of Hen & Chicken Lane, & lying east of Edward Edwards holding		

No.	Date of lease	Lessee	Area (Armstrong's survey of 1835)			Yearly rent			Description of premises	No. of houses 1837	Observations
			A	R	P	£	s.	d.			
247–71	18 Apr. 1810	Major Alexander Taylor	13	3		232	15	10	Houses & lands lying on the west side of Rathmines Road		Note. This content includes the lane XY and half the Public Road from W to V.
272–9	8 Oct. 1824	Revd William Stafford & others	2	2	36	34	2	6	The ground on which the Roman Catholic Chapel stands, on the east side of Rathmines Road.		
280–2	11 May 1826	Terence Dolan, Gent.	1	2	1	60	0	0	Houses & gardens on Richmond Hill, west side of the Half Mile Road		
283–6	22 Jan. 1830	Joseph Stringer Esq.	1	2	15	130	18	0	Houses and gardens in Richmond Hill, and east side of Rathmines Road		
287	1 Dec. 1824	Alexander Feviar	0	0	35	36	8	0	Houses & gardens on the east side of Rathmines Road		
288	1 Feb. 1809	Henry Charles Sirr									
289	1 Sept. 1829	Thomas Bradley, timber merchant	0	0	34	30	0	0	Houses & gardens east side of Rathmines Road		Note. This plot containing 34 perches is in Mr Barnards original lease.
290–8	31 Jul. 1808	William Barnard	5	0	7	91	11	8	Houses & premises on the east side of Rathmines Road		Note. This extent of 5 a. 0 r. 7 p. is exclusive of Mr Bradley's plot & exclusive of any part of the Public Road.
299–301	25 Mar. 1830	Mrs Mary Holohan	3	3	22	41	7	2	Fields between Rathmines Road & the Half mile road		
302–24	31 Aug. 1705	Joseph Fade, linen draper	15	2	19	20	0	0	South side of Mount Pleasant, called the lands of Cullens Wood	94 at 7d. each	
325–60	10 Feb. 1711	John Boland, farmer	36	2	8	55	7	0	Houses & lands surrounding the Church of Rathmines and Rathmines Castle		
361	20 Dec. 1701	Jeffry Gibton	1	3	15	5	0	0	A field lying west of the Double Mills		
362	6 Apr. 1734	George Rook	1[-]	0	30	5	7	0	A field lying south of Weavers Square		
363–4	30 Nov. 1703	Arthur Emerson	2	1	14	6	0	0	Five fields at Cow Parlour Lane		
365–9	6 Apr. 1691	Arthur Emerson	3	0	8	15	9	9	Premises at Ardee Street and Sterling Street	26 at 7d. each	
370–1	9 Apr. 1783	James Horan							See larger map		
372–6	19 Jun. 1703	Thomas Cooke	1	1	16	23	0	0	Premises in Black Pitts including the convent and part of the garden thereof		
377–85	23 Jul. 1701	Joseph Harriett	4	0	38	27	1	0	Premises in Black Pitts & including part of convent garden		
386–405	18 Nov. 1719	George Edkins	17	0	35	40	0	0	Ropers Rest House and lands thereto belonging		
406–9	20 Mar. 1720	Edward Edwards	10	2	36	20	0	0	Part of Portobello Barracks in 1849	32 at 7d. each	

115

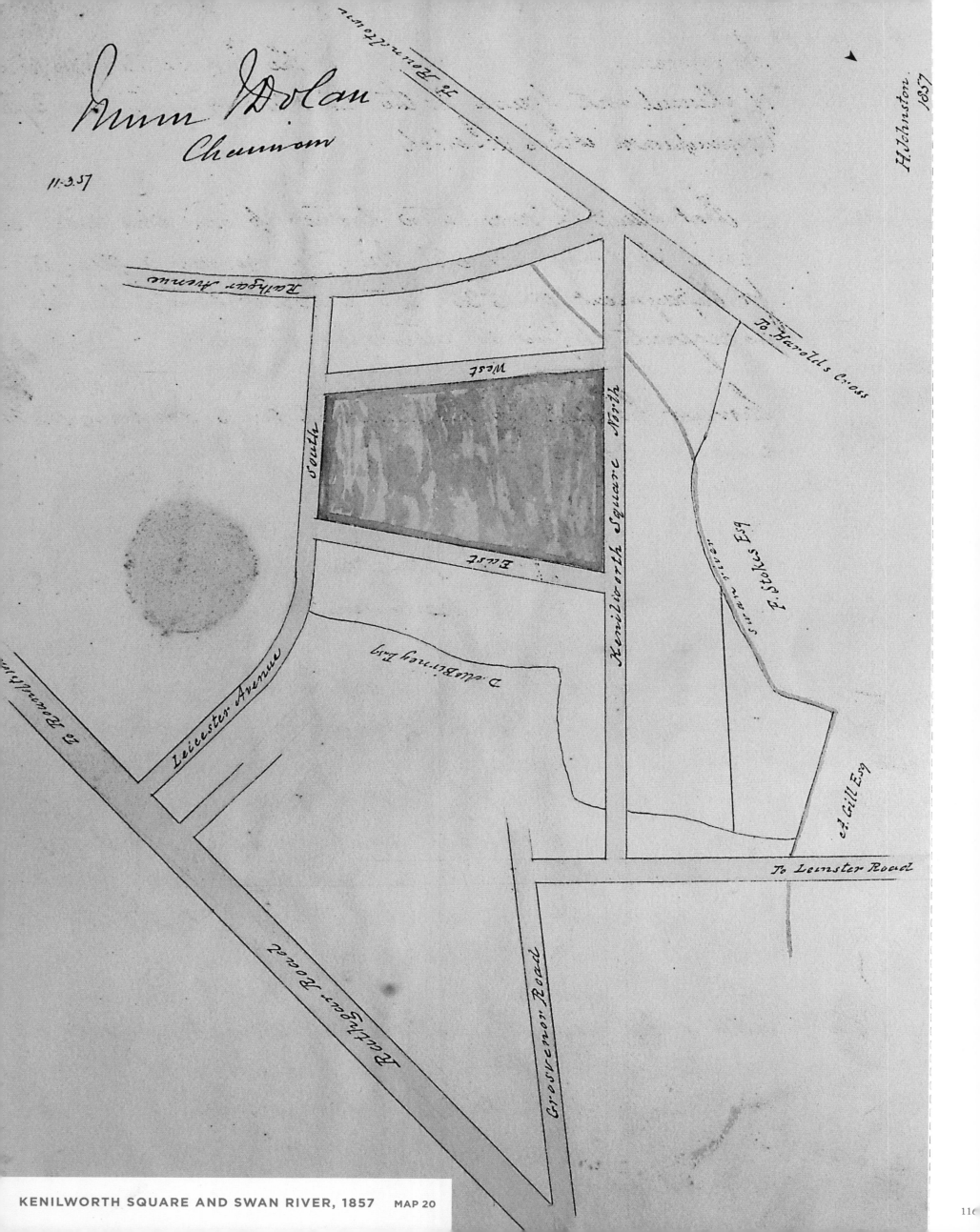

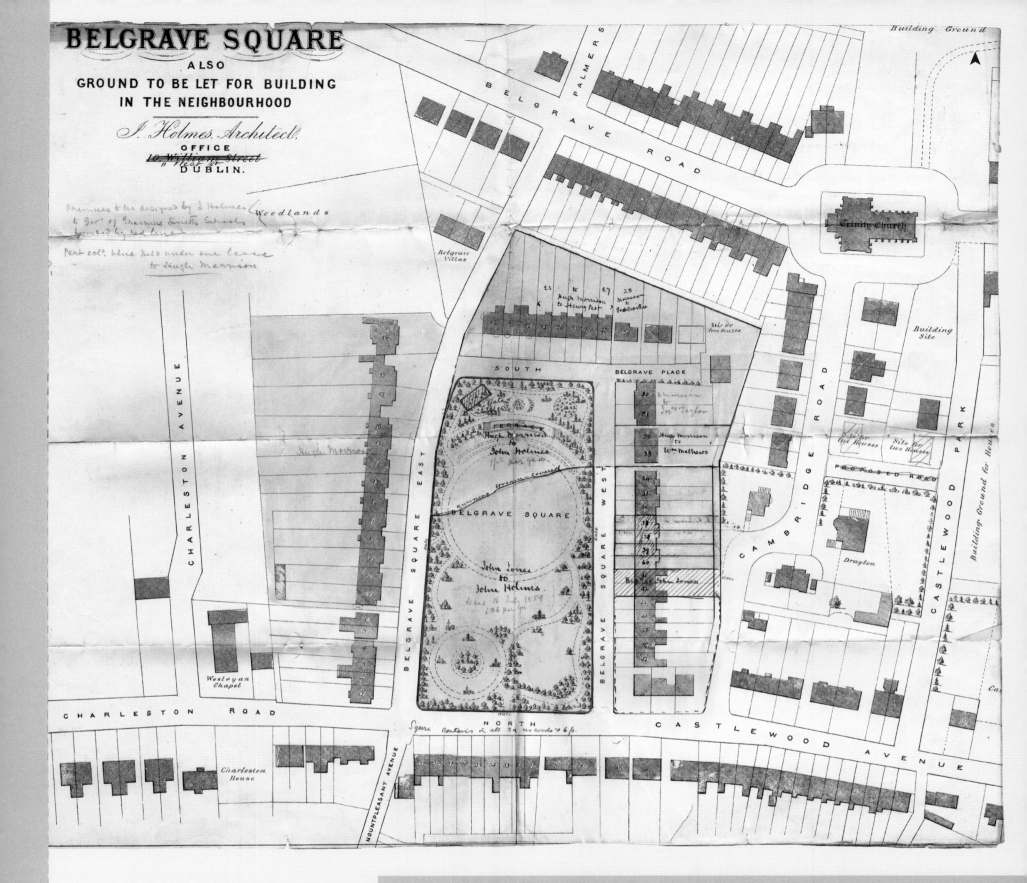

BELGRAVE SQUARE, 1872–97   MAP 21

117

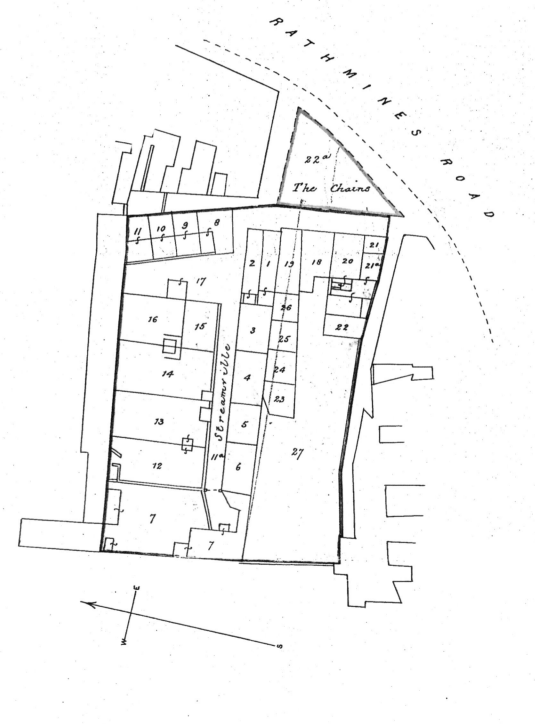

Map referred to in this Deed

NOTE— The premises, the interests in which are conveyed by this deed are colored Red— the remaining premises acquired by the Commissioners being surrounded by a Yellow border.

Scale 40 Feet to an Inch

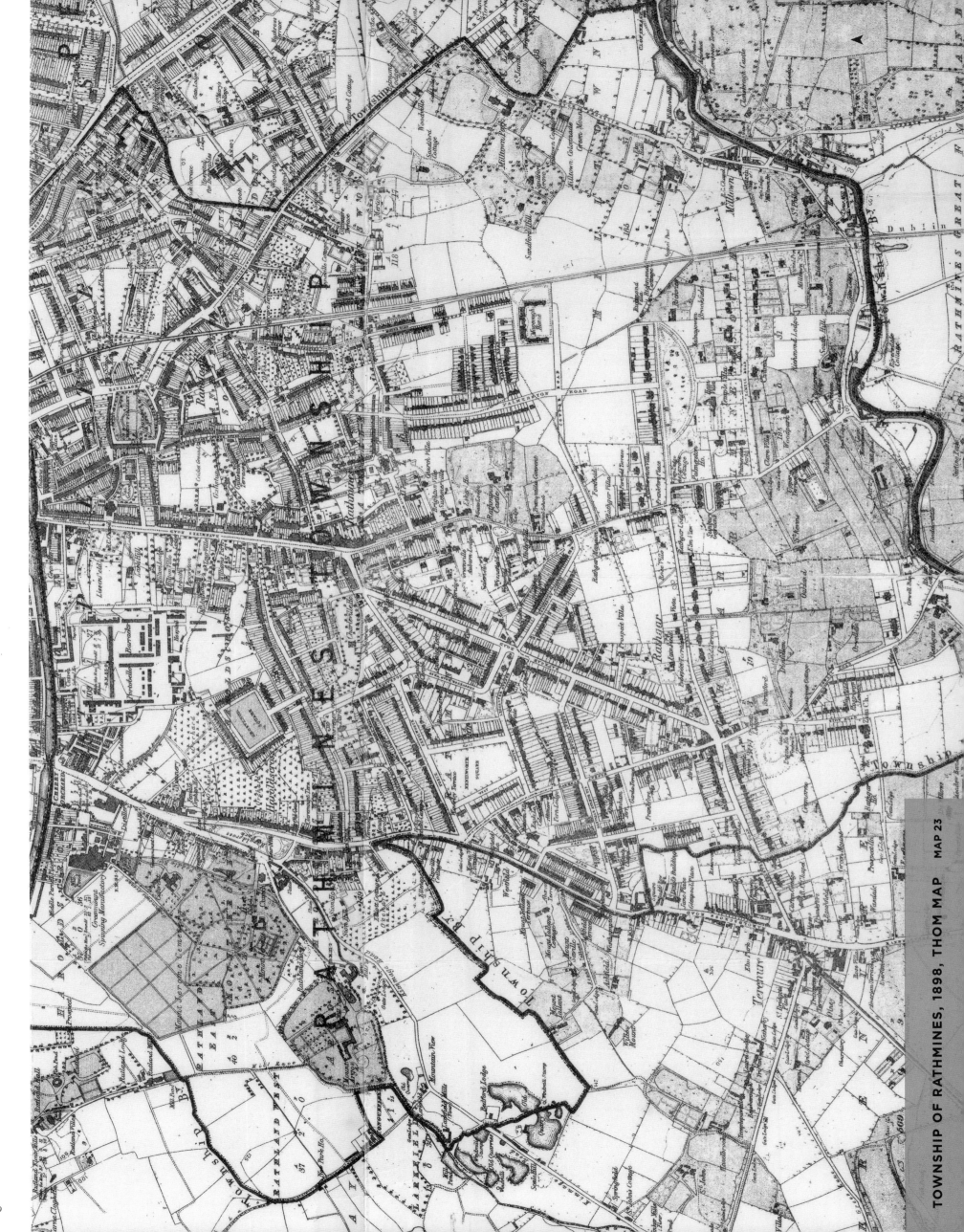

TOWNSHIP OF RATHMINES, 1898, THOM MAP   MAP 23

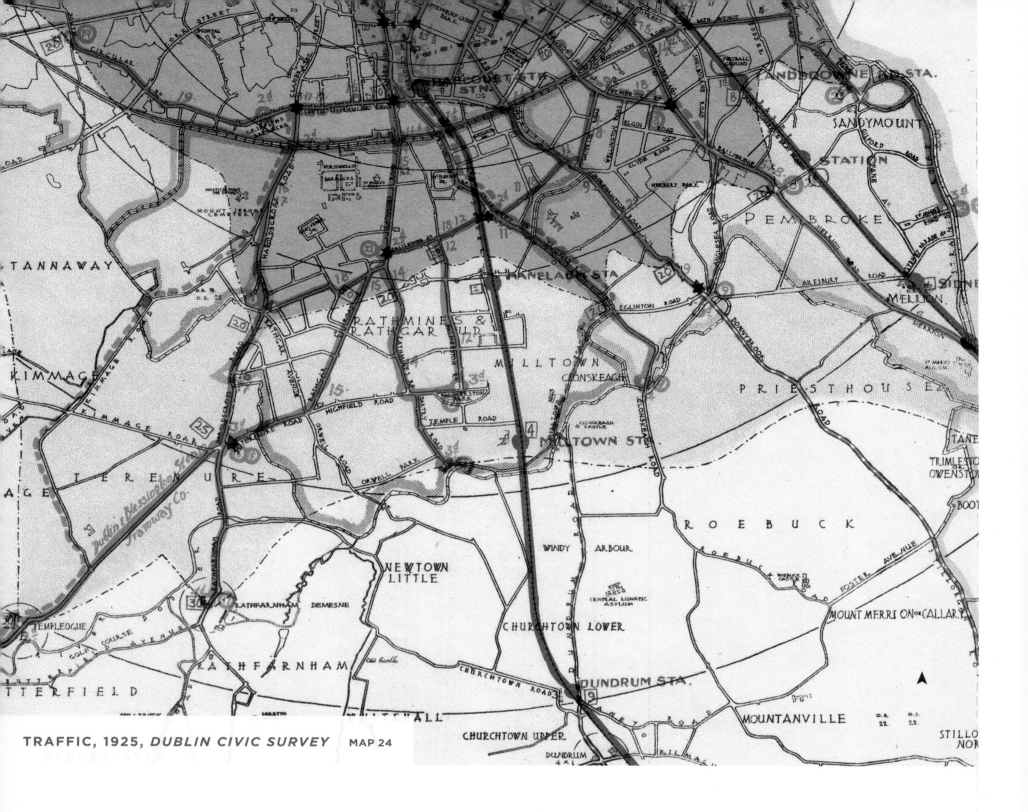

TRAFFIC, 1925, *DUBLIN CIVIC SURVEY* | MAP 24

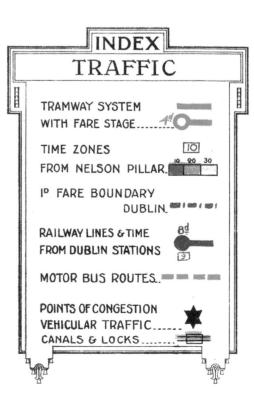

INDEX
TRAFFIC

TRAMWAY SYSTEM
WITH FARE STAGE

TIME ZONES
FROM NELSON PILLAR

1ᴰ FARE BOUNDARY
DUBLIN

RAILWAY LINES & TIME
FROM DUBLIN STATIONS

MOTOR BUS ROUTES

POINTS OF CONGESTION
VEHICULAR TRAFFIC
CANALS & LOCKS

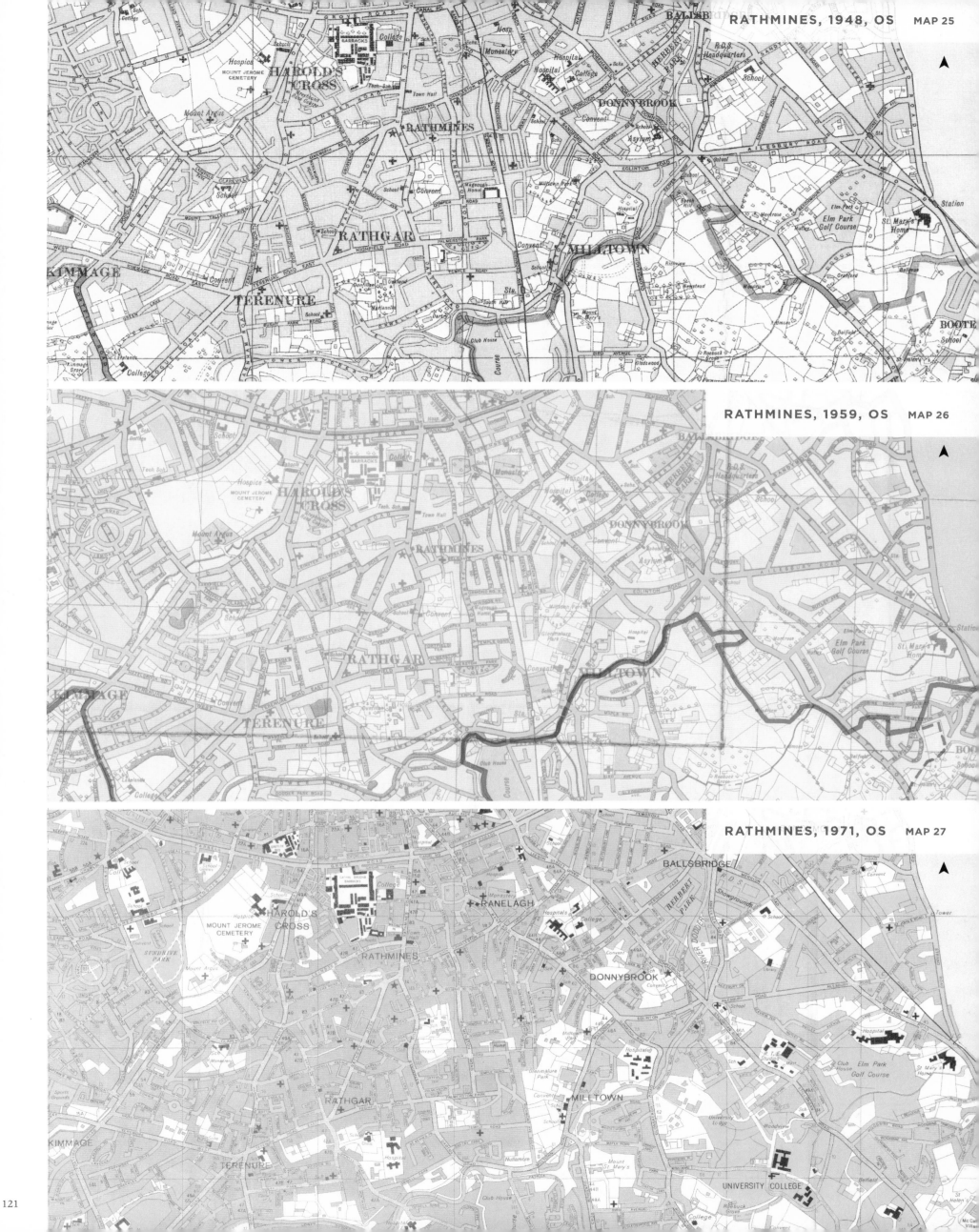

RATHMINES, 1948, OS   MAP 25

RATHMINES, 1959, OS   MAP 26

RATHMINES, 1971, OS   MAP 27

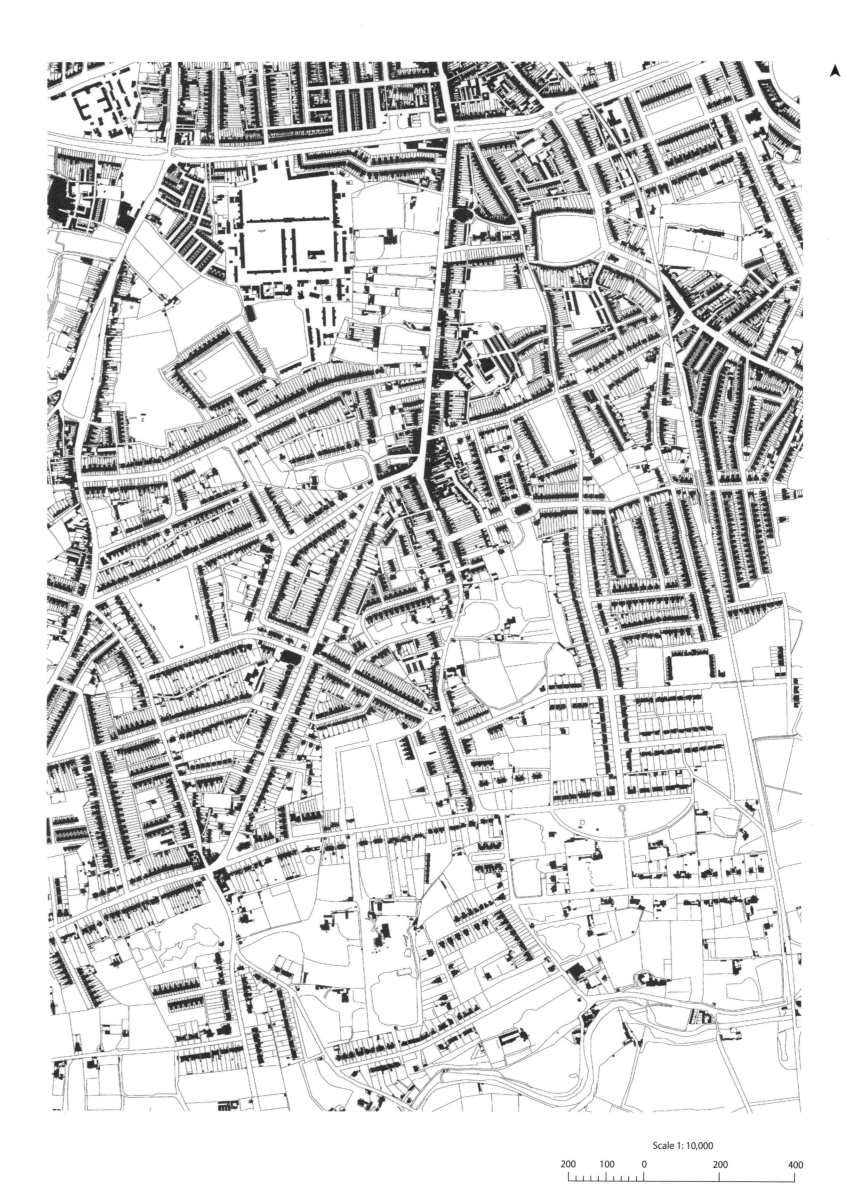

Scale 1 : 10,000

200   100   0   200   400

Metres

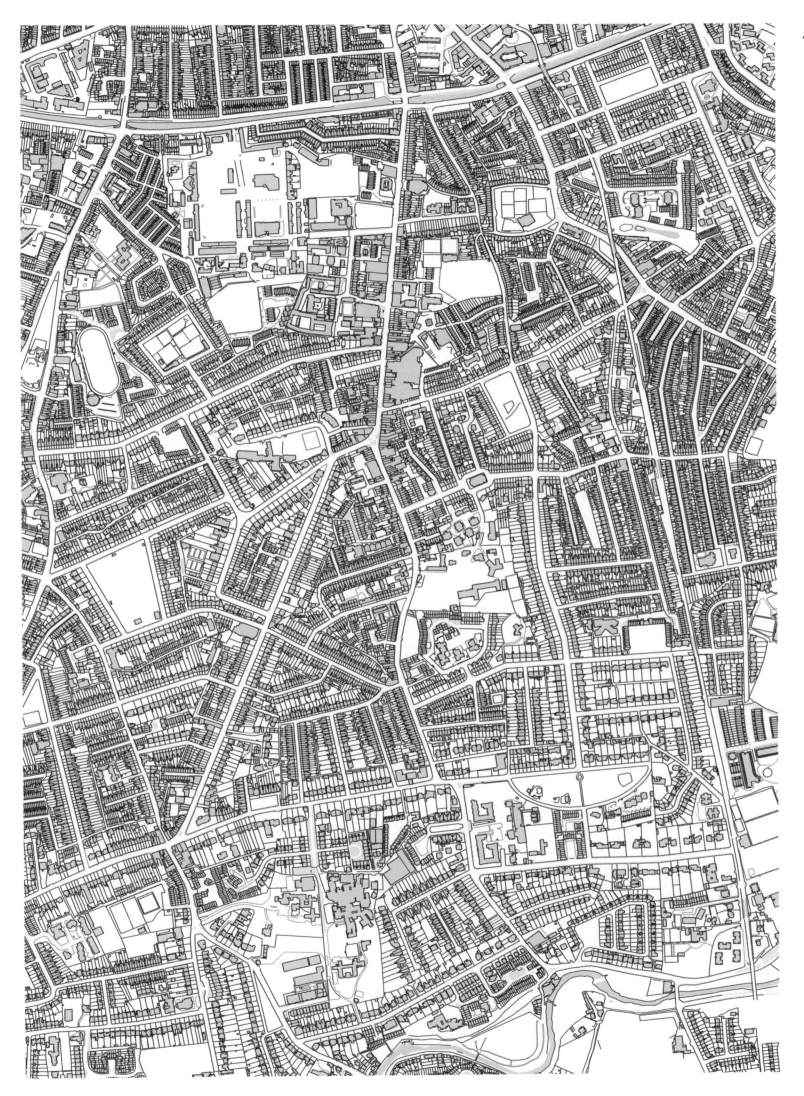

Scale 1: 10,000

200   100   0   200   400

Metres

Previous pages: Rathmines Road Lower, looking south, *c.* 1910 (National Library of Ireland)

Further notes

Period reconstructions and thematic maps
Figs 1–9, pp 8–29

For the suburbs series, four reconstructions aim to show the development of the chosen area of study from its origins down to the present day (for Rathmines, Figs 1, 2, 5 and 9). Two further maps focus on a selected street or area but may be utilised in a broadly comparative way between suburbs — one tracing the development of a chosen street and another plotting the valuation of buildings in *c.* 1900 (for Rathmines, Figs 4 and 7 respectively). Additional maps are included to highlight topographical features or themes specific to the suburb in question. For Rathmines, these focus on the Meath and Palmerston estates (Fig. 3), developments associated with the Rathmines and Rathgar township commissioners / Urban District Council (Fig. 6) and the civic nucleus of the late nineteenth century (Fig. 8).

Figs 1 and 2 show key topographical features in Rathmines from the medieval / early modern period to the late eighteenth century at a scale of 1:10,000. Sites, taken from the Topographical information section and select historic maps are depicted with standard symbols and lines that do not reflect actual dimensions. Where there is a doubt about location, a question mark (for sites) or dashed lines (for roads or boundaries) are used.

Fig. 1 is a composite map that shows features across the medieval and early modern eras. It uses a base of modern contours at 3 m intervals. Modern placenames are included in grey; contemporary placenames are depicted in black. Rivers have been plotted according to Sweeney and the first-edition OS maps (1843). The extent of Cullenswood is conjectural and is based on documentary and placename evidence from the Meath papers.

Fig. 2 is based on John Rocque's county map (1760). Roads, buildings, gardens, fields and plots have been mapped using the first-edition OS maps (1843) as a guide.

Placenames have been taken from Rocque and the Topographical information. Rivers have been plotted according to Sweeney and the first-edition OS maps.

Figs 5 and 9 show the approximate extent of the built-up area at different stages during the nineteenth and twentieth centuries at a scale of 1:8000, using key Ordnance Survey maps from 1843 to 1908 and 1908 to *c.* 2019. Streets, roads, lanes, rail/tram lines and buildings with their associated plots are shaded according to their main phase of development. Where properties include extensive garden or parkland, shading has been generalised and limited to the main building and immediate area. The map does not necessarily indicate the age of individual buildings/features, depicted on the 1907–8 or *c.* 2019 base maps, that may have been redeveloped or demolished since their initial construction.

Topographical information
pp 35–79

Primary source material is listed to approximately 1970. Features originating after this date are included only in exceptional circumstances.

The list of early spellings in section **1** seeks to give a representative selection of placename forms. It is confined to the earliest and latest examples noted of the variants deemed to be the most significant. Where necessary the earliest noted attestation of the commonest spelling in each of these categories is also given.

Street names are listed in alphabetical order in section **10**. The first entry for each street gives its present-day name according to the most authoritative source, with versions in Irish taken from the Placename Database of Ireland (Logainm), where available. This is followed in the right-hand column by the nearest main thoroughfare in brackets and the street's first identifiable appearance, named or unnamed, in a map or other record and the various names subsequently applied to it in chronological order of occurrence.

Entries under each heading in sections **11–22** are arranged in chronological order by categories: for example, mills are listed before cloth manufactories, because the oldest mill pre-dates the oldest cloth manufactory. In general, dates of initiation and cessation are specified as such. Where these are unknown, the first and last recorded dates are given and references of intermediate date are omitted except where corroborative evidence appears necessary. In source-citations, a pair of years joined by a hyphen includes all intervening years for which that source is available: thus 1843–1908 (OS) means all Ordnance Survey maps from 1843 to 1907–8 inclusive.

The section on residence (**22**) is not intended to embrace more than a small fraction of the dwelling houses in the suburb. The main criteria for inclusion are (1) contribution to the townscape, past or present; (2) significance in defining critical stages in the history of urban or suburban housing; (3) abundance of documentation, especially for houses representative of a large class of dwellings. Biographical associations are not in themselves a ground for inclusion. Only residences that can be located to at least a street location, or that are named in two or more primary sources, have been included.

Sites are located, where possible, according to their orientation to the nearest street and by grid reference (these relate to the eastings and northings shown on Map 3, pp 92–3). 'Site unknown' is stated for features that cannot be precisely placed along a street, with 'location unknown' being used in cases where no locational evidence has been found. Grid references are given in Irish Transverse Mercator co-ordinates. They indicate the approximate centre of the feature in question.

Abbreviated source-references are explained in the bibliography and general abbreviations on pp 132–41.

List of illustrations

Maps and plates listed on pp 85–6

ii–iii, 43	'Hen and Chicken Lane, Harold's Cross', looking east to Rathmines, 1817, by C.M. Nairn. Reproduced courtesy of the National Library of Ireland, PD 1969 TX 92.
viii–ix	*Plan of Dublin, Baile Átha Cliath*, by Geographia Ltd (London, [*c.* 1935]), extract. Reproduced courtesy of University College Dublin Library.
4–5	Rathmines Road Lower, looking north, *c.* 1910, from Lawrence Photographic Collection. Reproduced courtesy of the National Library of Ireland, L_ROY_05953.
32–3, 54	'Cullen's Castle, near Cullen's wood', 1772, by Gabriel Beranger. Reproduced courtesy of the National Library of Ireland, PD 1958 TX 72.
40	Dartry Road, tram depot, mid-20th cent. Postcard, reproduced courtesy of the author.
42	Grosvenor Square, early 20th cent., from Fergus O'Connor Collection. Reproduced courtesy of the National Library of Ireland, OCO 321.
45	Leinster Road, looking west, early 20th cent. Postcard, reproduced courtesy of the author.
46	Rathmines Road Lower, looking south, early 20th cent. Postcard, reproduced courtesy of the author.
47	Rathmines College, Rathmines Road Upper, early 20th cent. Postcard, reproduced courtesy of the author.
49 (top)	Rathmines Road Lower, looking north, *c.* 1910, from Lawrence Photographic Collection. Reproduced courtesy of the National Library of Ireland, L_ROY_08548.
49 (bottom), 124–5	Rathmines Road Lower, looking south, *c.* 1910, from Lawrence Photographic Collection. Reproduced courtesy of the National Library of Ireland, L_ROY_08547.
52	Holy Trinity Church, Church Avenue, 1833 (*Dublin Penny Journal* 14.9.1833). Reproduced courtesy of the National Library of Ireland.
53 (top)	'Front elevation of a R.C. Chapel, designed for the parish of Rathmines', *c.* 1830. Reproduced courtesy of the Irish Architectural Archive.
53 (bottom)	Grosvenor Hall, Grosvenor Road, early 20th cent., from Lawrence Photographic Collection. Reproduced courtesy of the National Library of Ireland, L_CAB_07275.
55	Portobello Barracks, Rathmines Road Lower, *c.* 1900. Reproduced courtesy of the National Library of Ireland, L_ROY_08903.
56 (top)	Town hall (old), 1878, by J. O'Connell. Reproduced courtesy of the National Library of Ireland, MS 7994.

56 (bottom)	Town hall (new) and gated Leinster Square, *c.* 1910, from Eason Photographic Collection. Reproduced courtesy of the National Library of Ireland, Eas 1936.
58 (top)	Grubb's astronomical works, Observatory Lane, 1875. Available at https://phaidra.univie.ac.at/o:103093 (last accessed 28 July 2021). Reproduced courtesy of the Department of Astrophysics at the University of Vienna.
58 (bottom)	Tayto factory, Mountpleasant Avenue Upper, 1958. © Irish Photo Archive/© Lensmen Photographic Archive.
59	Junction Rathmines Road Lower/Upper, *c.* 1920, from Eason Photographic Collection. Reproduced courtesy of the National Library of Ireland, Eas 1934.
60	Kelso Laundry, Rathmines Road Lower, 1933, G. & T. Crampton Photograph Archive. Reproduced courtesy of University College Dublin Library.
61	Portobello Bridge and the Grand Canal viewed from Grove Road, 1812–47, by S.F. Brocas. Reproduced courtesy of the National Library of Ireland, PD 1963 TX (34b).
62	'Clanbrassil Bridge, Harold's Cross', 1817, by C.M. Nairn. Reproduced courtesy of the National Library of Ireland, PD 1969 TX 57.
63	Address to Frederick Stokes on his retirement from the chairmanship of Rathmines and Rathgar Township Board, including illustration of Rathmines Road Lower, looking south, 1878, by J. O'Connell. Reproduced courtesy of the National Library of Ireland, MS 7994.
64	School in Rathmines Castle (old), 1789 (*Gentleman's Magazine*, lix, pl. III, fig. 3). Reproduced courtesy of the National Library of Ireland, ET A324.
65	St Mary's National School, playground, Richmond Hill, early 20th cent., from Dixon Slides Collection. Reproduced courtesy of Dublin City Library and Archive.
67	Rathmines public library, *c.* 1920, from Fergus O'Connor Collection. Reproduced courtesy of the National Library of Ireland, OCO 320.
68	'Palace Rink', skating rink, Rathmines Road Lower, 1909–13. Postcard, reproduced courtesy of the author.
69	Kenilworth Bowling Club, in Grosvenor Square, early 20th cent., from Eason Photographic Collection. Reproduced courtesy of the National Library of Ireland, Eas 1846.
71	Rathmines, looking south-west from the Grand Canal at Portobello, from 'La Touche Bridge, Portobello Hotel', 1809, by Thomas Snagg. Reproduced courtesy of the National Museum of Ireland.
72	Rathmines Castle (new), Rathmines Road Upper, 1833 (*Dublin Penny Journal* 14.9.1833). Reproduced courtesy of the National Library of Ireland.
75	Kensington Lodge, Grove Park, 1882 (*Irish Builder* 15.8.1882). Reproduced courtesy of the National Library of Ireland.
78 (top)	Belfield Terrace, Rathmines Road Upper, *c.* 1910, from Eason Photographic Collection. Reproduced courtesy of the National Library of Ireland, Eas 1937.
78 (bottom)	Fortescue Terrace, RC church, Rathmines Road Lower, *c.* 1910, from Eason Photographic Collection. Reproduced courtesy of the National Library of Ireland, Eas 1914.
80–1	Traffic map from *The Dublin civic survey report* (Liverpool, 1925). Reproduced courtesy of Arnold Horner.

Selected bibliography
and key to abbreviations

(Other abbreviations are explained in the general list for the series on pp 137–41)

Alen's reg.	*Calendar of Archbishop Alen's register, c. 1172–1534*, ed. Charles McNeill (Dublin, 1950).
Anglo-Celt	*The Anglo-Celt* (Cavan, 1846–).
Annual rept	*Sixth annual report of the Poor Law Commissioners* (London, 1840).
Applotment bk	Tithe applotment books, 1823–37. NAI.
Archer	Archer, Joseph, *Statistical survey of the County Dublin* (Dublin, 1801).
Armstrong 1–4	(1) Armstrong, W.A., Maps and rental of the estate of the Right Honourable Earl of Meath in and adjacent to the city of Dublin, 1808–50. Meath papers G34; (2) Armstrong, W.A., Maps and rental of the estate of the Right Honourable Earl of Meath in and adjacent to the city of Dublin, 1808–50. Meath papers G35; (3) Armstrong, W.A., 'A map of part of the lands of Cullinswood in the county of Dublin now let to Major Taylor being part of the estate of the Earl of Meath', 1810. Meath papers, box 158 (Map 11); (4) Armstrong, W.A., 'Part of the estate of the Right Hon. the Earl of Meath in the south suburbs of the city of dublin', 1836. Survey and Mapping Department, Dublin City Council.
Ball	Ball, F. Elrington, *A history of the County Dublin: the people, parishes and antiquities from the earliest times to the close of the eighteenth century* (5 vols, Dublin, 1903; repr. 1995).
Barry	Barry, Charles, *Plan of Rathmines school* (Dublin, 1795).
Belgrave Sq. map	'Belgrave Square, also ground to be let for building in the neighbourhood, J. Holmes, Architect', 1872–97. Erasmus Smith Trust Archive, High School, Dublin, EE/1369 (2).
Beranger	Beranger, Gabriel, 'Cullen's Castle, near Cullen's wood', 1772. NLI, PD 1958 TX 72.
BNL	*Belfast News-Letter* (Belfast, 1737–).
Boundary comm.	*Royal commission for inquiring into number and boundaries of poor law unions and electoral divisions in Ireland*, HC 1850 [1278], xxvi.
Bradley	Bradley, John, 'Some reflections on the problem of Scandinavian settlement in the hinterland of Dublin during the ninth century' in John Bradley, A.J. Fletcher and Anngret Simms (eds), *Dublin in the medieval world: studies in honour of Howard B. Clarke* (Dublin, 2009), pp 39–62.

Brownrigg	Brownrigg, John, 'A survey of part of the farm of St Sepulchers in the county of Dublin let by his grace Robert, lord archbishop of Dublin to Mrs Frances Usher', 1782. RCB, Dublin Diocesan Collection. (Map 8).
Brunskill	Brunskill, H.O., 'The battle of Rathmines: 2 August 1649' in *DHR*, ii (1939), pp 18–29.
	Burton, Nathanial, *Letters from Harold's Cross, 1850* (Dublin, 1979).
Campbell	Campbell, Thomas, *City of Dublin surveyed by Mr Thomas Campbell under the directions of Major Taylor* ([Dublin], 1811).
Comerford	Comerford, Patrick, 'The synagogues of Dublin', available at www.patrickcomerford.com/2019/10/the-synagogues-of-dublin-16-leicester.html (last accessed 21 Apr. 2021).
Cooke	*Cooke's Royal map of Dublin* (Dublin, 1822).
Corcoran	Corcoran, Michael, *Through streets broad and narrow: a history of Dublin trams* (Leicester, 2000).
Court bk	*Court book of the liberty of St Sepulchre within the jurisdiction of the archbishop of Dublin, 1586–1590*, ed. Herbert Wood (Dublin, 1930).
Curtis, J.	Curtis, Joe, *Harold's Cross: a history* (Dublin, 2016).
Curtis, M., 2015	Curtis, Maurice, *Rathgar: a history* (Dublin, 2015).
Curtis, M., 2019	Curtis, Maurice, *The little book of Rathmines* (Stroud, 2019).
DCC flat schemes	Dublin City Council flat schemes. Database compiled by Dublin City Council Architects Department. DCLA.
Duff et al.	Duff, Thomas, Joseph Hegarty and Matthew Hussey, *The story of the Dublin Institute of Technology* (Dublin, 2000).
Dungan	Dungan, Myles, *If you want to know who we are: the Rathmines and Rathgar Musical Society, 1913–2013* (Dublin, 2013).
Evening Echo	*Evening Echo* (Dublin, 1892–).
Evening Herald	*Evening Herald* (Dublin, 1891–).
Evening Press	*Evening Press* (Dublin, 1954–95).
FJ	*Freeman's Journal* (Dublin, 1763–1924).
FLJ	*Finns Leinster Journal* (Kilkenny, 1767–1828).
Galavan	Galavan, Susan, *Dublin's bourgeois homes: building the Victorian suburbs, 1850–1901* (London, 2017).
Garland	Garland website, available at www.garlandconsultancy.com/news-and-resources/news/2016/03/10/a-history-of-garland-house (last accessed 21 Apr. 2021).
Gentleman's magazine	*Gentleman's magazine and historical chronicle* (London, 1736–1833).
Gough and Quinn	Gough, Michael and R.F. Quinn, 'Religious-owned lands in Dublin' in *Studies: an Irish Quarterly Review*, lxxvi:304 (1987), pp 387–402.
Greene	Greene, John, 'A survey of part of the farme of St Sepulchers lyeing in the barony of Newcastle and county of Dublin belonging to … William lord archbishop of Dublin', 1717. RCB, Dublin Diocesan Collection. (Map 7).
Grimes	Grimes, Brendan, *Majestic shrines and graceful sanctuaries: the church architecture of Patrick Byrne, 1783–1864* (Dublin, 2009).
	Haden, C.W., *The demesne of Old Rathmines: an historical survey of Upper Rathmines, Dartry and Milltown* (Dublin, 1988).
Hofman	Hofman, Wemmechien, 'A snapshot of life in Harold's Cross cottages, 1884–1940' in *DHR*, lxix (2016), pp 59–70.
Ir. Daily Ind.	*Irish Daily Independent* (Dublin, 1891–).
Ir. Independent	*Irish Independent* (Dublin, 1905–).

Ir. Monthly	*Irish Monthly* (Dublin, 1873–1954).
Ir. Press	*Irish Press* (Dublin, 1931–95).
Ir. Times	*The Irish Times* (Dublin, 1859–).
Iveagh Trust website	Iveagh Trust website, available at www.theiveaghtrust.ie (last accessed 21 Apr. 2021).
Jesuit or Catholic Sentinel	*Jesuit or Catholic Sentinel* (Boston, 1829–34).
Joyce	Joyce, W. St J., *The neighbourhood of Dublin: its topography, antiquities and historical associations* (Dublin, 1921).
Kelly	Kelly, Deirdre, *Four roads to Dublin: the history of Rathmines, Ranelagh and Leeson Street* (Dublin, 1995).
Kerry Evening Post	*Kerry Evening Post* (Tralee, 1774–).
Kerryman	*Kerryman* (Tralee, 1904–).
Laoide	Laoide, Seosamh, *Post-sheanchas* (Dublin, 1905).
Lavin	Lavin, Anne, 'Leinster Square (with Prince Arthur Terrace) Rathmines: an early suburban speculative terraced housing development 1830–52' (Masters in Urban and Building Conservation, UCD, 1995).
Leask	Leask, H.G., *Christ Church Rathgar: the story of one hundred years* (Dublin, 1962).
Leinster Exp.	*Leinster Express* (Maryborough [Portlaoise], 1831–).
Leitrim Obs.	*Leitrim Observer* (Carrick-on-Shannon, 1889–).
Levistone Cooney	Levistone Cooney, D.A., 'A small school in Rathmines' in *DHR*, xlv (1992), pp 41–54.
Little	Little, Seán, 'Rathmines in history' in *St Mary's College Annual* (1979), pp 33–53.
Local electoral area rept 2013	*Local electoral area boundary committee report 2013* (Dublin, 2013), available at www.boundarycommittee.ie/2008_Reports.htm (last accessed 21 Apr. 2021).
Local electoral area rept 2018	*Local electoral area boundary committee no. 2 report 2018* (Dublin, 2018), available at www.boundarycommittee.ie (last accessed 21 Apr. 2021).
Maher	Maher, W.A., *A history of St Mary's College, Rathmines, Dublin, 1890–1990* (Dublin, 1994).
McDevitt	McDevitt, Murrough (ed.), *Leinster Cricket Club: celebrating 150 years of sport* (Dublin, 2002).
Meath papers	Meath estate papers, Kilruddery House, Co. Wicklow. Private collection. Used by permission.
Memorials	*Memorials of the great civil war in England from 1646 to 1652: edited from original letters in the Bodleian Library*, ed. Henry Carey (2 vols, London, 1842).
Meyler	Meyler, W.T., *Saint Catherine's bells: an autobiography* (2 vols, Dublin, 1868).
Mills, 1889a	Mills, James, 'Notices of the manor of St Sepulchre, Dublin, in the fourteenth century' in *JRSAI*, ix (1889), pp 31–41.
Mills, 1889b	Mills, James, 'Notices of the manor of St Sepulchre, Dublin, in the fourteenth century (continued)' in *JRSAI*, ix (1889), pp 119–26.
Moffat	Moffat, C.B., 'The Rev. Charles William Benson, M.A., LL.D.' in *The Irish Naturalist*, xxviii:6 (1919), pp 73–8.
Montgomery	Montgomery, Bob, *Motor assembly in Ireland* (Dublin, 2018).
Mun. bound. comm.	*Municipal boundaries commission (Ireland)*. Part II, 1881 [C. 2827].
Munster Exp.	*Munster Express* (Waterford, 1860–).
Murphy	Murphy, F.J., 'Dublin trams, 1872–1959' in *DHR*, xxxiii (1979), pp 2–9.
Musical Times	*Musical Times* (London, 1844–).

Nairn 1, 2	Nairn, C.M. (1) 'Hen and Chicken Lane Harold's Cross', 1817. NLI, PD 1969 TX 92; (2) 'Clanbrassil Bridge, Harold's Cross', 1817. NLI, PD 1969 TX 57.
Nation	*The Nation* (Dublin, 1842–1900).
Nenagh Guardian	*Nenagh Guardian* (Nenagh, 1838–).
Ní Thiarnaigh	Ní Thiarnaigh, Éilís, 'St Louis Convent and high school: 100 years in Rathmines' in *DHR*, lxvii (2014), pp 42–53.
Noonan	Noonan, Chris, 'The beginnings of Opus Dei in Ireland leading to the establishment of its first corporate apostolate, Nullamore University residence, Dublin in 1954' in *Studia et Documenta*, xiii (2019), pp 177–241.
O Brolchain	O Brolchain, Honor, 'From bootmaking to building: the Plunketts and the Crannys in 19th century Dublin 4 and 6', available at www.honorobrolchain.ie/talks/from-bootmaking-to-building/ (last accessed 19 Apr. 2021).
O'Carroll	O'Carroll, Ciarán, *Church of Mary Immaculate Refuge of Sinners Rathmines, Dublin 6* (Dublin, 2000).
	O'Connell, Angela, *The servants' church: a history of the church of the Three Patrons in the parish of Rathgar* (Dublin, 2004).
OS	Ordnance Survey. Large-scale maps: Dublin city, scale 1:1056, manuscript, sheets 37–48, 1838, with revisions to 1843 (NAI, OS 140) (Maps 16, 17); Rathmines and Rathgar township, scale 1:1056, printed, sheets xviii.85–8, 95–8, xxii.5–8, 15–18, 26–8, surveyed 1876–7, revised 1882; Dublin city, scale 1:1000, sheet 3328.4, surveyed in 1967; sheets 3328.5, 9, 15; 3329.1, 6, 11, 16, surveyed in 1968. Maps of the parish of St Peter, scale 1:2500, surveyed in 1863–7 [*c.* 1864] (Map 2). Maps of Co. Dublin: scale 1:10,560, sheets 18, 22, surveyed in 1837 (engraved in 1837), sheet 18 corrected, printed 1843, revised 1875 (engraved 1876); sheet 22 corrected, printed 1844, revised 1869 (engraved 1871) (Maps 18, 19); scale 1:2500, sheets xviii.15, xxii.3, surveyed in 1837, revised in 1907–8 (Map 4), 1936 (Map 5); scale 1:5000, surveyed in *c.* 2019 (Map 3).
OSN	Ordnance Survey name books, Dublin city and county, 1836. NAI, OS 144. Typescript copy, DCLA.
Palmerston papers	Palmerston papers. University of Southampton, Broadlands archives, BR 137–152.
Palmerston rent book	Palmerston estate, Dublin rent book, 1790, 1791. NLI, MS 1566.
Parkes	Parkes, Susan, *Kildare Place: the history of the Church of Ireland training college, 1811–1969* (Dublin, 1984).
Quane	Quane, Michael, 'The Hibernian Royal Marine School, Dublin' in *DHR*, xxi (1967), pp 67–78.
Queen	*The Queen* (London, 1861–1970).
Rathmines Free Press	*Rathmines Free Press* (Dublin, 1922–4).
Refaussé and Clark	Refaussé, Raymond and Mary Clark (eds), *A catalogue of the maps of the estates of the archbishops of Dublin, 1654–1850* (Dublin, 2000).
RJS website	Rathgar Junior School website, available at www.rathgarjuniorschool.ie (last accessed 21 Apr. 2021).
Ronan	Ronan, M.V., *The reformation in Dublin* (London, 1926).
	Roundtree, Susan, 'Mountpleasant Square' in Mary Clark and Alastair Smeaton (eds), *The Georgian Squares of Dublin: an architectural history* (Dublin, 2006), pp 123–53.

RRTA	Rathmines and Rathgar Township archives. DCLA, UDC/1. Descriptive list by Mary Clark (1982), available at www.dublincity.ie/sites/default/files/media/file-uploads/2018-06/Rathmines-and-Rathgar-Township.pdf (last accessed 21 Apr. 2021).
RRTM (1–10)	Rathmines and Rathgar Township/Urban District Council Minute Books, 1847–1930. DCLA, UDC/1/Min 1/1–1/10.
Scannell	Scannell, James, 'From horse drawn trams to LUAS: a look at public transport in Dublin from the 1870s to the present time' in *DHR*, xxxiii (1979), pp 2–9.
Shepherd	Shepherd, W.E., *The Dublin and South Eastern Railway* (London, 1974).
Sherrard, Brassington and Greene	Sherrard, Brassington and Greene, 'Survey of part of the farm of Saint Sepulchre in the county of Dublin, belonging to the Very Reverend Richard Hastings Graves', 1826, copied 1830. Scale eighty feet to an inch. NAI, MS M 2574. (Map 14).
Smith	Smith, Elizabeth, 'Belgrave Square Rathmines: the development of its green space' in *DHR*, lxix (2016), pp 17–29.
Snagg	Snagg, Thomas, 'La Touche Bridge, Portobello Hotel', 1809. National Museum of Ireland, Dublin.
Sunday Ind.	*Sunday Independent* (Dublin, 1906–).
Sweeney	Sweeney, C.L., *The rivers of Dublin* (Dublin, 1991).
TH	*Tuam Herald* (Tuam, 1837–78, 1883–1923, 1927–).
Val. 1, 2, 3	Records of the General Valuation Office relating to Rathmines. (1) Valuation Office field and house books, 1845, NAI, OL 5.0945/47, 5.2716/17–71. (2) Printed tenement valuation, South Dublin Union, 1850. (3) Manuscript revision books and related maps, Rathmines, (scale 1:1056), Rathmines, 1850–1902. Valuation Office, Dublin.
	Walsh, Jed, *On the banks of the Dodder: Rathgar and Churchtown, an illustrated history* (Dublin, 2019).
Walsh	Walsh, John, *Higher education in Ireland, 1922–2016: politics, policy and power – a history of higher education in the Irish state* (London, 2018).
Wilson	Wilson, William, *This modern plan of the city and environs of Dublin* (London and Dublin, 1798).
Wyse Jackson	Wyse Jackson, Peter, 'The botanic garden of Trinity College Dublin 1687 to 1987' in *Botanical Journal of the Linnean Society*, xcv:4 (1987), pp 301–11.
Zimmerman	Zimmerman, Marc, *The history of Dublin cinemas* (Dublin, 2007).

General abbreviations

AAI	*Art and architecture of Ireland*, ed. Andrew Carpenter and others (5 vols, Dublin, New Haven and London, 2014).
Aalen and Whelan	Aalen, F.H.A. and Kevin Whelan (eds), *Dublin city and county: from prehistory to present: studies in honour of J.H. Andrews* (Dublin, 1992).
Abercrombie et al.	Abercrombie, Patrick, et al., *Dublin of the future: the new town plan* (Dublin, 1922).
AFM	*Annála ríoghachta Éireann: annals of the kingdom of Ireland by the Four Masters, from the earliest period to the year 1616*, ed. John O'Donovan (7 vols, Dublin, 1851).
ALC	*The annals of Loch Cé: a chronicle of Irish affairs from AD 1014 to AD 1590*, ed. W.M. Hennessy (2 vols, London, 1871).
Ancient records	*Calendar of ancient records of Dublin in the possession of the municipal corporation*, ed. J.T. Gilbert and R.M. Gilbert. 19 vols, Dublin, 1889–1944.
Ann. Clon.	*The annals of Clonmacnoise, being annals of Ireland from the earliest period to AD 1408, translated into English, AD 1627, by Conell Mageoghagan*, ed. Denis Murphy (Dublin, 1896).
Ann. Conn.	*Annála Connacht: the annals of Connacht (AD 1224–1544)*, ed. A.M. Freeman (Dublin, 1944).
Ann. Inisf.	*The annals of Inisfallen (MS Rawlinson B 503)*, ed. Seán Mac Airt (Dublin, 1951).
Ann. Tig.	*The annals of Tigernach*, ed. Whitley Stokes, facsimile repr. from *Revue Celtique*, xvi–xviii (1895–7) (2 vols, Lampeter, 1993).
Arch. Survey	Archaeological Survey of Ireland, National Monuments Service, Department of Culture, Heritage and the Gaeltacht, available at www.archaeology.ie (last accessed 21 Apr. 2021).
Archiseek	Archiseek website, available at www.archiseek.com (last accessed 21 Apr. 2021).
AU 1, 2	(1) *Annála Uladh, Annals of Ulster … : a chronicle of Irish affairs, 431 to 1541*, ed. W.M. Hennessy and Bartholomew MacCarthy (4 vols, 2nd edn, Dublin, 1998); (2) *The Annals of Ulster (to AD 1131)*, pt 1, *Text and translation*, ed. Seán Mac Airt and Gearóid Mac Niocaill (Dublin, 1983).
BL	British Library, London.
Bodl.	Bodleian Library, Oxford.

Bonar Law and Bonar Law	Bonar Law, Andrew and Charlotte Bonar Law, *A contribution towards a catalogue of the printed maps of Dublin city and county* (2 vols, Dublin, 2005).
Boundary com. rept	*Municipal boundaries commission (Ireland)*, pt III, *report and evidence*, HC 1881 [C.3089], 1.
Brooking	Brooking, Charles, *A map of the city and suburbs of Dublin. And also the archbishop and earl of Meaths liberties with the bounds of each parish, drawn from an actual survey*. With inset *A prospect of the city of Dublin from the north* (Dublin, 1728).
Cal. Carew MSS	*Calendar of the Carew manuscripts preserved in the archiepiscopal library at Lambeth, 1515–74* [etc.] (6 vols, London, 1867–73).
Cal. chart. rolls	*Calendar of the charter rolls, 1226–57* [etc.] (6 vols, London, 1903–27).
Cal. doc. Ire.	*Calendar of documents relating to Ireland, 1171–1251* [etc.] (5 vols, London, 1875–86).
Cal. exch. inq.	*Calendar of exchequer inquisitions, 1455–1699* [etc.] (Dublin, 1991–).
Cal. fine rolls	*Calendar of the fine rolls, 1271–1307* [etc.] (22 vols, London, 1911–62).
Cal. justic. rolls Ire.	*Calendar of the justiciary rolls or proceedings in the court of the justiciar of Ireland, 1295–1303* [etc.] (3 vols, Dublin, 1905–56).
Cal. papal letters	*Calendar of entries in the papal registers relating to Great Britain and Ireland: papal letters, 1198–1304* [etc.] (London and Dublin, 1893–).
Cal. pat. rolls	*Calendar of the patent rolls, 1216–25* [etc.] (London, 1901–).
Cal. pat. rolls Ire.	*Calendar of the patent and close rolls of chancery in Ireland* (3 vols, Dublin, 1861–3).
Cal. pat. rolls Ire., Jas I	*Irish patent rolls of James I: facsimile of the Irish record commissioners' calendar prepared prior to 1830* (Dublin, 1966).
Cal. SP dom.	*Calendar of state papers, domestic series, 1547–1580* [etc.] (London, 1856–).
Cal. SP Ire.	*Calendar of the state papers relating to Ireland, 1509–73* [etc.] (24 vols, London, 1860–1910).
Cal. treas. bks	*Calendar of treasury books* (32 vols, London, 1904–62).
Census, 1659	*A census of Ireland circa 1659*, ed. Séamus Pender (Dublin, 1939; repr. 2002).
Census, 1821 [etc.]	Printed census reports (for full references see W.E. Vaughan and A.J. Fitzpatrick, *Irish historical statistics, 1821–1971* (Dublin, 1978), pp 355–61).
Census returns, 1901 [etc.]	Unpublished census returns, NAI.
Chartae	*Chartae, privilegia et immunitates, being transcripts of charters and privileges to cities, towns, abbeys and other bodies corporate* … (Dublin, 1829–30).
Christ Church deeds	'Calendar to Christ Church deeds' in *PRI repts DK 20–4* (Dublin, 1888–92). Index in *PRI rept DK 27*, pp 3–101. Repr. with additional material and new index as *Christ Church deeds*, ed. M.J. McEnery and Raymond Refaussé (Dublin, 2001). Cited by deed number.
Chron. Scot.	*Chronicum Scotorum: a chronicle of Irish affairs … to AD 1135, with a supplement … from 1141 to 1150*, ed. W.M. Hennessy (London, 1866).
C. of I.	Church of Ireland.
Clarke	Clarke, H.B., *Dublin, part I, to 1610* (IHTA, no. 11) (Dublin, 2002).

Commons' jn. Ire.	*Journals of the House of Commons of the kingdom of Ireland*, printed in four ser. (for full lists, see H.D. Gribbon, 'Journals of the Irish House of Commons' in *An Leabharlann: the Irish Library*, 2nd ser., ii (1985), pp 52–5).
CS	*The civil survey, AD 1654–56*, ed. R.C. Simington (10 vols, Dublin, 1931–61).
D'Alton	D'Alton, John, *The history of the county of Dublin* (Dublin, 1838; repr. Cork, 1976).
Daly	Daly, Mary, *Dublin: the deposed capital: a social and economic history, 1860–1914* (Cork, 1984).
DCLA	Dublin City Library and Archive, Dublin.
De Gomme	[De Gomme, Bernard], 'The city and suburbs of Dublin, from Kilmainham to Rings-End wherein the rivers, streets, lanes, allys, churches, gates & c. are exactly described, 1673', scale 1760 yards to one English mile. National Maritime Museum, Greenwich, P/49 (11).
DHR	*Dublin Historical Record* (Dublin, 1938–).
DIA	Dictionary of Irish architects online, available at www.dia. ie (last accessed 21 Apr. 2021).
DIB	*Dictionary of Irish biography: from the earliest times to the year 2002*, ed. James McGuire and James Quinn (9 vols, Cambridge, 2009), available at www.dib.ie (last accessed 21 Apr. 2021).
Donnelly	Donnelly, Nicholas, *A short history of some Dublin parishes* (17 parts, Dublin, [*c.* 1905–16]; repr. Blackrock, 1983).
Dublin almanac	*The Dublin almanac and general advertiser of Ireland* (Dublin, 1834–50).
Dublin civic survey	*The Dublin civic survey report* (Liverpool, 1925).
Dublin guide	Lewis, Richard, *The Dublin guide: or a description of the city of Dublin …* (Dublin, 1787).
Duncan	Duncan, William, *Map of the county of Dublin* (8 sheets, Dublin, 1821). (Map 13).
Education repts	*Reports from the commissioners of the board of education in Ireland*, HC 1813 (47), v.
Electoral Act	The Electoral Acts, 1923–1980, available at www. irishstatutebook.ie (last accessed 21 Apr. 2021). Cited by act number.
Electoral rolls, 1908 [etc.]	Borough of the city of Dublin register of local government voters, 1908–15, Rathmines Ward, available at databases.dublincity.ie/advanced.php (last accessed 21 Apr. 2021).
Endowed schools rept	*Report of the commissioners for enquiring into the endowed schools in Ireland*, HC 1857–8 [2336], xxii, pt iv; 1881 [2831], xxxv, pt i.
Excavations	*Excavations 1969: summary accounts of archaeological excavations in Ireland* [etc.] (Dublin and Bray, 1969–76, 1985–), available at www.excavations.ie (last accessed 21 Apr. 2021).
Extents Ir. mon. possessions	*Extents of Irish monastic possessions, 1540–41, from manuscripts in the Public Record Office, London*, ed. N.B. White (Dublin, 1943).
Fairs and markets rept	*Report of the commissioners appointed to inquire into the state of the fairs and markets in Ireland*, HC 1852–3 [1674], xli.
Fiants	'Calendar of fiants of Henry VIII … Elizabeth' in *PRI repts DK 7–22* (Dublin, 1875–90); repr. as *The Irish fiants of the Tudor sovereigns …* (4 vols, Dublin, 1994).
Goodbody	Goodbody, Rob, *Dublin, part III, 1756 to 1847* (IHTA, no. 26) (Dublin, 2014).

Gwynn and Hadcock	Gwynn, Aubrey and R.N. Hadcock, *Medieval religious houses: Ireland* (London, 1970).
HC	House of commons sessional paper.
IAA	Irish Architectural Archive, Dublin.
IHS	*Irish Historical Studies* (Dublin, 1938–).
IHTA	*Irish historic towns atlas*, ed. J.H. Andrews, Anngret Simms, H.B. Clarke, Raymond Gillespie, Jacinta Prunty, Michael Potterton, Ruth McManus and Jonathan Wright (Dublin, 1986–).
IMC	Irish Manuscripts Commission.
Ir. Builder	*The Irish Builder and Engineer* (Dublin, 1867–), formerly *The Dublin Builder* (Dublin, 1859–66).
JRSAI	*Journal of the Royal Society of Antiquaries of Ireland* (Dublin, 1850–).
Lennon, 2008	Lennon, Colm, *Dublin, part II, 1610 to 1756* (*IHTA*, no. 19) (Dublin, 2008).
Lennon, 2018	Lennon, Colm, *Clontarf* (*IHTA*, Dublin suburbs, no. 2) (Dublin, 2018).
Lewis	Lewis, Samuel, *A topographical dictionary of Ireland* (2 vols with atlas, London, 1837).
Logainm	Logainm: Bunachar logainmneacha na hÉireann (Placenames Database of Ireland), available at www.logainm.ie (last accessed 21 Apr. 2021).
Lucas	Lucas, Richard, *A general directory of the kingdom of Ireland* … (Dublin, 1788).
Mac Niocaill	Mac Niocaill, Gearóid, *Na buirgéisí, xii–xv aois* (2 vols, Dublin, 1964).
McCullough	McCullough, Niall, *Dublin, an urban history: the plan of the city* (Dublin, 2007).
McManus	McManus, Ruth, *Dublin, 1910–1940: shaping the city and suburbs* (Dublin, 2002).
Mun. boundary repts	*Municipal corporation boundaries (Ireland) reports and plans*, HC 1837 (301), xxix.
Mun. corp. Ire. rept	*Municipal corporations (Ireland), appendices to the first report of the commissioners*, HC 1835, xxvii, xxviii; 1836, xxiv.
Murphy and Potterton	Murphy, Margaret and Michael Potterton, *The Dublin region in the Middle Ages: settlement, land-use and economy* (Dublin, 2010).
NAI	National Archives of Ireland, Dublin, formerly Public Record Office of Ireland.
NGI	National Gallery of Ireland, Dublin.
NHI	*A new history of Ireland*, ed. T.W. Moody, F.X. Martin, F.J. Byrne et al. (9 vols, Oxford, 1976–2005).
NIAH intro./survey	*National inventory of architectural heritage: an introduction to the architectural heritage of County Meath* [etc.] (Dublin, 2002–), survey available at www.buildingsofireland.ie (last accessed 21 Apr. 2021).
NLI	National Library of Ireland, Dublin.
Ó Maitiú	Ó Maitiú, Séamas, *Dublin's suburban towns, 1834–1930* (Dublin, 2003).
OSM	Ordnance Survey memoirs, RIA.
Parl. boundary repts	*Parliamentary representation: boundary reports, Ireland*, HC 1831–2 (519), xliii.
Parl. gaz.	*The parliamentary gazetteer of Ireland* (3 vols, London, 1846).
Petty	Petty, William, *Hiberniae delineatio quoad hactenus licuit perfectissima* … ([London], 1685).
Pigot	*Pigot's national commercial directory of Ireland* (Dublin, 1820 and 1824).

Pratt	Pratt, Henry, *A map of the kingdom of Ireland newly corrected and improved … with plans of the citys and fortified towns …* (London, [1708]; repr. Dublin, [1732]).
PRIA	*Proceedings of the Royal Irish Academy* (Dublin, 1836–).
Primary educ. returns	*Royal commission of inquiry, primary education (Ireland), vi, Educational census. Returns showing the number of children actually present in each primary school on 25th June 1868 …,* HC 1870 [C.6.v], xxviii, pt V.
PRI rept DK 1 [etc.]	*First [etc.] report of the deputy keeper of the public records in Ireland* (Dublin, 1869–).
PRONI	Public Record Office of Northern Ireland, Belfast.
Prunty	Prunty, Jacinta, *Maps and map-making in local history* (Dublin, 2004).
Publ. instr. rept 1	*First report of the commissioners on public instruction, Ireland,* HC 1835 [45, 46], xxxiii.
Publ. instr. rept 2	*Second report of the commissioners on public instruction, Ireland,* HC 1835 [47], xxxiv.
RC	Roman Catholic.
RCB	Representative Church Body Library, Dublin.
RD	Registry of Deeds, Dublin, memorials of deeds.
RIA	Royal Irish Academy, Dublin.
Rocque	Rocque, John, *An actual survey of the county of Dublin, 1760* (4 sheets, Dublin, 1760; repr. London, 1802). (Map 9).
Rot. pat. Hib.	*Rotulorum patentium et clausorum cancellariae Hiberniae calendarium* i, pt 1, *Hen. II–Hen. VII*, ed. Edward Tresham (Dublin, 1828).
Slater	*Slater's national commercial directory of Ireland* (Manchester, 1846 etc.).
Stat. Ire.	*The statutes at large passed in the parliaments held in Ireland* … (22 vols, Dublin, 1786–1801).
Taylor, A.	Taylor, Alexander, 'A sketch of the environs of Dublin', [*c.* 1802]. BL Add MS 32451D. (Map 10).
Taylor, J.	Taylor, John, *Taylor's map of the environs of Dublin* (Dublin, 1816). (Map 12).
Taylor and Skinner	Taylor, George and Andrew Skinner, *Maps of the roads of Ireland, surveyed in 1777* (London and Dublin, 1778).
TCD	Trinity College, Dublin.
Thom	*Thom's Irish almanac and official directory* (Dublin, 1844 etc.).
Thom map	'Map of the city of Dublin and its environs, constructed for Thom's almanac and official directory' in *Thom*, 1871 etc. UCD School of Geography, Planning and Environmental Policy, available at digital.ucd.ie / view / ucdlib:33009 (last accessed 21 Apr. 2021). (Map 23).
Thomas	Thomas, Avril, *The walled towns of Ireland* (2 vols, Dublin, 1992).
TNA:PRO	The National Archives: Public Record Office, Kew.
UJA	*Ulster Journal of Archaeology* (Belfast, 1853–).
Urb. Arch. Survey	Urban Archaeology Survey, National Monuments Service, Department of the Culture, Heritage and the Gaeltacht.
Walker 1	Walker, B.M. (ed.), *Parliamentary election results in Ireland, 1801–1922* (Dublin, 1978).
Walker 2	Walker, B.M. (ed.), *Parliamentary election results in Ireland, 1918–92* (Dublin, 1992).
Warburton *et al.*	Warburton, John, James Whitelaw and Robert Walsh, *History of the city of Dublin* (2 vols, London, 1818).
Watson	Watson, John, et al., *The gentleman and citizen's almanack* (Dublin, 1729–1844).

In this series

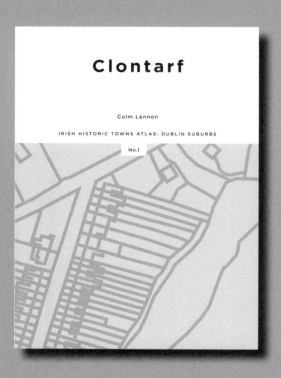

Clontarf is the first in the Dublin suburbs series. Clontarf's emergence from manor through township to suburb of Dublin is explained, and illustrated with thematic maps and views. A series of historic maps shows the topographical development of the district by land and by sea. Captured is 'a seaside place' seeking to maintain its own independent village identity, as detailed through topographical features of the natural and built environment, in the face of strong metropolitan influences on its fabric, society, administration and culture.

AVAILABLE AT RIA.IE

The Irish Historic Towns Atlas (IHTA) project was established in 1981 with the aim of recording the historical geography of a selection of Irish towns, both large and small. To date, thirty towns atlases have been published. In addition, the project has produced a number of ancillary publications, including pocket maps, guides to urban mapping and a set of proceedings of its annual seminar on 'Maps and texts'. The Dublin suburbs series, of which this volume is part, now complements the main towns atlas series.

The Irish Historic Towns Atlas project has played a major role in promoting Irish urban studies within a European scholarly milieu, through its active participation in the International Commission for the History of Towns. The Irish series is part of a larger project to facilitate the comparative study of towns in Europe based on a unified system of cartographical principles. Over 560 towns atlases have been published under the European project.

www.ihta.ie